Introduction to Python Programming

To learn more about OpenStax, visit openstaxtextbooks.com
Individual print copies and bulk orders can be purchased through our website.

Book and Cover Design © 2024 Open Stax Textbooks.
Textbook content produced by OpenStax is licensed under a CCA4

Senior Contributing Authors: Udayan Das, Saint Mary's College of California; Aubrey Lawson; Chris Mayfield, James Madison University; Narges Norouzi, UC Berkeley

Contributing Authors: Yamuna Rajasekhar; Reed Kanemaru.

Contact us:

info@openstaxtextbooks.com

Trademarks
The OpenStax name, OpenStax logo, OpenStax book covers, OpenStax CNX name, OpenStax CNX logo, OpenStax Tutor name, Openstax Tutor logo, Connexions name, Connexions logo, Rice University name, and Rice University logo are not subject to the license and may not be reproduced without the prior and express written consent

CONTENTS

1 Statements 7

Introduction 7
1.1 Background 8
1.2 Input/output 10
1.3 Variables 14
1.4 String basics 16
1.5 Number basics 20
1.6 Error messages 24
1.7 Comments 27
1.8 Why Python? 31
1.9 Chapter summary 34

2 Expressions 39

Introduction 39
2.1 The Python shell 40
2.2 Type conversion 42
2.3 Mixed data types 45
2.4 Floating-point errors 48
2.5 Dividing integers 51
2.6 The math module 54
2.7 Formatting code 60
2.8 Python careers 65
2.9 Chapter summary 67

3 Objects 71

Introduction 71
3.1 Strings revisited 71
3.2 Formatted strings 76
3.3 Variables revisited 79
3.4 List basics 83
3.5 Tuple basics 85
3.6 Chapter summary 88

4 Decisions 91

Introduction 91
4.1 Boolean values 91
4.2 If-else statements 96

4.3 Boolean operations   100
4.4 Operator precedence   104
4.5 Chained decisions   107
4.6 Nested decisions   113
4.7 Conditional expressions   116
4.8 Chapter summary   118

5 Loops   121

Introduction   121
5.1 While loop   121
5.2 For loop   125
5.3 Nested loops   129
5.4 Break and continue   133
5.5 Loop else   137
5.6 Chapter summary   140

6 Functions   145

Introduction   145
6.1 Defining functions   145
6.2 Control flow   149
6.3 Variable scope   153
6.4 Parameters   158
6.5 Return values   163
6.6 Keyword arguments   168
6.7 Chapter summary   170

7 Modules   173

Introduction   173
7.1 Module basics   174
7.2 Importing names   177
7.3 Top-level code   180
7.4 The help function   184
7.5 Finding modules   189
7.6 Chapter summary   194

8 Strings   197

Introduction   197
8.1 String operations   197
8.2 String slicing   200
8.3 Searching/testing strings   204
8.4 String formatting   209

8.5 Splitting/joining strings   217
8.6 Chapter summary   220

9 Lists   223

Introduction   223
9.1 Modifying and iterating lists   223
9.2 Sorting and reversing lists   226
9.3 Common list operations   229
9.4 Nested lists   231
9.5 List comprehensions   234
9.6 Chapter summary   238

10 Dictionaries   241

Introduction   241
10.1 Dictionary basics   241
10.2 Dictionary creation   243
10.3 Dictionary operations   245
10.4 Conditionals and looping in dictionaries   250
10.5 Nested dictionaries and dictionary comprehension   256
10.6 Chapter summary   260

11 Classes   265

Introduction   265
11.1 Object-oriented programming basics   265
11.2 Classes and instances   267
11.3 Instance methods   272
11.4 Overloading operators   276
11.5 Using modules with classes   281
11.6 Chapter summary   283

12 Recursion   287

Introduction   287
12.1 Recursion basics   287
12.2 Simple math recursion   289
12.3 Recursion with strings and lists   292
12.4 More math recursion   294
12.5 Using recursion to solve problems   297
12.6 Chapter summary   301

13 Inheritance 303

Introduction 303
13.1 Inheritance basics 303
13.2 Attribute access 306
13.3 Methods 310
13.4 Hierarchical inheritance 316
13.5 Multiple inheritance and mixin classes 320
13.6 Chapter summary 323

14 Files 327

Introduction 327
14.1 Reading from files 327
14.2 Writing to files 331
14.3 Files in different locations and working with CSV files 335
14.4 Handling exceptions 339
14.5 Raising exceptions 344
14.6 Chapter summary 347

15 Data Science 349

Introduction 349
15.1 Introduction to data science 349
15.2 NumPy 352
15.3 Pandas 354
15.4 Exploratory data analysis 362
15.5 Data visualization 368
15.6 Summary 375

Answer Key 379

Index 403

1 Statements

Figure 1.1 credit: Larissa Chu, CC BY 4.0

Chapter Outline

1.1 Background
1.2 Input/output
1.3 Variables
1.4 String basics
1.5 Number basics
1.6 Error messages
1.7 Comments
1.8 Why Python?
1.9 Chapter summary

Introduction

Computers and programs are everywhere in today's world. Programs affect many aspects of daily life and society as a whole. People depend on programs for communication, shopping, entertainment, health care, and countless other needs. Learning how to program computers opens the door to many careers and opportunities for building a better world.

Programs consist of statements to be run one after the other. A **statement** describes some action to be carried out.

The statement `print("Good morning")` instructs Python to output the message `"Good morning"` to the user. The statement `count = 0` instructs Python to assign the integer `0` to the variable `count`.

This chapter introduces statements for input and output, assigning variables, and basic arithmetic. Making mistakes is a normal part of programming, and the chapter includes advice on understanding error messages. The chapter ends with a short history of Python and discusses why Python has become so popular today.

1.1 Background

Learning Objectives

By the end of this section you should be able to
- Name two examples of computer programs in everyday life.
- Explain why Python is a good programming language to learn.

Computer programs

A **computer** is an electronic device that stores and processes information. Examples of computers include smartphones, tablets, laptops, desktops, and servers. Technically, a **program** is a sequence of instructions that a computer can run. Programs help people accomplish everyday tasks, create new technology, and have fun.

The goal of this book is to teach introductory programming and problem solving. Writing programs is a creative activity, inherently useful, and rewarding! No prior background in computer science is necessary to read this book. Many different types of programs exist, as shown in the illustration below. This book will focus on general purpose programs that typically run "behind the scenes."

> **CHECKPOINT**
>
> Online music streaming
>
> Access multimedia content (https://openstax.org/books/introduction-python-programming/pages/1-1-background)

> **CONCEPTS IN PRACTICE**
>
> Computers and programs
>
> 1. How many types of programs were described in the animation?
>   a. 3
>   b. 4
>   c. 5
>
> 2. What type of program will this book explain how to write?
>   a. a tool that summarizes an individual's music preferences
>   b. a mobile app for managing and sharing playlists of songs
>   c. a website that shows the top artists for the past five years
>
> 3. Which of the following devices is an example of a computer?
>   a. wired headphones that plug into a smartphone
>   b. remote control that pauses or skips the current song
>   c. wi-fi speaker that streams music from Amazon
>
> 4. Reading this book requires a strong background in mathematics.
>   a. true
>   b. false

> **EXPLORING FURTHER**
>
> Later chapters of this book show how to write analysis programs using real data. Example libraries that provide access to online streaming services include Spotipy (https://openstax.org/r/100spotipy), Pytube (https://openstax.org/r/100pytube), and Pydora (https://openstax.org/r/100pydora). Python-related tools often have the letters "py" in their name.

The Python language

This book introduces Python (https://openstax.org/r/100python), one of the top programming languages today. Leading tech giants like Google, Apple, NASA, Instagram, Pixar, and others use Python extensively.

One reason why Python is popular is because many libraries exist for doing real work. A **library** is a collection of code that can be used in other programs. Python comes with an extensive Standard Library (https://openstax.org/r/100pythlibrary) for solving everyday computing problems like extracting data from files and creating summary reports. In addition, the community develops many other libraries for Python. Ex: Pandas (https://openstax.org/r/100pandas) is a widely used library for data analysis.

Another reason why Python is popular is because the syntax is concise and straightforward. The **syntax** of a language defines how code must be structured. Syntax rules define the keywords, symbols, and formatting used in programs. Compared to other programming languages, Python is more concise and straightforward.

> **EXAMPLE 1.1**
>
> **Hello world in Python and Java**
>
> By tradition, Hello World (https://openstax.org/r/100helloworld) is the first program to write when learning a new language. This program simply displays the message "Hello, World!" to the user. The hello world program is only one line in Python:
>
> ```python
> print("Hello, World!")
> ```
>
> In contrast, the hello world program is five lines in Java (a different language).
>
> ```java
> public class Hello {
>   public static void main(String[] args) {
>     System.out.println("Hello, World!");
>   }
> }
> ```
>
> However, conciseness is not the only consideration for which language is used. In different situations different languages may be more appropriate. Ex: Java is often used in Android development.

> **CHECKPOINT**
>
> **Counting lines in a file**
>
> Access multimedia content (https://openstax.org/books/introduction-python-programming/pages/1-1-background)

> **CONCEPTS IN PRACTICE**
>
> Python vs Java syntax
>
> 5. In general, Python programs are _____ than Java programs.
>   a. faster
>   b. longer
>   c. shorter
>
> 6. In the example programs above, what syntax required by Java is not required by Python?
>   a. semicolons
>   b. parentheses
>   c. quote marks

> **TRY IT**
>
> Favorite song
>
> The program below asks for your name and displays a friendly greeting. Run the program and see what happens. In the error message, EOF stands for End of File.
>
> - Many of the programs in this chapter expect input from the user. Enter your name in the Input box below the code. Run the program again, and see what changes.
> - Copy the following lines to the end of the program: `print("What is your favorite song?")` `song = input()` `print("Cool! I like", song, "too.")`
> - The modified program reads two lines of input: `name` and `song`. Add your favorite song to the Input box below your name, and run the program again.
>
> The next section of the book will explain how `print()` and `input()` work. Feel free to experiment with this code until you are ready to move on.
>
> Access multimedia content (https://openstax.org/books/introduction-python-programming/pages/1-1-background)

1.2 Input/output

Learning objectives

By the end of this section you should be able to

- Display output using the `print()` function.
- Obtain user input using the `input()` function.

Basic output

The `print()` function displays output to the user. **Output** is the information or result produced by a program. The `sep` and `end` options can be used to customize the output. Table 1.1 shows examples of `sep` and `end`.

Multiple values, separated by commas, can be printed in the same statement. By default, each value is separated by a space character in the output. The `sep` option can be used to change this behavior.

By default, the `print()` function adds a newline character at the end of the output. A **newline** character tells the display to move to the next line. The end option can be used to continue printing on the same line.

Code	Output
`print("Today is Monday.")` `print("I like string beans.")`	Today is Monday. I like string beans.
`print("Today", "is", "Monday")` `print("Today", "is", "Monday", sep="...")`	Today is Monday Today...is...Monday
`print("Today is Monday, ", end="")` `print("I like string beans.")`	Today is Monday, I like string beans.

`print("Today", "is", "Monday", sep="? ",`
`end="!!")`
`print("I like string beans.")`
	Today? is? Monday!!I like string beans.

Table 1.1 Example uses of print().

CHECKPOINT

Displaying output to the user

Access multimedia content (https://openstax.org/books/introduction-python-programming/pages/1-2-inputoutput)

CONCEPTS IN PRACTICE

The print() function

1. Which line of code prints Hello world! as one line of output?
    a. `print(Hello world!)`
    b. `print("Hello", "world", "!")`
    c. `print("Hello world!")`

2. Which lines of code prints Hello world! as one line of output?
    a. `print("Hello")`
       `print(" world!")`
    b. `print("Hello")`
       `print(" world!", end="")`
    c. `print("Hello", end="")`
       `print(" world!")`

3. What output is produced by the following statement?

   `print("555", "0123", sep="-")`

a. `555 0123`
b. `5550123-`
c. `555-0123`

> **DO SPACES REALLY MATTER?**
>
> Spaces and newline characters are not inherently important. However, learning to be precise is an essential skill for programming. Noticing little details, like how words are separated and how lines end, helps new programmers become better.

Basic input

Computer programs often receive input from the user. **Input** is what a user enters into a program. An input statement, `variable = input("prompt")`, has three parts:

1. A **variable** refers to a value stored in memory. In the statement above, *variable* can be replaced with any name the programmer chooses.
2. The **input()** function reads one line of input from the user. A function is a named, reusable block of code that performs a task when called. The input is stored in the computer's memory and can be accessed later using the variable.
3. A **prompt** is a short message that indicates the program is waiting for input. In the statement above, *"prompt"* can be omitted or replaced with any message.

> **CHECKPOINT**
>
> Obtaining input from the user
>
> Access multimedia content (https://openstax.org/books/introduction-python-programming/pages/1-2-inputoutput)

> **CONCEPTS IN PRACTICE**
>
> The input() function
>
> 4. Which line of code correctly obtains and stores user input?
>   a. `input()`
>   b. `today_is = input`
>   c. `today_is = input()`
>
> 5. Someone named Sophia enters their name when prompted with
>
>    ```
>    print("Please enter your name: ")
>    name = input()
>    ```
>
>   What is displayed by `print("You entered:", name)`?
>   a. `You entered: name`
>   b. `You entered: Sophia`

c. You entered:, Sophia

6. What is the output if the user enters "six" as the input?

   ```
   print("Please enter a number: ")
   number = input()
   print("Value =", number)
   ```

   a. Value = six
   b. Value = 6
   c. Value = number

TRY IT

Frost poem

Write a program that uses multiple `print()` statements to output the following poem by Robert Frost (https://openstax.org/r/100robertfrost). Each `print()` statement should correspond to one line of output.

Tip: You don't need to write the entire program all at once. Try writing the first `print()` statement, and then click the Run button. Then write the next `print()` statement, and click the Run button again. Continue writing and testing the code incrementally until you finish the program.

```
I shall be telling this with a sigh
Somewhere ages and ages hence:
Two roads diverged in a wood, and I--
I took the one less traveled by,
And that has made all the difference.
```

Access multimedia content (https://openstax.org/books/introduction-python-programming/pages/1-2-inputoutput)

TRY IT

Name and likes

Write a program that asks the following two questions (example input in bold):

Shakira
   What do you like? **singing**

   What is your name? Shakira
   What do you like? singing

Output a blank line after reading the input. Then output the following message based on the input:

```
Shakira likes singing
```

```
Shakira likes singing
```

Access multimedia content (https://openstax.org/books/introduction-python-programming/pages/1-2-inputoutput)

1.3 Variables

Learning objectives

By the end of this section you should be able to

- Assign variables and print variables.
- Explain rules for naming variables.

Assignment statement

Variables allow programs to refer to values using names rather than memory locations. Ex: age refers to a person's age, and `birth` refers to a person's date of birth.

A statement can set a variable to a value using the **assignment operator** (=). Note that this is different from the equal sign of mathematics. Ex: `age = 6` or `birth = "May 15"`. The left side of the assignment statement is a variable, and the right side is the value the variable is assigned.

CHECKPOINT

Assigning and using variables

Access multimedia content (https://openstax.org/books/introduction-python-programming/pages/1-3-variables)

CONCEPTS IN PRACTICE

Assigning and using variables

1. Which line of code correctly retrieves the value of the variable, `city`, after the following assignment?

   ```
   city = "Chicago"
   ```

   a. `print("In which city do you live?")`
   b. `city = "London"`
   c. `print("The city where you live is", city)`

2. Which program stores and retrieves a variable correctly?
   a. `print("Total =", total)`
      `total = 6`
   b. `total = 6`
      `print("Total =", total)`
   c. `print("Total =", total)`

```
    total = input()
```

3. Which is the assignment operator?
   a. :
   b. ==
   c. =

4. Which is a valid assignment?
   a. `temperature = 98.5`
   b. `98.5 = temperature`
   c. `temperature - 23.2`

Variable naming rules

A variable name can consist of letters, digits, and underscores and be of any length. The name cannot start with a digit. Ex: `101class` is invalid. Also, letter case matters. Ex: `Total` is different from `total`. Python's style guide recommends writing variable names in **snake case**, which is all lowercase with underscores in between each word, such as `first_name` or `total_price`.

A name should be short and descriptive, so words are preferred over single characters in programs for readability. Ex: A variable named `count` indicates the variable's purpose better than a variable named `c`.

Python has reserved words, known as **keywords**, which have special functions and cannot be used as names for variables (or other objects).

False	await	else	import	pass
None	break	except	in	raise
True	class	finally	is	return
and	continue	for	lambda	try
as	def	from	nonlocal	while
assert	del	global	not	with
asynch	elif	if	or	yield

Table 1.2 Keywords

CONCEPTS IN PRACTICE

Valid variable names

5. Which can be used as a variable name?
   a. median
   b. class

c. `import`

6. Why is the name, `2nd_input`, not a valid variable name?
   a. contains an underscore
   b. starts with a digit
   c. is a keyword

7. Which would be a good name for a variable storing a zip code?
   a. `z`
   b. `var_2`
   c. `zip_code`

8. Given the variable name, `DogBreed`, which improvement conforms to Python's style guide?
   a. `dog_breed`
   b. `dogBreed`
   c. `dog-breed`

TRY IT

Final score

Write a Python computer program that:

- Creates a variable, `team1`, assigned with the value `"Liverpool"`.
- Creates a variable, `team2`, assigned with the value `"Chelsea"`.
- Creates a variable `score1`, assigned with the value `4`.
- Creates a variable, `score2`, assigned with the value `3`.
- Prints `team1`, `"versus"`, and `team2` as a single line of output.
- Prints `"Final score: "`, `score1`, `"to"`, `score2` as a single line of output.

Access multimedia content (https://openstax.org/books/introduction-python-programming/pages/1-3-variables)

1.4 String basics

Learning objectives

By the end of this section you should be able to

- Use the built-in `len()` function to get a string's length.
- Concatenate string literals and variables using the + operator.

Quote marks

A string is a sequence of characters enclosed by matching single (') or double (") quotes. Ex: `"Happy birthday!"` and `'21'` are both strings.

To include a single quote (') in a string, enclose the string with matching double quotes ("). Ex: `"Won't this work?"` To include a double quote ("), enclose the string with matching single quotes ('). Ex: `'They said "Try it!", so I did'`.

Valid string	Invalid string
`"17"` or `'17'`	`17`
`"seventeen"` or `'seventeen'`	`seventeen`
`"Where?"` or `'Where?'`	`"Where?'`
`"I hope you aren't sad."`	`'I hope you aren't sad.'`
`'The teacher said "Correct!" '`	`"The teacher said "Correct!" "`

Table 1.3 Rules for strings.

> **CONCEPTS IN PRACTICE**
>
> Valid and invalid strings
>
> 1. Which of the following is a string?
>   a. `Hello!`
>   b. `29`
>   c. `"7 days"`
>
> 2. Which line of code assigns a string to the variable email?
>   a. `"fred78@gmail.com"`
>   b. `"email = fred78@gmail.com"`
>   c. `email = "fred78@gmail.com"`
>
> 3. Which is a valid string?
>   a. `I know you'll answer correctly!`
>   b. `'I know you'll answer correctly!'`
>   c. `"I know you'll answer correctly!"`
>
> 4. Which is a valid string?
>   a. `You say "Please" to be polite`
>   b. `"You say "Please" to be polite"`
>   c. `'You say "Please" to be polite'`

len() function

A common operation on a string object is to get the string length, or the number of characters in the string. The **len()** function, when called on a string value, returns the string length.

> **CHECKPOINT**
>
> Using len() to get the length of a string
>
> Access multimedia content (https://openstax.org/books/introduction-python-programming/pages/

1-4-string-basics)

CONCEPTS IN PRACTICE

Applying len() function to string values

5. What is the return value for `len("Hi Ali")`?
   a. 2
   b. 5
   c. 6

6. What is the length of an empty string variable (`""`)?
   a. undefined
   b. 0
   c. 2

7. What is the output of the following code?

   ```
   number = "12"
   number_of_digits = len(number)
   print("Number", number, "has", number_of_digits, "digits.")
   ```

   a. `Number 12 has 12 digits.`
   b. `Number 12 has 2 digits.`
   c. `Number 12 has number_of_digits digits.`

Concatenation

Concatenation is an operation that combines two or more strings sequentially with the concatenation operator (+). Ex: `"A" + "part"` produces the string `"Apart"`.

CHECKPOINT

Concatenating multiple strings

Access multimedia content (https://openstax.org/books/introduction-python-programming/pages/1-4-string-basics)

CONCEPTS IN PRACTICE

String concatenation

8. Which produces the string `"10"`?
   a. `1 + 0`
   b. `"1 + 0"`
   c. `"1" + "0"`

9. Which produces the string `"Awake"`?

a. `"wake" + "A"`
b. `"A + wake"`
c. `"A" + "wake"`

10. A user enters `"red"` after the following line of code.

    `color = input("What is your favorite color?")`

    Which produces the output `"Your favorite color is red!"`?
    a. `print("Your favorite color is " + color + !)`
    b. `print("Your favorite color is " + "color" + "!")`
    c. `print("Your favorite color is " + color + "!")`

11. Which of the following assigns `"one-sided"` to the variable holiday?
    a. `holiday = "one" + "sided"`
    b. `holiday = one-sided`
    c. `holiday = "one-" + "sided"`

TRY IT

Name length

Write a program that asks the user to input their first and last name separately. Use the following prompts (example input in bold):

```
What is your first name? Alan
What is your last name? Turing
```

The program should then output the length of each name. Based on the example input above, the output would be:

```
Your first name is 4 letters long
Your last name is 6 letters long
```

Access multimedia content (https://openstax.org/books/introduction-python-programming/pages/1-4-string-basics)

TRY IT

Punctuation

Write a Python computer program that:

- Assigns the string `"Freda"` to a variable, name.

- Assigns the string "happy" to a variable, `feel`.
- Prints the string "Hi Freda!" with a single `print()` function using the variable name.
- Prints the string "I'm glad you feel happy." with a single `print()` function using the variable `feel`.

Access multimedia content (https://openstax.org/books/introduction-python-programming/pages/1-4-string-basics)

1.5 Number basics

Learning objectives

By the end of this section you should be able to

- Use arithmetic operators to perform calculations.
- Explain the precedence of arithmetic operators.

Numeric data types

Python supports two basic number formats, integer and floating-point. An integer represents a whole number, and a floating-point format represents a decimal number. The format a language uses to represent data is called a **data type**. In addition to integer and floating-point types, programming languages typically have a string type for representing text.

CHECKPOINT

Integer and floating-point

Access multimedia content (https://openstax.org/books/introduction-python-programming/pages/1-5-number-basics)

CONCEPTS IN PRACTICE

Integers, floats, and strings

Assume that x = 1, y = 2.0, and s = "32".

1. What is the output of the following code?

   ```
   print(x, type(x))
   ```

   a. 1 'int'.
   b. 1.0 <class 'float'>.
   c. 1 <class 'int'>.

2. What is the output of the following code?

   ```
   print(y, type(y))
   ```

   a. 2.0 <class 'int'>
   b. 2.0 <class 'float'>
   c. 2 <class 'int'>

3. What is the type of the following value?

   `"12.0"`

   a. `string`
   b. `int`
   c. `float`

Basic arithmetic

Arithmetic operators are used to perform mathematical operations like addition, subtraction, multiplication, and division.

Four basic arithmetic operators exist in Python:

1. Addition (+)
2. Subtraction (-)
3. Multiplication (*)
4. Division (/)

CHECKPOINT

Examples of arithmetic operators

Access multimedia content (https://openstax.org/books/introduction-python-programming/pages/1-5-number-basics)

CONCEPTS IN PRACTICE

Applying arithmetic operators

Assume that `x = 7`, `y = 20`, and `z = 2`.

4. Given the following lines of code, what is the output of the code?

   ```
   c = 0
   c = x - z
   c = c + 1
   print(c)
   ```

   a. 1
   b. 5
   c. 6

5. What is the value of a?

   `a = 3.5 - 1.5`

   a. `2`
   b. `2.0`

c. 2.5

6. What is the output of `print(x / z)`?
   a. 3
   b. 3.0
   c. 3.5

7. What is the output of `print(y / z)`?
   a. 0
   b. 10
   c. 10.0

8. What is the output of `print(z * 1.5)`?
   a. 2
   b. 3
   c. 3.0

Operator precedence

When a calculation has multiple operators, each operator is evaluated in order of **precedence**. Ex: `1 + 2 * 3` is 7 because multiplication takes precedence over addition. However, `(1 + 2) * 3` is 9 because parentheses take precedence over multiplication.

Operator	Description	Example	Result
`()`	Parentheses	`(1 + 2) * 3`	9
`**`	Exponentiation	`2 ** 4`	16
`+, -`	Positive, negative	`-math.pi`	-3.14159
`*, /`	Multiplication, division	`2 * 3`	6
`+, -`	Addition, subtraction	`1 + 2`	3

Table 1.4 Operator precedence from highest to lowest.

CHECKPOINT

Order of operations in an arithmetic expression

Access multimedia content (https://openstax.org/books/introduction-python-programming/pages/1-5-number-basics)

CONCEPTS IN PRACTICE

Multiple arithmetic operators

9. What is the value of `4 * 3 ** 2 + 1`?
   a. 37
   b. 40
   c. 145

10. Which part of `(1 + 3) ** 2 / 4` evaluates first?
    a. `4 ** 2`
    b. `1 + 3`
    c. `2 / 4`

11. What is the value of `-4 ** 2`?
    a. -16
    b. 16

12. How many operators are in the following statement?

    `result = -2 ** 3`

    a. 1
    b. 2
    c. 3

TRY IT

Values and types

Write a Python computer program that:

1. Defines an integer variable named `'int_a'` and assigns `'int_a'` with the value `10`.
2. Defines a floating-point variable named `'float_a'` and assigns `'float_a'` with the value `10.0`.
3. Defines a string variable named `'string_a'` and assigns `'string_a'` with the string value `"10"`.
4. Prints the value of each of the three variables along with their type.

Access multimedia content (https://openstax.org/books/introduction-python-programming/pages/1-5-number-basics)

TRY IT

Meters to feet

Write a Python computer program that:

1. Assigns the integer value `10` to a variable, `meters`.
2. Assigns the floating-point value `3.28` to a variable, `meter2feet`.
3. Calculates 10 meters in feet by multiplying `meter` by `meter2feet`. Store the result in a variable, `feet`.

4. Prints the content of variable feet in the output.

Access multimedia content (https://openstax.org/books/introduction-python-programming/pages/1-5-number-basics)

1.6 Error messages

Learning objectives

By the end of this section you should be able to

- Identify the error type and line number in error messages.
- Correct syntax errors, name errors, and indentation errors.

How to read errors

A natural part of programming is making mistakes. Even experienced programmers make mistakes when writing code. Errors may result when mistakes are made when writing code. The computer requires very specific instructions telling the computer what to do. If the instructions are not clear, then the computer does not know what to do and gives back an error.

When an error occurs, Python displays a message with the following information:

1. The line number of the error.
2. The type of error (Ex: SyntaxError).
3. Additional details about the error.

Ex: Typing `print "Hello!"` without parentheses is a syntax error. In Python, parentheses are required to use `print`. When attempting to run `print "Hello!"`, Python displays the following error:

```
Traceback (most recent call last):
  File "/home/student/Desktop/example.py", line 1
    print "Hello"
                ^
SyntaxError: Missing parentheses in call to 'print'. Did you mean print("Hello")?
```

The caret character (^) shows where Python found the error. Sometimes the error may be located one or two lines before where the caret symbol is shown because Python may not have discovered the error until then. **Traceback** is a Python report of the location and type of error. The word traceback suggests a programmer trace back in the code to find the error if the error is not seen right away.

Learning to read error messages carefully is an important skill. The amount of technical jargon can be overwhelming at first. But this information can be very helpful.

CHECKPOINT

Incorrect variable name

Access multimedia content (https://openstax.org/books/introduction-python-programming/pages/1-6-error-messages)

> **CONCEPTS IN PRACTICE**
>
> Parts of an error
>
> Given the following error message:
>
> ```
> Traceback (most recent call last):
>   File "/home/student/Desktop/example.py", line 2
>     print "test"
>           ^
> SyntaxError: Missing parentheses in call to 'print'. Did you mean print("test")?
> ```
>
> 1. What is the filename of the program?
>   a. Desktop
>   b. example.py
>   c. test
>
> 2. On which line was the error found?
>   a. 1
>   b. 2
>   c. 3
>
> 3. What type of error was found?
>   a. missing parentheses
>   b. SyntaxError
>   c. traceback

Common types of errors

Different types of errors may occur when running Python programs. When an error occurs, knowing the type of error gives insight about how to correct the error. The following table shows examples of mistakes that anyone could make when programming.

Mistake	Error message	Explanation
`print("Have a nice day!"`	`SyntaxError: unexpected EOF while parsing`	The closing parenthesis is missing. Python is surprised to reach the end of file (EOF) before this line is complete.
`word = input("Type a word: )`	`SyntaxError: EOL while scanning string literal`	The closing quote marks are missing. As a result, the string does not terminate before the end of line (EOL).
`print("You typed:", wird)`	`NameError: name 'wird' is not defined`	The spelling of word is incorrect. The programmer accidentally typed the wrong key.

Table 1.5 Simple mistakes.

Mistake	Error message	Explanation
`prints("You typed:", word)`	`NameError: name 'prints' is not defined`	The spelling of `print` is incorrect. The programmer accidentally typed an extra letter.
`  print("Hello")`	`IndentationError: unexpected indent`	The programmer accidentally typed a space at the start of the line.
`    print("Goodbye")`	`IndentationError: unexpected indent`	The programmer accidentally pressed the Tab key at the start of the line.

Table 1.5 Simple mistakes.

CONCEPTS IN PRACTICE

Types of errors

For each program below, what type of error will occur?

4. ```
   print("Breakfast options:")
    print("A. Cereal")
    print("B. Eggs")
    print("C. Yogurt")
   choice = input("What would you like? ")
   ```

   a. IndentationError
   b. NameError
   c. SyntaxError

5. ```
   birth = input("Enter your birth date: )
   print("Happy birthday on ", birth)
   ```

   a. IndentationError
   b. NameError
   c. SyntaxError

6. ```
   print("Breakfast options:")
   print(" A. Cereal")
   print(" B. Eggs")
   print(" C. Yogurt")
   choice = intput("What would you like? ")
   ```

   a. IndentationError
   ```

b. `NameError`
  c. `SyntaxError`

TRY IT

Three errors

The following program has three errors.

- Run the program to find the first error, and correct the corresponding line of code.
- Then run the program again to find and correct the second error.
- Keep running and correcting the program until no errors are found.

Access multimedia content (https://openstax.org/books/introduction-python-programming/pages/1-6-error-messages)

TRY IT

Wrong symbols

This code is based on an earlier example, but the code contains several mistakes.

- One line is missing required punctuation, and another line uses incorrect symbols.
- Run the program to find the first error, and correct the corresponding line of code.
- Keep running and correcting the program until no errors are found.

Access multimedia content (https://openstax.org/books/introduction-python-programming/pages/1-6-error-messages)

1.7 Comments

Learning objectives

By the end of this section you should be able to

- Write concise, meaningful comments that explain intended functionality of the code.
- Write a docstring (more verbose comment) that describes the program functionality.

The hash character

Comments are short phrases that explain what the code is doing. Ex: Lines 1, 8, and 10 in the following program contain comments. Each comment begins with a hash character (`#`). All text from the hash character to the end of the line is ignored when running the program. In contrast, hash characters inside of strings are treated as regular text. Ex: The string `"Item #1: "` does not contain a comment.

When writing comments:

- The `#` character should be followed by a single space. Ex: `# End of menu` is easier to read than `#End of menu`.
- Comments should explain the purpose of the code, not just repeat the code itself. Ex: `# Get the user's preferences` is more descriptive than `# Input item1 and item2`.

EXAMPLE 1.2

Program with three comments

```
1   # Display the menu options
2   print("Lunch Menu")
3   print("----------")
4   print("Burrito")
5   print("Enchilada")
6   print("Taco")
7   print("Salad")
8   print()  # End of menu
9
10  # Get the user's preferences
11  item1 = input("Item #1: ")
12  item2 = input("Item #2: ")
```

CONCEPTS IN PRACTICE

Simple comments

1. The main purpose of writing comments is to _____.
   a. avoid writing syntax errors
   b. explain what the code does
   c. make the code run faster

2. Which symbol is used for comments in Python?
   a. #
   b. /*
   c. //

3. Which comment is formatted correctly?
   a. 0 spaces:
      `#Get the user input`
   b. 1 space:
      `# Get the user input`
   c. 2 spaces:
      `#  Get the user input`

Code quality

The example program above had two parts: (1) display the menu options, and (2) get the user's preferences. Together, the blank lines and comments show the overall structure of the program.

Programmers spend more time reading code than writing code. Therefore, making code easier for others to read and understand is important. Two ways to improve code quality include:

- Separate each part (lines that have a similar purpose) with a blank line.

- Write a comment before each part. Not every line needs a comment.

CHECKPOINT

Comments in a program

Access multimedia content (https://openstax.org/books/introduction-python-programming/pages/1-7-comments)

CONCEPTS IN PRACTICE

Code quality

4. Which comment is most useful for the following code?

   ```
   print("You said:", adj1 + " " + noun1)
   ```

   a. `# Append adj1 and noun1`
   b. `# Print out a bunch of stuff`
   c. `# Show the resulting phrase`

5. Where should a blank line be inserted?

   ```
   1  name = input("Whose birthday is today? ")
   2  print("Happy birthday to", name)
   3  print("Everyone cheer for", name)
   ```

   a. After line 1
   b. After line 2
   c. After line 3

6. To temporarily prevent a line from being run, one might . . .
   a. introduce a syntax error in the line.
   b. remove the line from the program.
   c. insert a # at the beginning of the line.

Documentation

Python programs may optionally begin with a string known as a docstring. A **docstring** is documentation written for others who will use the program but not necessarily read the source code. Most of the official documentation at docs.python.org (https://openstax.org/r/100docstrings) is generated from docstrings.

Documentation can be long, so docstrings are generally written as multi-line strings (`"""`). Common elements of a docstring include a one-line summary, a blank line, and a longer description.

CHECKPOINT

Vacations docstring

Access multimedia content (https://openstax.org/books/introduction-python-programming/pages/1-7-comments)

CONCEPTS IN PRACTICE

Documentation

7. The main purpose of writing docstrings is to . . .
   a. summarize the program's purpose or usage.
   b. explain how each part of the code works.
   c. maintain a list of ideas for new features.

8. Which of the following is NOT a docstring?
   a. `"""Vacations Madlib."""`
   b. `"""Vacations Madlib. This program asks the user for two adjectives and two nouns, which are then used to print a funny story about a vacation. """`
   c. ```
      # Vacations Madlib.
      #
      # This program asks the user for two adjectives
      # and two nouns, which are then used to print
      # a funny story about a vacation.
      ```

9. Which docstring is most useful for this program?
   a. `"""Vacations Madlib."""`
   b. `"""Vacations Madlib. This program asks the user for two adjectives and two nouns, which are then used to print a funny story about a vacation. """`
   c. `"""Vacations Madlib. This program asks the user for two adjectives and two nouns, which are then used to print a funny story about a vacation. The code uses four variables to store the user input: two for the adjectives, and two for the nouns. The output is displayed on seven lines, beginning with a blank line after the input. """`

## TRY IT

### Whose birthday

Add two comments to the following program: one for the input, and one for the output. Separate the input and output with a blank line. Then, compare your comments with the sample solution, and ask yourself the following questions:

- Are your comments longer or shorter? Why?
- Is the formatting of your comments correct?

Access multimedia content (https://openstax.org/books/introduction-python-programming/pages/1-7-comments)

## TRY IT

### Gravity calculation

Write a docstring for the following program. The first line of the docstring should explain, in one short
      ```

sentence, what the program is. The second line of the docstring should be blank. The third and subsequent lines should include a longer explanation of what the program does. At the end of the docstring, add a line that says "Author: " followed by your name.

Access multimedia content (https://openstax.org/books/introduction-python-programming/pages/1-7-comments)

1.8 Why Python?

Learning objectives

By the end of this section you should be able to

- Name two historical facts about how Python was first created.
- Describe two ways Python is considered a popular language.

Historical background

Python has an interesting history. In 1982, Guido van Rossum (https://openstax.org/r/100vanRossum), the creator of Python, started working at CWI (https://openstax.org/r/100CWI), a Dutch national research institute. He joined a team that was designing a new programming language, named ABC, for teaching and prototyping. ABC's simplicity was ideal for beginners, but the language lacked features required to write advanced programs.

Several years later, van Rossum joined a different team at CWI working on an operating system. The team needed an easier way to write programs for monitoring computers and analyzing data. Languages common in the 1980's were (and still are) difficult to use for these kinds of programs. van Rossum envisioned a new language that would have a simple syntax, like ABC, but also provide advanced features that professionals would need.

At first, van Rossum started working on this new language as a hobby during his free time. He named the language Python because he was a fan of the British comedy group Monty Python (https://openstax.org/r/100MontyPython). Over the next year, he and his colleagues successfully used Python many times for real work. van Rossum eventually decided to share Python with the broader programming community online. He freely shared Python's entire source code so that anyone could write and run Python programs.

Python's first release, known as Version 0.9.0, appeared in 1991, about six years after C++ and four years before Java. van Rossum's decisions to make the language simple yet advanced, suitable for everyday tasks, and freely available online contributed to Python's long-term success.

CHECKPOINT

Key decisions

Access multimedia content (https://openstax.org/books/introduction-python-programming/pages/1-8-why-python)

CONCEPTS IN PRACTICE

Python history

1. The Python programming language was named after a ____.

a. British comedy group
   b. Dutch programmer
   c. non-venomous snake

2. Which programming language came first?
   a. Java
   b. Python

3. Which sentence best describes the beginning of Python?
   a. CWI hired Guido van Rossum to design a new programming language to compete with C++.
   b. Python started out as a hobby and became open source after several years of development.
   c. van Rossum posted Python's source code online after working on the language for one year.

EXPLORING FURTHER

For more details about Python's history, see "A brief history of Python (https://openstax.org/r/100history)" by Vasilisa Sheromova, and "History and Philosophy of Python (https://openstax.org/r/100sheromova)" by Bernd Klein.

Popularity of Python

Over the years, Python has become a nonprofit organization with a thriving community. Millions of programmers around the world use Python for all kinds of interesting projects. Hundreds of thousands of Python libraries have been released as open source software. The Python community is very active and supportive online, answering questions and sharing code.

One way to see Python's popularity is the TIOBE index (https://openstax.org/r/100TIOBE). TIOBE is a Dutch company that provides products and services for measuring software code quality. Since 2001, TIOBE has tracked the popularity of programming languages and posted the results online. Figure 1.2 shows the TIOBE index over time for five of the most popular languages.

The TIOBE index is based on the number of search engine results for each language. The percentage refers to how many results belong to that language. Python has been among the top 10 languages every year since 2004. In October 2021, Python became the #1 language on the TIOBE index. No other language but C and Java had been #1 for the previous 20 years.

Another way to see Python's popularity is to analyze how frequently Python is discussed online. Stack Overflow (https://openstax.org/r/100overflow) is a question-and-answer website for programmers. Figure 1.3 shows the number of questions asked each month that were tagged with Python, JavaScript, and so forth. In recent years, Python has become the most asked about language in programming forums.

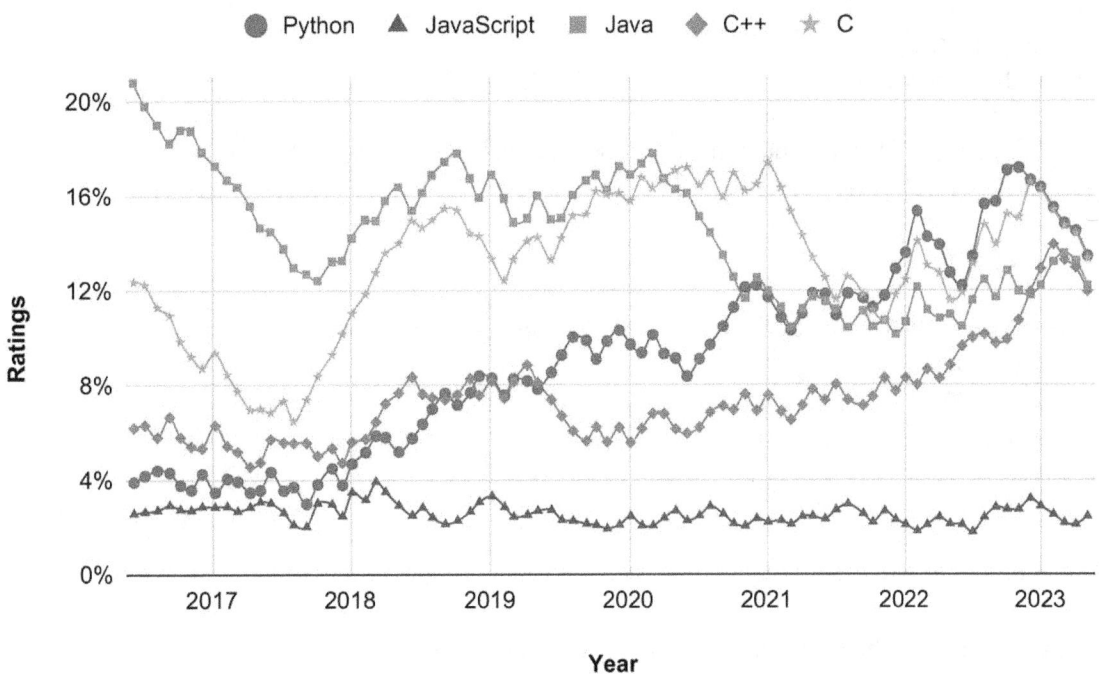

Figure 1.2 TIOBE programming community index. Source: www.tiobe.com (https://www.tiobe.com/tiobe-index/)

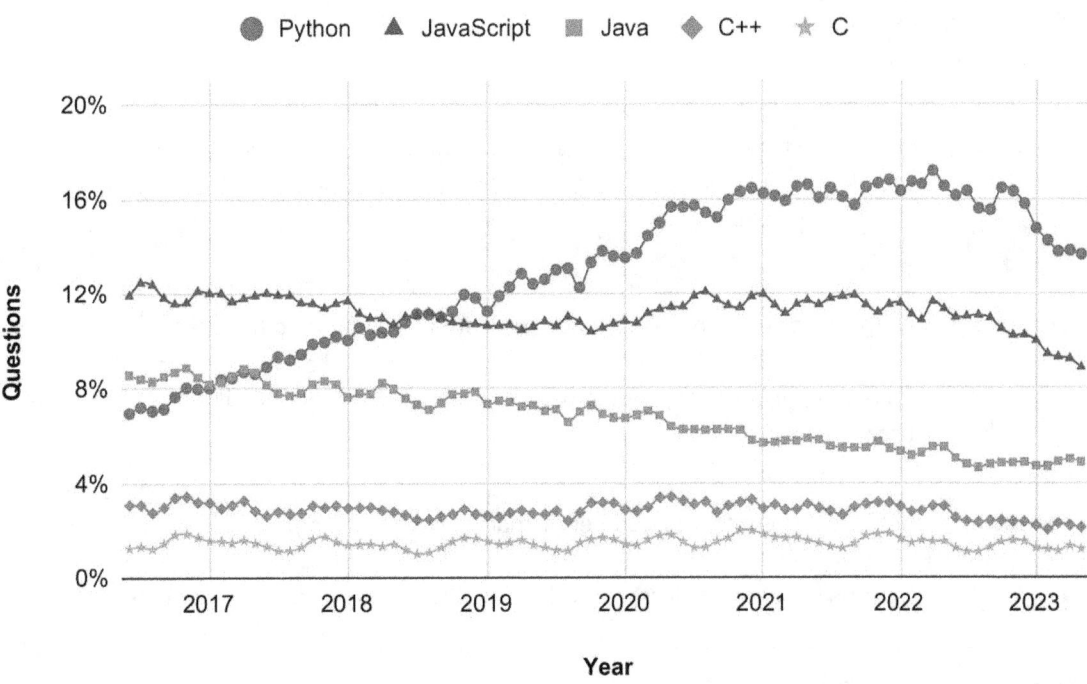

Figure 1.3 Stack Overflow questions per month. Source: data.stackexchange.com (https://data.stackexchange.com/)

CONCEPTS IN PRACTICE

Python popularity

4. According to the TIOBE Index, which two languages were most popular from 2001 to 2021?

a. C and C++
   b. Java and C
   c. Python and JavaScript

5. In what year did Python become the most asked about language on Stack Overflow?
   a. 2018
   b. 2019
   c. 2020

6. How long has TIOBE been tracking programming language popularity?
   a. since 1991
   b. since 2001
   c. since 2015

1.9 Chapter summary

This chapter introduced the basics of programming in Python, including:

- `print()` and `input()`.
- Variables and assignment.
- Strings, integers, and floats.
- Arithmetic, concatenation.
- Common error messages.
- Comments and docstrings.

At this point, you should be able to write programs that ask for input, perform simple calculations, and output the results. The programming practice below ties together most topics presented in the chapter.

Function	Description
`print(values)`	Outputs one or more values, each separated by a space, to the user.
`input(prompt)`	If present, `prompt` is output to the user. The function then reads a line of input from the user.
`len(string)`	Returns the length (the number of characters) of a string.
`type(value)`	Returns the type (or class) of a value. Ex: `type(123)` is `<class 'int'>`.
Operator	**Description**
`=` (Assignment)	Assigns (or updates) the value of a variable. In Python, variables begin to exist when assigned for the first time.

Table 1.6 Chapter 1 reference.

Function	Description
+ (Concatenation)	Appends the contents of two strings, resulting in a new string.
+ (Addition)	Adds the values of two numbers.
- (Subtraction)	Subtracts the value of one number from another.
* (Multiplication)	Multiplies the values of two numbers.
/ (Division)	Divides the value of one number by another.
** (Exponentiation)	Raises a number to a power. Ex: 3**2 is three squared.
Syntax	**Description**
# (Comment)	All text is ignored from the # symbol to the end of the line.
' or " (String)	Strings may be written using either kind of quote. Ex: 'A' and "A" represent the same string. By convention, this book uses double quotes (") for most strings.
""" """ (Docstring)	Used for documentation, often in multi-line strings, to summarize a program's purpose or usage.

Table 1.6 Chapter 1 reference.

TRY IT

Fun facts

Write a program that assigns a variable named number to any integer of your choice. Ex: number = 74. Then, use this variable to calculate and output the following results:

```
74 squared is 5476
74 cubed is 405224
One tenth of 74 is 7.4
```

```
74 plus 123 is 197
74 minus 456 is -382
```

Run the program multiple times, using a different integer each time. Your output should be mathematically correct for any integer that you choose.

The point of this exercise is to perform basic arithmetic within a print statement. Do not use any other variables besides number. Your program should have only one assignment statement (at the beginning).

Access multimedia content (https://openstax.org/books/introduction-python-programming/pages/1-9-chapter-summary)

TRY IT

Mad lib

A mad lib is a word game in which one person asks others for words to substitute into a pre-written story. The story is then read aloud with the goal of making people laugh.

This exercise is based the Vacations Mad Lib (https://openstax.org/r/100madlibs) available on the Printables (https://openstax.org/r/100printable) section of MadLibs.com. Write a program that asks the user to input two adjectives and two nouns (user input in bold):

tranquil
```
    Adjective: scandalous
    Noun: pancake
    Noun: field

    Adjective: tranquil
    Adjective: scandalous
    Noun: pancake
    Noun: field
```

Use `input()` to display each prompt exactly as shown. The user's input should be on the same line as the prompt. Each colon must be followed by exactly one space. After reading the input, the program should output the following three lines:

tranquil `place with your` **scandalous** `family.`
```
    Usually you go to some place that is near a/an pancake or up on a/an field.

    A vacation is when you take a trip to some tranquil place with your scandalous family.
    Usually you go to some place that is near a/an pancake or up on a/an field.
```

Notice that the first line should be completely blank. Replace the bold words (from the above example) with the actual words input by the user.

Your final program should have four input statements, three print statements, and at least two comments.

For completeness, write an appropriate docstring at the top of the program.

Access multimedia content (https://openstax.org/books/introduction-python-programming/pages/1-9-chapter-summary)

2 Expressions

Figure 2.1 credit: modification of work "Grace Hopper at Univac I console", courtesy of the Computer History Museum

Chapter Outline

2.1 The Python shell
2.2 Type conversion
2.3 Mixed data types
2.4 Floating-point errors
2.5 Dividing integers
2.6 The math module
2.7 Formatting code
2.8 Python careers
2.9 Chapter summary

 Introduction

A computer program is a sequence of statements that run one after the other. In Python, many statements consist of one or more expressions. An **expression** represents a single value to be computed. Ex: The expression 3*x - 5 evaluates to 7 when x is 4. Learning to recognize expressions opens the door for programming all kinds of interesting calculations.

Expressions are often a combination of literals, variables, and operators. In the previous example, 3 and 5 are literals, x is a variable, and * and - are operators. Expressions can be arbitrarily long, consisting of many calculations. Expressions can also be as short as one value. Ex: In the assignment statement x = 5, the literal 5 is an expression.

The Statements chapter introduced simple expressions like 1 * 2 and "Hi " + "there". This chapter explores other kinds of expressions for working with numbers and strings. The first section shows a great way to experiment with expressions using a Python shell. Later sections present more details about integers and floating-point numbers, explain how to import and use the math module, and show how to make long lines of code easier to read.

2.1 The Python shell

Learning objectives

By the end of this section you should be able to
- Use a Python shell to run statements and expressions interactively.
- Explain the function of the up and down arrow keyboard shortcuts.

The interpreter

Python is a high-level language, meaning that the source code is intended for humans to understand. Computers, on the other hand, understand only low-level machine code made up of 1's and 0's. Programs written in high-level languages must be translated into machine code to run. This translation process can happen all at once, or a little at a time, depending on the language.

Python is an interpreted language: the source code is translated one line at a time while the program is running. The Python **interpreter** translates source code into machine code and runs the resulting program. If and when an error occurs, the interpreter stops translating the source code and displays an error message.

Most development environments include a Python shell for experimenting with code interactively. A **shell**, also called a console or terminal, is a program that allows direct interaction with an interpreter. The interpreter usually runs an entire program all at once. But the interpreter can run one line of code at a time within a Python shell.

CHECKPOINT

Running a Python shell

Access multimedia content (https://openstax.org/books/introduction-python-programming/pages/2-1-the-python-shell)

CONCEPTS IN PRACTICE

Using a Python shell

1. Python is a ____ language.
    a. high-level
    b. low-level

2. Which of the following is the most basic line of code the interpreter can run?
    a. `print(1 + 1)`
    b. `1 + 1`
    c. `1`

3. What result does the shell display after running the line `name = input()`?
    a. the name that was input
    b. nothing (except for >>>)

The arrow keys

A Python shell is convenient for exploring and troubleshooting code. The user can try something, look at the results, and then try something else. When an error occurs, an error message is displayed, but the program keeps running. That way, the user can edit the previous line and correct the error interactively.

The acronym REPL (pronounced "rep ul") is often used when referring to a shell. **REPL** stands for "read-eval-print loop," which describes the repetitive nature of a shell:

1. **R**ead/input some code
2. **E**valuate/run the code
3. **P**rint any results
4. **L**oop back to step 1

Most shells maintain a history of every line of code the user types. Pressing the up or down arrow key on the keyboard displays the history. The **up arrow** displays the previous line; the **down arrow** displays the next line. That way, the user can repeat a line without having to type the line again.

CHECKPOINT

Correcting a typo

Access multimedia content (https://openstax.org/books/introduction-python-programming/pages/2-1-the-python-shell)

CONCEPTS IN PRACTICE

Using the arrow keys

4. Which arrow keys were needed to edit the typo?
    a. only the up arrow key
    b. the up and down arrows
    c. the up and left arrows

5. What keys would the user press to go back two lines?
    a. press the up arrow twice
    b. press the down arrow twice
    c. press the left arrow twice

TRY IT

Exploring the shell

Running code interactively is a great way to learn how Python works. Open a Python shell on your computer, or use the one at python.org/shell (https://openstax.org/r/100pythonshell). Then enter any Python code, one line at a time, to see the result. Here are a few expressions to try:

- `x = 5`
- `3*x - 5`
- `3 * (x-5)`
- `x`
- `type(1)`
- `type('1')`

- `str(1)`
- `int('1')`
- `abs(-5)`
- `abs(5)`
- `len("Yo")`
- `len("HoHo")`
- `round(9.49)`
- `round(9.50)`

Note: These functions (`type`, `str`, `int`, `len`, and `round`) will be explored in more detail later in the chapter. You can read more about the built-in functions (https://openstax.org/r/100builtin) in the Python documentation.

TRY IT

Correcting mistakes

Open a Python shell on your computer, or use the one at python.org/shell (https://openstax.org/r/100pythonshell). Run the following two statements in the shell:

- `x = 123`
- `y = 456`

Making mistakes is common while typing in a shell. The following lines include typos and other errors. For each line: (1) run the line in a shell to see the result, (2) press the up arrow to repeat the line, and (3) edit the line to get the correct result.

- `print("Easy as", X)`
- `print("y divided by 2 is", y / 0)`
- `name = intput("What is your name? ")`
- `print(name, "is", int(name), "letters long.")`
- `print("That's all folks!)`

The expected output, after correcting typos, should look like:

- `Easy as 123`
- `y divided by 2 is 228.0`
- `(no error/output)`
- `Stacie is 6 letters long.`
- `That's all folks!`

2.2 Type conversion

Learning objectives

By the end of this section you should be able to
- Explain how the interpreter uses implicit type conversion.
- Use explicit type conversion with `int()`, `float()`, and `str()`.

Implicit type conversion

Common operations update a variable such that the variable's data type needs to be changed. Ex: A GPS first assigns distance with 250, an integer. After a wrong turn, the GPS assigns distance with 252.5, a float. The Python interpreter uses **implicit type conversion** to automatically convert one data type to another. Once distance is assigned with 252.5, the interpreter will convert distance from an integer to a float without the programmer needing to specify the conversion.

CHECKPOINT

Example: Book ratings

Access multimedia content (https://openstax.org/books/introduction-python-programming/pages/2-2-type-conversion)

CONCEPTS IN PRACTICE

Implicit type conversion in practice

Consider the example above.

1. What is book_rating's data type on line 7?
    a. float
    b. integer

2. What would book_rating's data type be if update = 1.0 instead of 0.5?
    a. float
    b. integer

3. What is the data type of x after the following code executes?

   ```
   x = 42.0
   x = x * 1
   ```

    a. float
    b. integer

Explicit type conversion

A programmer often needs to change data types to perform an operation. Ex: A program should read in two values using input() and sum the values. Remember input() reads in values as strings. A programmer can use **explicit type conversion** to convert one data type to another.

- **int()** converts a data type to an integer. Any fractional part is removed. Ex: int(5.9) produces 5.
- **float()** converts a data type to a float. Ex: float(2) produces 2.0.
- **str()** converts a data type to a string. Ex: str(3.14) produces "3.14".

CHECKPOINT

Example: Ordering pizza

Access multimedia content (https://openstax.org/books/introduction-python-programming/pages/2-2-type-conversion)

CONCEPTS IN PRACTICE

Example: Ordering pizza

Consider the example above.

4. Which function converts the input number of slices to a data type that can be used in the calculation?
   a. `float()`
   b. `input()`
   c. `int()`

5. How could line 3 be changed to improve the program overall?
   a. Use `float()` instead of `int()`.
   b. Add `1` to the result of `int()`.
   c. Add `str()` around `int()`.

CONCEPTS IN PRACTICE

Using int(), float(), and str()

Given x = `4.5` and y = `int(x)`, what is the value of each expression?

6. y
   a. 4
   b. 5

7. `str(x)`
   a. 4.5
   b. "4.5"

8. `float(y)`
   a. 4.0
   b. 4.5

TRY IT

Grade average

The following program computes the average of three predefined exam grades and prints the average twice. Improve the program to read the three grades from input and print the average first as a float, and then as an integer, using explicit type conversion. Ignore any differences that occur due to rounding.

Access multimedia content (https://openstax.org/books/introduction-python-programming/pages/2-2-type-conversion)

TRY IT

Cups of water

The following program should read in the ounces of water the user drank today and compute the number of cups drank and the number of cups left to drink based on a daily goal. Assume a cup contains 8 ounces. Fix the code to calculate `cups_drank` and `cups_left` and match the following:

- `ounces` is an integer representing the ounces the user drank.
- `cups_drank` is a float representing the number of cups of water drank.
- `cups_left` is an integer representing the number of cups of water left to drink (rounded down) out of the daily goal of 8 cups.

Access multimedia content (https://openstax.org/books/introduction-python-programming/pages/2-2-type-conversion)

TRY IT

Product as float

The following program reads two integers in as strings. Calculate the product of the two integers, and print the result as a float.

Access multimedia content (https://openstax.org/books/introduction-python-programming/pages/2-2-type-conversion)

2.3 Mixed data types

Learning objectives

By the end of this section you should be able to

- Identify the data types produced by operations with integers, floats, and strings.
- Use operators and type conversions to combine integers, floats, and strings.

Combining integers and floats

Programmers often need to combine numbers of different data types. Ex: A program computes the total for an online shopping order:

```
quantity = int(input())
price = float(input())
total = quantity * price
print(total)
```

`quantity` is an integer, and `price` is a float. So what is the data type of `total`? For input 3 and 5.0, total is a float, and the program prints `15.0`.

Combining an integer and a float produces a float. A float is by default printed with at least one figure after the decimal point and has as many figures as needed to represent the value. Note: Division using the / operator always produces a float.

CHECKPOINT

Operations combining integers and floats

Access multimedia content (https://openstax.org/books/introduction-python-programming/pages/2-3-mixed-data-types)

CONCEPTS IN PRACTICE

Operations combining integers and floats

1. `8 * 0.25`
    a. `2`
    b. `2.0`

2. `2 * 9`
    a. `18`
    b. `18.0`

3. `20 / 2`
    a. `10`
    b. `10.0`

4. `7 / 2`
    a. `3.0`
    b. `3.5`

5. `12.0 / 4`
    a. `3`
    b. `3.0`

6. `8 - 1.0`
    a. `7.0`
    b. `7`

7. `5 - 0.25`
    a. `4.5`
    b. `4.75`

Combining numeric types and strings

Easy type conversion in Python can lead a programmer to assume that any data type can be combined with another. Ex: Noor's program reads in a number from input and uses the number in a calculation. This results in an error in the program because the `input()` function by default stores the number as a string. Strings and numeric data types are incompatible for addition, subtraction, and division. One of the operands needs to be explicitly converted depending on the goal of arithmetic or string concatenation.

The * operator also serves as the repetition operator, which accepts a string operand and an integer operand and repeats the string. Ex: `"banjo" * 3` produces `"banjobanjobanjo"`.

CHECKPOINT

Adding a string and an integer

Access multimedia content (https://openstax.org/books/introduction-python-programming/pages/2-3-mixed-data-types)

CONCEPTS IN PRACTICE

Operations combining numeric types and strings

8. `int('34') + 56`
   a. `'3456'`
   b. `90`
   c. `'90'`

9. `str(12) + ' red roses'`
   a. `'12 red roses'`
   b. `'12'`
   c. `Error`

10. `'50' * 3`
    a. `'150'`
    b. `150`
    c. `'505050'`

11. `str(5.2) + 7`
    a. `12.2`
    b. `'12.2'`
    c. `Error`

12. `80.0 + int('100')`
    a. `180`
    b. `180.0`
    c. `'180'`

13. `str(3.14) + '159'`
    a. `162.14`
    b. `'3.14159'`
    c. `Error`

14. `2.0 * 'this'`

a. `'this'`
b. `'thisthis'`
c. `Error`

TRY IT

After the point

Write a program that reads in a string of digits that represents the digits after the decimal point of a number, num. Concatenate the input string together with `'.'` and num, and print the result. Ex: If input is 345, the program will print `2.345`.

Access multimedia content (https://openstax.org/books/introduction-python-programming/pages/2-3-mixed-data-types)

TRY IT

Print n times

Write a program that reads in two strings, `str1` and `str2`, and an integer, `count`. Concatenate the two strings with a space in between and a newline (`"\n"`) at the end. Print the resulting string `count` times.

Access multimedia content (https://openstax.org/books/introduction-python-programming/pages/2-3-mixed-data-types)

2.4 Floating-point errors

Learning objectives

By the end of this section you should be able to

- Explain numerical inaccuracies related to floating-point representation.
- Use the `round()` function to mitigate floating-point errors in output.

Floating-point errors

Computers store information using 0's and 1's. All information must be converted to a string of 0's and 1's. Ex: 5 is converted to 101. Since only two values, 0 or 1, are allowed the format is called binary.

Floating-point values are stored as binary by Python. The conversion of a floating point number to the underlying binary results in specific types of floating-point errors.

A **round-off error** occurs when floating-point values are stored erroneously as an approximation. The difference between an approximation of a value used in computation and the correct (true) value is called a round-off error.

Ex: Storing the float $(0.1)_{10}$ results in binary values that actually produce $(0.1000000000000000055511151231257827021181583404541015625)_{10}$ when converted back, which is not exactly equal to $(0.1)_{10}$.

| ```
# Print floats with 30 decimal places
print(f'{0.1:.30f}') # prints 0.1
print(f'{0.2:.30f}') # prints 0.2
print(f'{0.4:.30f}') # prints 0.4
``` | 0.100000000000000005551115123126<br>0.200000000000000011102230246252<br>0.400000000000000022204460492503 |

Table 2.1 Round-off error. (The example above shows a formatted string or f-string, which are introduced in the Objects chapter.)

An **overflow error** occurs when a value is too large to be stored. The maximum and minimum floating-point values that can be represented are 1.8×10^{308} and -1.8×10^{308}, respectively. Attempting to store a floating-point value outside the range $(-1.8 \times 10^{308}, 1.8 \times 10^{308})$ leads to an overflow error.

Below, 3.0^{256} and 3.0^{512} can be represented, but 3.0^{1024} is too large and causes an overflow error.

| ```
print('3.0 to the power of 256 =',
3.0**256)
print('3.0 to the power of 512 = ',
3.0**512)
print('3.0 to the power of 1024 = ',
3.0**1024)
``` | ```
3.0 to the power of 256 =
1.3900845237714473e+122
3.0 to the power of 512 =
1.9323349832288915e+244
3.0 to the power of 1024 =
Traceback (most recent call last):
  File "<stdin>", line 3, in <module>
    print('3.0 to the power of 1024 = ',
3.0**1024)
OverflowError: (34, 'Numerical result out
of range')
``` |

Table 2.2 Overflow error.

> **CONCEPTS IN PRACTICE**
>
> Floating-point errors
>
> For each situation, which error occurs?
>
> 1. The statement `result = 2.0 * (10.0 ** 500)` assigns the variable result with too large of a value.
>   a. round-off
>   b. overflow
>
> 2. `0.123456789012345678901234567890 * 0.1` produces `0.01234567890123456843087801360`.
>   a. round-off
>   b. overflow
```

Floating point round() function

Python's **round()** function is used to round a floating-point number to a given number of decimal places. The function requires two arguments. The first argument is the number to be rounded. The second argument decides the number of decimal places to which the number is rounded. If the second argument is not provided, the number will be rounded to the closest integer. The `round()` function can be used to mitigate floating-point errors.

Ex:
- `round(2.451, 2) = 2.45`
- `round(2.451) = 2`

CHECKPOINT

Examples of round() function

Access multimedia content (https://openstax.org/books/introduction-python-programming/pages/2-4-floating-point-errors)

CONCEPTS IN PRACTICE

Examples of round() function

3. What is the output of `round(6.6)`?
   a. 6
   b. 6.6
   c. 7

4. What is the output of `round(3.5, 2)`?
   a. 3
   b. 3.5
   c. 3.50

5. What is the output of `round(12)`?
   a. 12.0
   b. 12
   c. 12.00

6. What is the output of `round(0.1, 1)`?
   a. 0.1
   b. 0.10
   c. 0.1000000000000000055511151231257827021181583404541015625

TRY IT

Inaccurate tips

The following code calculates the tip amount, given a bill amount and the tip ratio. Experiment with the following bill amounts and tip ratios and see if any inaccuracies may result in calculating the tip amount.

- bill amount: 22.70 and 33.33
- tip ratio: 0.15, 0.18, and 0.20

Access multimedia content (https://openstax.org/books/introduction-python-programming/pages/2-4-floating-point-errors)

TRY IT

Area of a triangle

Complete the following steps to calculate a triangle's area, and print the result of each step. The area of a triangle is $\frac{bh}{2}$, where b is the base and h is the height.

1. Calculate the area of a triangle with base = 7 and height = 3.5.
2. Round the triangle's area to one decimal place.
3. Round the triangle's area to the nearest integer value.

Access multimedia content (https://openstax.org/books/introduction-python-programming/pages/2-4-floating-point-errors)

2.5 Dividing integers

Learning objectives

By the end of this section you should be able to

- Evaluate expressions that involve floor division and modulo.
- Use the modulo operator to convert between units of measure.

Division and modulo

Python provides two ways to divide numbers:

- **True division** (/) converts numbers to floats before dividing. Ex: `7 / 4` becomes `7.0 / 4.0`, resulting in `1.75`.
- **Floor division** (//) computes the quotient, or the number of times divided. Ex: `7 // 4` is 1 because 4 goes into 7 one time, remainder 3. The **modulo operator** (%) computes the remainder. Ex: `7 % 4` is 3.

Note: The % operator is traditionally pronounced "mod" (short for "modulo"). Ex: When reading `7 % 4` out loud, a programmer would say "seven mod four."

CHECKPOINT

Quotient and remainder

Access multimedia content (https://openstax.org/books/introduction-python-programming/pages/2-5-dividing-integers)

CONCEPTS IN PRACTICE

Division and modulo

What is the value of each expression?

1. `13 / 5`
   a. `2`
   b. `2.6`
   c. `3`

2. `13 % 5`
   a. `2`
   b. `2.6`
   c. `3`

3. `1 // 4`
   a. `0`
   b. `0.25`
   c. `1`

4. `2 % 0`
   a. `0`
   b. `2`
   c. `Error`

Unit conversions

Division is useful for converting one unit of measure to another. To convert centimeters to meters, a variable is divided by 100. Ex: 300 centimeters divided by 100 is 3 meters.

Amounts often do not divide evenly as integers. 193 centimeters is 1.93 meters, or 1 meter and 93 centimeters. A program can use floor division and modulo to separate the units:

- The quotient, 1 meter, is `193 // 100`.
- The remainder, 93 centimeters, is `193 % 100`.

Programs often use floor division and modulo together. If one line of code floor divides by m, the next line will likely modulo by m. The unit m by which an amount is divided is called the **modulus**. Ex: When converting centimeters to meters, the modulus is 100.

CHECKPOINT

Money and time

Access multimedia content (https://openstax.org/books/introduction-python-programming/pages/2-5-dividing-integers)

2.5 • Dividing integers

CONCEPTS IN PRACTICE

Unit conversions

5. What is the modulus for converting minutes to hours?
   a. 40
   b. 60
   c. 280

6. A program has the line pounds = ounces // 16. What is likely the next line of code?
   a. ounces = ounces % 16
   b. pounds = ounces % 16
   c. ounces = ounces - pounds * 16

TRY IT

Arrival time

Having a mobile device can be a lifesaver on long road trips. Programs like Google Maps find the shortest route and estimate the time of arrival. The time of arrival is based on the current time plus how long the trip will take.

Write a program that (1) inputs the current time and estimated length of a trip, (2) calculates the time of arrival, and (3) outputs the results in hours and minutes. Your program should use the following prompts (user input in bold):

```
13
    Current minute (0-59)? 25
    Trip time (in minutes)? 340

    Current hour (0-23)? 13
    Current minute (0-59)? 25
    Trip time (in minutes)? 340
```

In this example, the current time is 13:25 (1:25pm). The trip time is 340 minutes (5 hours and 40 minutes). 340 minutes after 13:25 is 19:05 (7:05pm). Your program should output the result in this format:

```
    Arrival hour is 19
    Arrival minute is 5
```

The arrival hour must be between 0 and 23. Ex: Adding 120 minutes to 23:00 should be 1:00, not 25:00. The arrival minute must be between 0 and 59. Ex: Adding 20 minutes to 8:55 should be 9:15, not 8:75.

Hint: Multiply the current hour by 60 to convert hours to minutes. Then, calculate the arrival time, in total minutes, as an integer.

Your code must not use Python keywords from later chapters, such as `if` or `while`. The solution requires only addition, multiplication, division, and modulo.

Access multimedia content (https://openstax.org/books/introduction-python-programming/pages/2-5-dividing-integers)

TRY IT

Change machine

Self-checkout aisles are becoming increasingly popular at grocery stores. Customers scan their own items, and a computer determines the total purchase amount. Customers who pay in cash insert dollar bills, and a machine automatically dispenses change in coins.

That's where this program comes into the story. Your task is to calculate how many of each coin to dispense. Your program should use the following prompts (user input in bold):

18.76
```
    Cash payment? 20

    Total amount? 18.76
    Cash payment? 20
```

You may assume that the cash paid will always be a whole number (representing dollar bills) that is greater than or equal to the total amount. The program should calculate and output the amount of change due and how many dollars, quarters, dimes, nickels, and pennies should be dispensed:

```
    Change Due $1.24

     Dollars: 1
    Quarters: 0
       Dimes: 2
     Nickels: 0
     Pennies: 4
```

Hint: Calculate the total change, in cents, as an integer. Use the `round()` function to avoid floating-point errors.

Your code must not use Python keywords from later chapters, such as `if` or `while`. The solution requires only subtraction, multiplication, division, and modulo.

Access multimedia content (https://openstax.org/books/introduction-python-programming/pages/2-5-dividing-integers)

2.6 The math module

Learning objectives

By the end of this section you should be able to

- Distinguish between built-in functions and math functions.
- Use functions and constants defined in the math module.

Importing modules

Python comes with an extensive standard library (https://openstax.org/r/100pythlibrary) of modules. A **module** is previously written code that can be imported in a program. The **import statement** defines a variable for accessing code in a module. Import statements often appear at the beginning of a program.

The standard library also defines built-in functions such as `print()`, `input()`, and `float()`. A **built-in function** is always available and does not need to be imported. The complete list of built-in functions (https://openstax.org/r/100builtin) is available in Python's official documentation.

A commonly used module in the standard library is the math module (https://openstax.org/r/100mathmodule). This module defines functions such as `sqrt()` (square root). To call `sqrt()`, a program must `import math` and use the resulting math variable followed by a dot. Ex: `math.sqrt(25)` evaluates to `5.0`.

The following program imports and uses the math module, and uses built-in functions for input and output.

EXAMPLE 2.1

Calculating the distance between two points

```
import math

x1 = float(input("Enter x1: "))
y1 = float(input("Enter y1: "))
x2 = float(input("Enter x2: "))
y2 = float(input("Enter y2: "))

distance = math.sqrt((x2-x1)**2 + (y2-y1)**2)
print("The distance is", distance)
```

CHECKPOINT

Importing math in a Python shell

Access multimedia content (https://openstax.org/books/introduction-python-programming/pages/2-6-the-math-module)

CONCEPTS IN PRACTICE

Built-in functions and math module

1. In the above example, when evaluating math, why did the interpreter raise a `NameError`?
    a. The math module was not available.

b. The variable pie was spelled incorrectly.
  c. The math module was not imported.

2. Which of these functions is builtin and does not need to be imported?
   a. `log()`
   b. `round()`
   c. `sqrt()`

3. Which expression results in an error?
   a. `math.abs(1)`
   b. `math.log(1)`
   c. `math.sqrt(1)`

Mathematical functions

Commonly used math functions and constants are shown below. The complete math module listing (https://openstax.org/r/100mathmodule) is available in Python's official documentation.

Constant	Value	Description
`math.e`	$e = 2.71828 ...$	Euler's number: the base of the natural logarithm.
`math.pi`	$\pi = 3.14159 ...$	The ratio of the circumference to the diameter of a circle.
`math.tau`	$\tau = 6.28318 ...$	The ratio of the circumference to the radius of a circle. Tau is equal to 2π.

Table 2.3 Example constants in the math module.

Function	Description	Examples
Number-theoretic		
`math.ceil(x)`	The ceiling of x: the smallest integer greater than or equal to x.	`math.ceil(7.4)` → 8 `math.ceil(-7.4)` → -7
`math.floor(x)`	The floor of x: the largest integer less than or equal to x.	`math.floor(7.4)` → 7 `math.floor(-7.4)` → -8
Power and logarithmic		
`math.log(x)`	The natural logarithm of x (to base e).	`math.log(math.e)` → 1.0 `math.log(0)` → ValueError: math domain error

Table 2.4 Example functions in the math module.

Function	Description	Examples
math.log(x, base)	The logarithm of x to the given base.	math.log(8, 2) → 3.0 math.log(10000, 10) → 4.0
math.pow(x, y)	x raised to the power y. Unlike the ** operator, math.pow() converts x and y to type float.	math.pow(3, 0) → 1.0 math.pow(3, 3) → 27.0
math.sqrt(x)	The square root of x.	math.sqrt(9) → 3.0 math.sqrt(-9) → ValueError: math domain error
Trigonometric		
math.cos(x)	The cosine of x radians.	math.cos(0) → 1.0 math.cos(math.pi) → -1.0
math.sin(x)	The sine of x radians.	math.sin(0) → 0.0 math.sin(math.pi/2) → 1.0
math.tan(x)	The tangent of x radians.	math.tan(0) → 0.0 math.tan(math.pi/4) → 0.999 (Round-off error; the result should be 1.0.)

Table 2.4 Example functions in the math module.

CONCEPTS IN PRACTICE

Using math functions and constants

4. What is the value of math.tau/2?
   a. approximately 2.718
   b. approximately 3.142
   c. approximately 6.283

5. What is the value of math.sqrt(100)?
   a. the float 10.0
   b. the integer 10
   c. ValueError: math domain error

6. What is πr^2 in Python syntax?
   a. pi * r**2

    b. `math.pi * r**2`
    c. `math.pi * r*2`

7. Which expression returns the integer 27?
    a. `3 ** 3`
    b. `3.0 ** 3`
    c. `math.pow(3, 3)`

TRY IT

Quadratic formula

In algebra, a quadratic equation is written as $ax^2 + bx + c = 0$. The coefficients a, b, and c are known values. The variable x represents an unknown value. Ex: $2x^2 + 3x - 5 = 0$ has the coefficients $a = 2$, $b = 3$, and $c = -5$. The quadratic formula provides a quick and easy way to solve a quadratic equation for x:

$$x = \frac{-b \pm \sqrt{b^2 - 4ac}}{2a}$$

The plus-minus symbol indicates the equation has two solutions. However, Python does not have a plus-minus operator. To use this formula in Python, the formula must be separated:

$$x_1 = \frac{-b + \sqrt{b^2 - 4ac}}{2a}$$
$$x_2 = \frac{-b - \sqrt{b^2 - 4ac}}{2a}$$

Write the code for the quadratic formula in the program below. Test your program using the following values for *a*, *b*, and *c*:

Provided input			Expected output	
a	b	c	x1	x2
1	0	-4	2.0	-2.0
1	2	-3	1.0	-3.0
2	1	-1	0.5	-1.0

Table 2.5

Provided input			Expected output
0	1	1	division by zero
1	0	1	math domain error

Table 2.5

Access multimedia content (https://openstax.org/books/introduction-python-programming/pages/2-6-the-math-module)

TRY IT

Cylinder formulas

In geometry, the surface area and volume of a right circular cylinder can be computed as follows:

$$A = 2\pi rh + 2\pi r^2$$

$$V = \pi r^2 h$$

Write the code for these two formulas in the program below. Hint: Your solution should use both math.pi and math.tau. Test your program using the following values for r and h:

Provided input		Expected output	
r	h	area	volume
0	0	0.0	0.0
1	1	12.57	3.14
1	2	18.85	6.28
2.5	4.8	114.67	94.25
3.1	7.0	196.73	211.33

Table 2.6

If you get an error, try to look up what that error means.

Access multimedia content (https://openstax.org/books/introduction-python-programming/pages/2-6-the-math-module)

2.7 Formatting code

Learning objectives

By the end of this section you should be able to

- Identify good spacing for expressions and statements.
- Write multi-line statements using implicit line joining.

Recommended spacing

Most spaces in Python code are ignored when running programs; however, spaces at the start of a line are very important. The following two programs are equivalent:

- Good spacing:

```
name = input("Enter someone's name: ")
place = input("Enter a famous place: ")
print(name, "should visit", place + "!")
```

- Poor spacing:

```
name=input ("Enter someone's name: " )
place =input("Enter a famous place: ")
print( name,"should visit" , place+ "!")
```

One might argue that missing or extra spaces do not matter. After all, the two programs above run exactly the same way. However, the "poor spacing" version is more difficult to read. Code like `name=input` and `place+` might lead to confusion.

Good programmers write code that is as easy to read as possible. That way, other programmers are more likely to understand the code. To encourage consistency, the Python community has a set of guidelines about where to put spaces and blank lines, what to name variables, how to break up long lines, and other important topics.

> **PYTHON STYLE GUIDE**
>
> PEP 8 (https://openstax.org/r/100PEP8) is the official style guide for Python. **PEP** stands for Python Enhancement Proposal. Members of the Python community write PEPs to document best practices and propose new features. The table below is based on guidelines from PEP 8 under the heading Whitespace in Expressions and Statements (https://openstax.org/r/100whitespace).

Guideline	Example	Common Mistakes
Parentheses: no space before or after.	`print("Go team!")`	`print ("Go team!")` `print( "Go team!" )`
Commas: no space before, one space after.	`print("Hello", name)`	`print("Hello" , name)` `print("Hello",name)`

Assignment: one space before and after the =.	`name = input("Your name? ")`	`name=input("Your name? ")`
		`name= input("Your name? ")`
		`name =input("Your name? ")`

Concatenation: one space before and after the +.	`print("Hi", name + "!")`	`print("Hi", name+"!")`
		`print("Hi", name+ "!")`
		`print("Hi", name +"!")`

Arithmetic: use space to show lower precedence.	`x**2 + 5*x - 8`	`x ** 2 + 5 * x - 8`
		`x ** 2+5 * x-8`
		`x**2+5*x-8`

Table 2.7 Guidelines for spaces.

CONCEPTS IN PRACTICE

Recommended spacing

1. Which statement is formatted properly?
   a. `name = input("What is your name? ")`
   b. `name = input ("What is your name? ")`
   c. `name = input( "What is your name? " )`

2. Which statement is formatted properly?
   a. `name=name+"!"`
   b. `name = name+"!"`
   c. `name = name + "!"`

3. Which statement is formatted properly?
   a. `print("Hello",name)`
   b. `print("Hello", name)`
   c. `print("Hello " , name)`

4. Which expression is formatted properly?

a. b**2 - 4*a*c
b. b ** 2 - 4 * a * c
c. b**2 - 4*a * c

Automatic concatenation

Long strings make Python programs difficult to read. Ex: This program prints the first sentence of the US Declaration of Independence (https://openstax.org/r/100declaration):

print("The unanimous Declaration of the thirteen united States of America, When in the Course of human events, it becomes necessary for one people to dissolve the political bands which have connected them with another, and to assume among the powers of the earth, the separate and equal station to which the Laws of Nature and of Nature's God entitle them, a decent respect to the opinions of mankind requires that they should declare the causes which impel them to the separation.")

PEP 8 recommends that each line of code be less than 80 characters long. That way, programmers won't need to scroll horizontally to read the code. The above program can be rewritten by breaking up the original string:

```
print("The unanimous Declaration of the thirteen united States of "
      "America, When in the Course of human events, it becomes "
      "necessary for one people to dissolve the political bands "
      "which have connected them with another, and to assume among "
      "the powers of the earth, the separate and equal station to "
      "which the Laws of Nature and of Nature's God entitle them, a "
      "decent respect to the opinions of mankind requires that they "
      "should declare the causes which impel them to the separation.")
```

For convenience, Python automatically concatenates multiple strings. The + operator is not required in this situation.

CHECKPOINT

String concatenation

Access multimedia content (https://openstax.org/books/introduction-python-programming/pages/2-7-formatting-code)

CONCEPTS IN PRACTICE

String literal concatenation

5. Which line prints the word "grandmother"?
   a. print(grandmother)
   b. print("grand" "mother")
   c. print("grand", "mother")

6. What string is equivalent to "Today is" "a holiday"?

a. `'Today isa holiday'`
b. `'Today is a holiday'`
c. `'Today is" "a holiday'`

7. If name is `"Ada"`, what does `print("Hello," name)` output?
   a. `Hello,Ada`
   b. `Hello, Ada`
   c. `SyntaxError`

Multi-line statements

Most statements in a Python program need only one line of code. But occasionally longer statements need to span multiple lines. Python provides two ways to write multi-line statements:

- Explicit line joining, using \ characters:

  ```
  decl = "The unanimous Declaration of the thirteen united States of " \
         "America, When in the Course of human events, it becomes " \
         "necessary for one people to dissolve the political bands..."
  ```

- Implicit line joining, using parentheses:

  ```
  decl = ("The unanimous Declaration of the thirteen united States of "
          "America, When in the Course of human events, it becomes "
          "necessary for one people to dissolve the political bands...")
  ```

Implicit line joining is more common, since many statements and expressions use parentheses anyway. PEP 8 recommends avoiding the use of explicit line joining whenever possible.

CONCEPTS IN PRACTICE

Multi-line statements

8. Which character is used for explicit line joining?
   a. /
   b. \
   c. |

9. What is the best way to print a very long string?
   a. Break up the string into multiple smaller strings.
      ```
      print("..." # first part of string
      "..." # next part of string
      "...")
      ```
   b. Print the string using multiple print statements.
      ```
      print("...") # first part of string
      print("...") # next part of string
      print("...")
      ```

c. Assign the string to a variable and print the variable.
   ```
   text = "..." # the entire string
   print(text)
   ```

10. Which example consists of two statements?
    a. `print("Happy `
       `"New Year")`
    b. `saying = ("Happy `
       `"New Year")`
    c. `saying= "Happy `
       `"New Year"`

TRY IT

Spaced out

The following code works correctly but is formatted poorly. In particular, the code does not include spaces recommended by PEP 8. Furthermore, two of the lines are about 90 characters long. Reformat the code to follow the guidelines in this section. Be careful not to change the behavior of the code itself.

Access multimedia content (https://openstax.org/books/introduction-python-programming/pages/2-7-formatting-code)

TRY IT

Five quotes

Write a program that prints the following five quotes (source: BrainyQuote (https://openstax.org/r/100brainyquote)) from Guido van Rossum, the creator of Python. Your program should have exactly five print statements, one for each quote:

```
    1. "If you're talking about Java in particular, Python is about the best fit
you can get amongst all the other languages. Yet the funny thing is, from a
language point of view, JavaScript has a lot in common with Python, but it is sort
of a restricted subset."
    2. "The second stream of material that is going to come out of this project is
a programming environment and a set of programming tools where we really want to
focus again on the needs of the newbie. This environment is going to have to be
extremely user-friendly."
    3. "I have this hope that there is a better way. Higher-level tools that
actually let you see the structure of the software more clearly will be of
tremendous value."
    4. "Now, it's my belief that Python is a lot easier than to teach to students
programming and teach them C or C++ or Java at the same time because all the
details of the languages are so much harder. Other scripting languages really don't
work very well there either."
```

5. "I would guess that the decision to create a small special purpose language or use an existing general purpose language is one of the toughest decisions that anyone facing the need for a new language must make."

Notice that all of these lines are longer than 80 characters, and some contain single quote marks. Format the code using multi-line statements and escape sequences as necessary.

Access multimedia content (https://openstax.org/books/introduction-python-programming/pages/2-7-formatting-code)

2.8 Python careers

Learning objectives

By the end of this section you should be able to

- Summarize how Python is used in fields other than CS and IT.
- Describe two different kinds of applications made with Python.

Fields and applications

Learning Python opens the door to many programming-related careers. Example job titles include software engineer, data scientist, web developer, and systems analyst. These jobs often require a degree in computer science (CS), information technology (IT), or a related field. However, programming is not limited to these fields and careers.

Many professionals use Python to support the work they do. Python programs can automate tasks and solve problems quickly. Table 2.8 shows a few examples of Python outside of computing fields. Knowing how to program is a useful skill that can enhance any career.

Python is a versatile language that supports many kinds of applications. Table 2.9 shows a few examples of programs that can be written in Python. Given Python's usefulness and popularity, Python is a great language to learn. A supportive community of professionals and enthusiasts is ready to help.

Field	Example use of Python
Business	An accountant writes a Python program to generate custom sales reports.
Education	A teacher writes a Python program to organize homework submissions.
Fine arts	An artist writes a Python program to operate an interactive art display.
Humanities	A linguist writes a Python program to analyze changes in slang word usage.
Science	A biologist writes a Python program to analyze DNA sequences for cancer.

Table 2.8 Python outside of CS and IT.

Application	Example use of Python
Artificial intelligence	An engineer develops models to support image and voice recognition. Ex: TensorFlow library (https://openstax.org/r/100tensorflow).
Data visualization	A statistician creates charts to make sense of large amounts of data. Ex: Matplotlib library (https://openstax.org/r/100matplotlib).
General purpose	Most programs in this book are general. Ex: Read inputs, perform calculations, print results.
Scientific computing	Python is very useful for conducting experiments and analyzing data. Ex: The SciPy project (https://openstax.org/r/100scipyproject).
Web development	Python can run interactive websites. Ex: Instagram is built with Django (https://openstax.org/r/100django), a Python framework.

Table 2.9 Applications built with Python.

CONCEPTS IN PRACTICE

Fields and applications

1. Which of the following fields use Python to support their work?
   a. geography
   b. health care
   c. political science
   d. all of the above

2. Which of the following Python libraries creates charts and plots?
   a. Matplotlib
   b. SciPy
   c. TensorFlow

3. Which of the following applications were built with Python?
   a. Facebook
   b. Instagram
   c. WhatsApp

EXPLORING FURTHER

For more examples of applications that can be built with Python, see "Top 12 Fascinating Python Applications in Real-World" (https://openstax.org/r/100top12apps) by Rohit Sharma. For more information about Python related careers, see "What Does a Python Developer Do?" (https://openstax.org/r/100careers) in BrainStation's career guide.

2.9 Chapter summary

Highlights from this chapter include:

- Expressions and statements can be run interactively using a shell.
- Input strings can be converted to other types. Ex: `int(input())`.
- Strings can be concatenated with other types. Ex: `"$" + str(cost)`.
- Floats are subject to round-off and overflow errors.
- Integers can be divided exactly using `//` and `%`.
- Modules like `math` provide many useful functions.
- Formatting long lines helps improve readability.

At this point, you should be able to write programs that ask for input of mixed types, perform mathematical calculations, and output results with better formatting. The programming practice below ties together most topics presented in the chapter.

Function	Description
`abs(x)`	Returns the absolute value of x.
`int(x)`	Converts x (a string or float) to an integer.
`float(x)`	Converts x (a string or integer) to a float.
`str(x)`	Converts x (a float or integer) to a string.
`round(x, ndigits)`	Rounds x to `ndigits` places after the decimal point. If `ndigits` is omitted, returns the nearest integer to x.
Operator	**Description**
`s * n` (Repetition)	Creates a string with n copies of s. Ex: `"Ha" * 3` is `"HaHaHa"`.
`x / y` (Real division)	Divides x by y and returns the entire result as a float. Ex: `7 / 4` is `1.75`.
`x // y` (Floor division)	Divides x by y and returns the quotient as an integer. Ex: `7 // 4` is `1`.
`x % y` (Modulo)	Divides x by y and returns the remainder as an integer. Ex: `7 % 4` is `3`.

Table 2.10 Chapter 2 reference.

TRY IT

Baking bread

The holidays are approaching, and you need to buy ingredients for baking many loaves of bread. According to a recipe by King Arthur Flour (https://openstax.org/r/100kingarthurflr), you will need the following ingredients for each loaf:

- 1 1/2 teaspoons instant yeast
- 1 1/2 teaspoons salt
- 1 1/2 teaspoons sugar
- 2 1/2 cups all-purpose flour
- 2 cups sourdough starter
- 1/2 cup lukewarm water

Write a program that inputs the following variables: `bread_weight` (float), `serving_size` (float), and `num_guests` (int). The output will look like the following:

Note: The measures the program comes up with are exact, but to bake, the baker would have to use some approximation. Ex: 9.765625 cups all-purpose flour really means 9 and 3/4 cups.

```
For 25 people, you will need 3.90625 loaves of bread:
  5.859375 teaspoons instant yeast
  5.859375 teaspoons salt
  5.859375 teaspoons sugar
  9.765625 cups all-purpose flour
  7.8125 cups sourdough starter
  1.953125 cups lukewarm water
```

In the above output, `bread_weight` is 16.0 ounces, `serving_size` is 2.5 ounces, and `num_guests` is 25 people. Use these three variables to calculate the number of loaves needed.

Make sure your output matches the above example exactly. Notice that each line of the ingredients begins with two spaces.

Access multimedia content (https://openstax.org/books/introduction-python-programming/pages/2-9-chapter-summary)

TRY IT

Tip calculator

Google has a variety of search tricks (https://openstax.org/r/100googletricks) that present users with instant results. If you search on Google for tip calculator (https://openstax.org/r/100tipcalculatr), an interactive tool is included at the top of the results. The goal of this exercise is to implement a similar tip calculator.

Begin by prompting the user to input the following values (user input in bold):

```
43.21
    Percentage to tip: 18
    Number of people: 2

    Enter bill amount: 43.21
    Percentage to tip: 18
    Number of people: 2
```

Then calculate the tip amount and total amount for the bill, based on the user input. Output the results using this format:

```
Tip amount: $7.78
Total amount: $50.99

Tip per person: $3.89
Total per person: $25.49
```

Your program should output all dollar amounts rounded to two decimal places. The output should be exactly six lines, as shown above. Notice the blank line before each section of the output. Notice also the space before but not after the dollar sign.

Access multimedia content (https://openstax.org/books/introduction-python-programming/pages/2-9-chapter-summary)

3 Objects

Figure 3.1 credit: modification of work "Port of Melbourne", by Chris Phutully/Flickr, CC BY 2.0

Chapter Outline

3.1 Strings revisited
3.2 Formatted strings
3.3 Variables revisited
3.4 List basics
3.5 Tuple basics
3.6 Chapter summary

 Introduction

An **object** is a single unit of data in a Python program. So far, this book has introduced three types of objects: strings, integers, and floats. This chapter takes a closer look at how strings are represented and how integers and floats can be formatted. To better understand what an object actually is, the relationship between variables and objects is emphasized. The chapter also introduces two types of containers: lists and tuples. A **container** is an object that can hold an arbitrary number of other objects. At the end of this chapter, you will be able to solve more complex problems using fewer variables.

3.1 Strings revisited

Learning objectives

By the end of this section you should be able to

- Extract a specific character from a string using an index.
- Use escape sequences to represent special characters.

Indexes

A string is a sequence of zero or more characters. Each character has an index that refers to the character's position. Indexes are numbered from left to right, starting at 0. Indexes are also numbered from right to left, starting at -1.

> **CHECKPOINT**
>
> **String indexes**
>
> Access multimedia content (https://openstax.org/books/introduction-python-programming/pages/3-1-strings-revisited)

> **CONCEPTS IN PRACTICE**
>
> **String indexes**
>
> 1. What is the index of the second character in a string?
>   a. 1
>   b. 2
>   c. -2
>
> 2. If `s = "Python!"`, what is the value of `s[1] + s[-1]`?
>   a. `"P!"`
>   b. `"y!"`
>   c. `"yn"`
>
> 3. If `s = "Python!"`, what type of object is `s[0]`?
>   a. character
>   b. integer
>   c. string

Unicode

Python uses **Unicode**, the international standard for representing text on computers. Unicode defines a unique number, called a **code point**, for each possible character. Ex: "P" has the code point 80, and "!" has the code point 33.

The built-in `ord()` function converts a character to a code point. Ex: `ord("P")` returns the integer 80. Similarly, the built-in `chr()` function converts a code point to a character. Ex: `chr(33)` returns the string "!".

Unicode is an extension of **ASCII**, the American Standard Code for Information Interchange. Originally, ASCII defined only 128 code points, enough to support the English language. Unicode defines over one million code points and supports most of the world's written languages.

32	(space)	64	@	96	`
33	!	65	A	97	a
34	"	66	B	98	b
35	#	67	C	99	c
36	$	68	D	100	d
37	%	69	E	101	e
38	&	70	F	102	f
39	'	71	G	103	g
40	(	72	H	104	h
41	)	73	I	105	i
42	*	74	J	106	j
43	+	75	K	107	k
44	,	76	L	108	l
45	-	77	M	109	m
46	.	78	N	110	n
47	/	79	O	111	o
48	0	80	P	112	p
49	1	81	Q	113	q
50	2	82	R	114	r
51	3	83	S	115	s
52	4	84	T	116	t
53	5	85	U	117	u
54	6	86	V	118	v
55	7	87	W	119	w
56	8	88	X	120	x
57	9	89	Y	121	y
58	:	90	Z	122	z
59	;	91	[	123	{
60	<	92	\	124	|
61	=	93	]	125	}
62	>	94	^	126	~
63	?	95	_	127	(delete)

Table 3.1 Character values. This table shows code points 32 to 127 as defined by ASCII and Unicode. Code points 0 to 31 are non-printable characters that were used for telecommunications.

CONCEPTS IN PRACTICE

ord() and chr()

4. What is the code point for the letter A?
   a. 1
   b. 65

c. 97

5. What value does `ord("0")` return?
   a. `0`
   b. `48`
   c. `Error`

6. What does `chr(126)` return?
   a. `~`
   b. `"~"`
   c. `Error`

Special characters

An **escape sequence** uses a backslash (\) to represent a special character within a string.

Escape sequence	Meaning	Example	Screen output
\n	A newline character that indicates the end of a line of text.	`print("Escape\nsequence!")`	Escape sequence!
\t	A tab character; useful for indenting paragraphs or aligning text on multiple lines.	`print("Escape\tsequence!")`	Escape sequence!
\'	A single quote; an alternative to enclosing the string in double quotes.	`print('I\'ll try my best!')`	I'll try my best
\"	A double quote; an alternative to enclosing the string in single quotes.	`print("I heard you said \"Yes\"")`	I heard you said "Yes"
\\	A backslash character.	`print("This prints a \\")`	This prints a \

Table 3.2 Common escape sequences.

CONCEPTS IN PRACTICE

Tabs and newlines

7. Which of the following is an escape sequence?
   a. `t`
   b. `/t`
   c. `\t`

8. Which statement prints a backslash (\) to the screen?
   a. `print(\\)`
   b. `print(\"\")`
   c. `print("\\")`

9. Which statement prints `Enter` and `here` on separate lines?
   a. `print("Enter here")`
   b. `print("Enter" + \n + "here")`
   c. `print("Enter" + "\n" + "here")`

TRY IT

Hopper quote

Grace Hopper (https://openstax.org/r/100gracehopper) (1906–1992) was a famous computer scientist (and rear admiral in the US Navy!) who came up with the idea of machine-independent programming languages. She envisioned a programming language based on English and made many contributions that paved the way for modern programming languages, including Python.

Write a program that prints the following text, including the quotation marks. Your program may not use single quotes (') anywhere in the code. The last line must be indented with a tab character.

```
"To me programming is more than an important practical art.
It is also a gigantic undertaking in the foundations of knowledge."
        -- Grace Hopper
```

Access multimedia content (https://openstax.org/books/introduction-python-programming/pages/3-1-strings-revisited)

TRY IT

Shift cipher

During the Roman Empire, Julius Caesar (100–44 BCE) used a simple technique to encrypt private messages. Each letter of the message was replaced with the third next letter of the alphabet. Ex: If the message was CAT, the C became F, the A became D, and the T became W, resulting in the message FDW. This technique is known as a shift cipher because each letter is shifted by some amount. In Caesar's case, the amount was three, but other amounts (besides 0) would work too.

Write a program that prompts the user to input the following two values (example input in bold):

```
Enter a 3-letter word: CAT
Shift by how many letters? 3
```

The program should then shift each letter of the word by the desired amount. Based on the example above, the output would be:

```
The secret message is: FDW
```

Hint: Use the `ord()` function to convert each letter to an integer, add the shift amount to each integer, use the `chr()` function to convert each integer to a character, and concatenate the resulting characters.

Access multimedia content (https://openstax.org/books/introduction-python-programming/pages/3-1-strings-revisited)

3.2 Formatted strings

Learning objectives

By the end of this section you should be able to

- Use f-strings to simplify output with multiple values.
- Format numbers with leading zeros and fixed precision.

F-strings

A **formatted string literal** (or **f-string**) is a string literal that is prefixed with `"f"` or `"F"`. A **replacement field** is an expression in curly braces (`{}`) inside an f-string. Ex: The string `f"Good morning, {first} {last}!"` has two replacement fields: one for a first name, and one for a last name. F-strings provide a convenient way to combine multiple values into one string.

CHECKPOINT

Printing an f-string

Access multimedia content (https://openstax.org/books/introduction-python-programming/pages/3-2-formatted-strings)

CONCEPTS IN PRACTICE

Basic f-strings

1. What is the output of the following code?

   ```
   animal = "dog"
   ```

```
says = "bark"
print(f"My {animal} says {says} {says} {says}")
```

   a. `My dog bark bark bark bark`
   b. `My dog says bark bark bark`
   c. Error

2. What is the output of the following code?

```
temp = "hot"
food = "potato"
print("{temp} {food}")
```

   a. `{temp} {food}`
   b. `hot potato`
   c. Error

3. How can the following code be rewritten using an f-string?

```
print(x, "+", y, "=", x + y)
```

   a. `print(f"x + y = {x+y}")`
   b. `print(f"{x + y} = {x + y}")`
   c. `print(f"{x} + {y} = {x+y}")`

Formatting numbers

Programs often need to display numbers in a specific format. Ex: When displaying the time, minutes are formatted as two-digit integers. If the hour is 9 and the minute is 5, then the time is "9:05" (not "9:5").

In an f-string, a replacement field may include a format specifier introduced by a colon. A **format specifier** defines how a value should be formatted for display. Ex: In the string `f"{hour}:{minute:02d}"`, the format specifier for `minute` is `02d`.

Format	Description	Example	Result
d	Decimal integer (default integer format).	`f"{12345678:d}"`	`'12345678'`
,d	Decimal integer, with comma separators.	`f"{12345678:,d}"`	`'12,345,678'`
10d	Decimal integer, at least 10 characters wide.	`f"{12345678:10d}"`	`'  12345678'`
010d	Decimal integer, at least 10 characters wide, with leading zeros.	`f"{12345678:010d}"`	`'0012345678'`

Table 3.3 Example format specifiers. The table shows common ways that numbers can be formatted. Many more formatting options are available and described in Python's Format Specification Mini-Language (https://docs.python.org/3/library/string.html#formatspec).

Format	Description	Example	Result
f	Fixed-point (default is 6 decimal places).	`f"{math.pi:f}"`	`'3.141593'`
.4f	Fixed-point, rounded to 4 decimal places.	`f"{math.pi:.4f}"`	`'3.1416'`
8.4f	Fixed-point, rounded to 4 decimal places, at least 8 characters wide.	`f"{math.pi:8.4f}"`	`'  3.1416'`
08.4f	Fixed-point, rounded to 4 decimal places, at least 8 characters wide, with leading zeros.	`f"{math.pi:08.4f}"`	`'003.1416'`

Table 3.3 Example format specifiers. The table shows common ways that numbers can be formatted. Many more formatting options are available and described in Python's Format Specification Mini-Language (https://docs.python.org/3/library/string.html#formatspec).

CONCEPTS IN PRACTICE

Formatting numbers

4. What f-string formats a date as MM/DD/YYYY?
   a. `f"{month:02d}/{day:02d}/{year}"`
   b. `f"{month:2d}/{day:2d}/{year}"`
   c. `f"{month}/{day}/{year}"`

5. What statement displays the variable money rounded to two decimal places?
   a. `print(f"{money:2d}")`
   b. `print(f"{money:2f}")`
   c. `print(f"{money:.2f}")`

6. What format specifier displays a floating-point number with comma separators and rounded to two decimal places?
   a. `.2,f`
   b. `,.2f`
   c. `,d.2f`

TRY IT

Mad lib (f-string)

A mad lib (https://openstax.org/r/100fstring) is a funny story that uses words provided by a user. The following mad lib is based on four words (user input in bold):

```
Enter a name: Buster
Enter a noun: dog
```

```
Enter an adjective: super
Verb ending in -ing: swimming

Buster, the super dog, likes to go swimming.
```

Most of the code for this mad lib is already written. Complete the code below by writing the f-string.

Access multimedia content (https://openstax.org/books/introduction-python-programming/pages/3-2-formatted-strings)

TRY IT

Wage calculator

You just landed a part-time job and would like to calculate how much money you will earn. Write a program that inputs the time you start working, the time you stop working, and your hourly pay rate (example input in bold):

```
Starting hour: 9
Starting minute: 30
Stopping hour: 11
Stopping minute: 0
Hourly rate: 15
```

Based on the user input, your program should calculate and display the following results:

```
Worked 9:30 to 11:00
Total hours: 1.5
Payment: $22.50
```

For this exercise, you need to write code that (1) calculates the total payment and (2) formats the three output lines. Use f-strings and format specifiers to display two-digit minutes, one decimal place for hours, and two decimal places for payment. The input code has been provided as a starting point.

Assume the use of a 24-hour clock. Ex: 16:15 is used instead of 4:15pm.

Access multimedia content (https://openstax.org/books/introduction-python-programming/pages/3-2-formatted-strings)

3.3 Variables revisited

Learning objectives

By the end of this section you should be able to

- Distinguish between variables, objects, and references.
- Draw memory diagrams with integers, floats, and strings.

References to objects

In Python, every variable refers to an object. The assignment statement `message = "Hello"` makes the variable `message` refer to the object `"Hello"`. Multiple variables may refer to the same object. Ex: `greeting = message` makes `greeting` refer to the same object as `message`. A **memory diagram** shows the relationship between variables and objects.

CHECKPOINT

Example memory diagram

Access multimedia content (https://openstax.org/books/introduction-python-programming/pages/3-3-variables-revisited)

CONCEPTS IN PRACTICE

Variables and objects

1. How many assignment statements are in the above animation?
   a. 2
   b. 3
   c. 4

2. Which of the following best describes the objects assigned?
   a. two float objects
   b. two int objects, one float object
   c. one int object, one float object

3. What symbol is used to show a variable's current value?
   a. an arrow
   b. a small black box
   c. a rounded box

EXPLORING FURTHER

Python Tutor (https://openstax.org/r/100pythontutor) is a free online tool for visualizing code execution. A user can enter any Python code, click Visualize Execution, and then click the Next button to run the code one line at a time. Here is the rating and score example (https://openstax.org/r/100ratingscore) from the animation above.

Python Tutor is also useful for drawing memory diagrams similar to the ones in this book. Before clicking Visualize Execution, change the middle option from "inline primitives, don't nest objects [default]" to "render all objects on the heap (Python/Java)" as shown in the following screenshot:

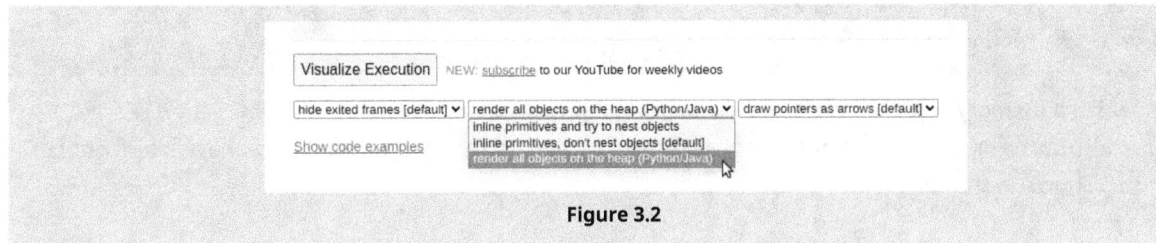

Figure 3.2

Properties of objects

Every object has an identity, a type, and a value:

- An object's **identity** is a unique integer associated with the object. Generally, this integer refers to the memory location where the object is stored. Once created, an object's identity never changes. The built-in `id()` function returns the object's identity.

- An object's **type** determines the possible values and operations of an object. Ex: Integers and floats can be "divided" using the / operator, but strings cannot. The built-in `type()` function returns the object's type.

- An object's **value** represents the current state of the object. Many objects, such as numbers and strings, cannot be modified once created. Some objects, such as lists (introduced later), are designed to be modified.

CHECKPOINT

Identity, type, and value

Access multimedia content (https://openstax.org/books/introduction-python-programming/pages/3-3-variables-revisited)

CONCEPTS IN PRACTICE

id() and type()

4. Which value might be returned by `id(rating)`?
   a. `9793344`
   b. `<class 'float'>`
   c. `10.0`

5. Which value might be returned by `type(rating)`?
   a. `10.0`
   b. `"float"`
   c. `<class 'float'>`

6. What expression returns the value of an object?
   a. `value(rating)`
   b. `rating`
   c. `"rating"`

EXPLORING FURTHER

As shown in a memory diagram, variables and objects are two separate ideas. Calling a function like `id()` or `type()` returns information about an object, not a variable. In fact, a variable doesn't have an identity or a type, as shown in this example:

```
>>> rating = 10   # Integer object somewhere in memory.
>>> type(rating)
<class 'int'>
>>> id(rating)
9793344
>>> rating = "ten"   # String object somewhere else in memory.
>>> type(rating)
<class 'str'>
>>> id(rating)
140690967388272
```

One might incorrectly think that the rating variable's type or identity changes. However, the only thing that changes is which object the rating variable refers to.

TRY IT

Three variables

1. Draw a memory diagram for the following code:

   ```
   a = 1
   b = 2
   c = b
   b = a
   a = c
   ```

2. Run the code on Python Tutor (https://openstax.org/r/100pythruncode) to check your answer.
3. Based on your diagram, answer these questions:
   - What is the final value of a, b, and c?
   - How many integer objects are created?

TRY IT

Different types

1. Draw a memory diagram for the following code:

   ```
   name = "Chocolate"
   length = len(name)
   ```

```
        price = 1.99
        lower = min(length, price)
        product = name
        name = name * 2
```

2. Run the code on Python Tutor (https://openstax.org/r/100pythruncode) to check your answer.
3. Based on your diagram, answer these questions:
    ○ What is the type and value of each object?
    ○ Which object does each variable reference?

3.4 List basics

Learning objectives

By the end of this section you should be able to

- Use indexes to access individual elements in a list.
- Use indexes to modify individual elements in a list.
- Use `len()` function to find the length of a list.
- Demonstrate that lists can be changed after creation.

Lists

A list object can be used to bundle elements together in Python. A list is defined by using square brackets [ ] with comma separated values within the square brackets. Ex: `list_1 = [1, 2, 4]`.

Empty lists can be defined in two ways:

- `list_1 = []`
- `list_1 = list()`

Lists can be made of elements of any type. Lists can contain integers, strings, floats, or any other type. Lists can also contain a combination of types. Ex: `[2, "Hello", 2.5]` is a valid list.

Python lists allow programmers to change the contents of the list in various ways.

CHECKPOINT

Lists

Access multimedia content (https://openstax.org/books/introduction-python-programming/pages/3-4-list-basics)

CONCEPTS IN PRACTICE

Lists

1. Which is the correct way to make a list of the numbers 3, 4, and 5?
    a. `new_list == [3, 4, 5]`
    b. `new_list = [3, 4, 5]`
    c. `new_list = (3, 4, 5)`

2. Which of the following is not a valid way to specify a list in Python?
   a. `my_list = [2, 2 3, 23]`
   b. `my_list = ["Jimmy", 2, "times"]`
   c. `my_list = ["C", "C++", "Python", "Java", "Rust", "Scala"]`

Using indexes

Individual list elements can be accessed directly using an index. Indexes begin at 0 and end at one less than the length of the sequence. Ex: For a sequence of 50 elements, the first position is 0, and the last position is 49.

The index number is put in square brackets `[ ]` and attached to the end of the name of the list to access the required element. Ex: `new_list[3]` accesses the 4th element in `new_list`. An expression that evaluates to an integer number can also be used as an index. Similar to strings, negative indexing can also be used to address individual elements. Ex: Index -1 refers to the last element and -2 the second-to-last element.

The `len()` function, when called on a list, returns the length of the list.

EXAMPLE 3.1

List indexes and len() function

The following code demonstrates the use of list indexes and the `len()` function. Line 6 shows the use of the `len()` function to get the length of the list. Line 10 shows how to access an element using an index. Line 14 shows how to modify a list element using an index.

```python
# Setup a list of numbers
    num_list = [2, 3, 5, 9, 11]
    print(num_list)

    # Print the length of the list
    print("Length: ", len(num_list))

    # Print the 4th element in the list
    # The number 3 is used to refer to the 4th element
    print("4th element:", num_list[3])

    # The desired value of the 4th element is actually 7
    # Update the value of the 4th element to 7
    num_list[3] = 7

    # The list of the first 5 prime numbers
    print(num_list)
```

The above code's output is:

```
[2, 3, 5, 9, 11]
Length: 5
4th element: 9
```

```
[2, 3, 5, 7, 11]
```

> **CONCEPTS IN PRACTICE**
>
> List indexes and the len() function
>
> 3. Which is the correct way to access the 17th element in a list called `cardList`?
>   a. `card_list[17]`
>   b. `16)card_list(16)`
>   c. `card_list[16]`
>
> 4. What is the correct way to modify the element `"Tom"` to `"Tim"` in the following list?
>
>   `name_list = ["Carla", "Monique", "Westin", "Tom"]`
>
>   a. `name_list[-1] = "Tim"`
>   b. `name_list[4] = "Tim"`
>   c. `name_list[end] = "Tim"`

> **TRY IT**
>
> List basics
>
> Write a program to complete the following:
>
> 1. Create a list with the following elements: 2, 23, 39, 6, -5.
> 2. Change the third element of the list (index 2) to 35.
> 3. Print the resulting list and the list's length.
>
> Access multimedia content (https://openstax.org/books/introduction-python-programming/pages/3-4-list-basics)

3.5 Tuple basics

Learning objectives

By the end of this section you should be able to

- Describe the features and benefits of a tuple.
- Develop a program that creates and uses a tuple successfully.
- Identify and discuss the mutability of a tuple.

Creating tuples and accessing elements

A **tuple** is a sequence of comma separated values that can contain elements of different types. A tuple must be created with commas between values, and conventionally the sequence is surrounded by parentheses.

Each element is accessed by index, starting with the first element at index 0.

| ```
tuple_1 = (2, 3, 4)
print(f'tuple_1: {tuple_1}')
print(tuple_1[1])
print()
data_13 = ('Aimee Perry', 96, [94, 100,
97, 93])
print(f'data_13: {data_13}')
print(data_13[2])
``` | ```
tuple_1: (2, 3, 4)
3

data_13: ('Aimee Perry', 96, [94, 100,
97, 93])
[94, 100, 97, 93]
``` |

Table 3.4 Example tuples.

CONCEPTS IN PRACTICE

Creating tuples and accessing elements

1. Consider the example above. Which accesses `tuple_1`'s first element?
   a. `tuple_1[0]`
   b. `tuple_1[1]`
   c. `tuple_1[2]`

2. Which creates a valid tuple?
   a. `tuple_2 = (42, 26, 13)`
   b. `tuple_3 = (42, 26, 13.5)`
   c. both

3. Which creates a tuple with three elements?
   a. `my_tuple = 'a', 'b', 'c'`
   b. `my_tuple = ['a', 'b', 'c']`
   c. `my_tuple = ('a', 'b', 'c')`

Tuple properties

How do tuples compare to lists? Tuples are ordered and allow duplicates, like lists, but have different mutability. An **immutable** object cannot be modified after creation. A **mutable** object can be modified after creation. Tuples are immutable, whereas lists are mutable.

CHECKPOINT

Mutability of a tuple vs. a list

Access multimedia content (https://openstax.org/books/introduction-python-programming/pages/3-5-tuple-basics)

CONCEPTS IN PRACTICE

Using tuples

4. Consider the final program in the example above. What is the value of `my_tuple`?
   a. `(0.693, 0.414, 3.142)`
   b. `(0.693, 1.414, 3.142)`
   c. `Error`

5. Why does the following code produce an error?

   ```
   tuple_1 = ('alpha', 'bravo', 'charlie')
   tuple_1.append('charlie')
   ```

   a. Append isn't allowed.
   b. Duplicates aren't allowed.
   c. Strings aren't allowed

6. A programmer wants to create a sequence of constants for easy reference that can't be changed anywhere in the program. Which sequence would be the most appropriate?
   a. list
   b. tuple

MUTABILITY AND PERFORMANCE

Tuples are immutable and have a fixed size, so tuples use less memory. Overall, tuples are faster to create and access, resulting in better performance that can be noticeable with large amounts of data.

TRY IT

Creating a tuple from a list

Suppose a programmer wants to create a tuple from a list to prevent future changes. The `tuple()` function creates a tuple from an object like a list. Ex: `my_tuple = tuple(my_list)` creates a tuple from the list `my_list`. Update the program below to create a tuple `final_grades` from the list grades.

Access multimedia content (https://openstax.org/books/introduction-python-programming/pages/3-5-tuple-basics)

TRY IT

Creating a tuple with user input

Write a program that reads in two strings and two integers from input and creates a tuple, `my_data`, with the four values.

Given input:

```
x
y
15
20
```

The output is:

```
my_data: ('x', 'y', 15, 20)
```

Access multimedia content (https://openstax.org/books/introduction-python-programming/pages/3-5-tuple-basics)

3.6 Chapter summary

Highlights from this chapter include:

- A **string** is a sequence of values that represents Unicode code points.
- An **index** refers to the position of a value in a sequence (string, list, tuple).
- Positive indexes range from 0 to length–1. Negative indexes range from –1 to –length.
- F-strings are a convenient way to print multiple outputs and format integers and floats.
- Variables refer to objects. Memory diagrams are useful for drawing variables and objects.
- A list object can be used to refer to multiple objects, by index, using the same variable.
- A tuple is similar to a list, but uses parentheses and cannot be changed once created.

Code	Description
`ord(c)`	Gets an integer representing the Unicode code point of a character.
`chr(i)`	Converts a Unicode code point (integer) into a One-character string.
`'\n'`	Escape sequence for the newline character.
`'\t'`	Escape sequence for the tab character.
`f"{number:.02d}"`	Creates a string by formatting an integer to be at least two digits.

Table 3.5 Chapter 3 reference.

Code	Description
`f"{number:.2f}"`	Creates a string by formatting a float to have two decimal places.
`id(object)`	Gets the identity (memory location) of an object.
`type(object)`	Gets the type (class name) of an object.
`my_list = ["a", "b", "c"]`	Creates a list of three strings.
`my_tuple = ("a", "b", "c")`	Creates a tuple of three strings.
`my_list[0]`	Gets the first element (`"a"`) of `my_tuple`.
`my_tuple[-1]`	Gets the last element (`"c"`) of `my_tuple`.

Table 3.5 Chapter 3 reference.

4 Decisions

Figure 4.1 credit: modification of work "Fork In The Road", by Ian Sane/Flickr, CC BY 2.0

Chapter Outline

- 4.1 Boolean values
- 4.2 If-else statements
- 4.3 Boolean operations
- 4.4 Operator precedence
- 4.5 Chained decisions
- 4.6 Nested decisions
- 4.7 Conditional expressions
- 4.8 Chapter summary

Introduction

The Python interpreter follows a single path of execution when executing a program. What if a programmer wants to define multiple possible paths? Ex: Instead of always taking the left path, a program uses the path width to decide which path to take. If the left path is wider, take the right path. Else, take the left path.

A **branch** is a group of statements that execute based on a condition. The Expressions chapter introduced expressions. This chapter explores how expressions can be used as conditions to make decisions in programs.

4.1 Boolean values

Learning objectives

By the end of this section you should be able to

- Explain a Boolean value.
- Use bool variables to store Boolean values.
- Demonstrate converting integers, floats, and strings to Booleans.
- Demonstrate converting Booleans to integers, floats, and strings.
- Use comparison operators to compare integers, floats, and strings.

bool data type

People often ask binary questions such as yes/no or true/false questions. Ex: Do you like pineapple on pizza? Ex: True or false: I like pineapple on pizza. The response is a Boolean value, meaning the value is either true or false. The **bool** data type, standing for Boolean, represents a binary value of either true or false. `true` and `false` are keywords, and capitalization is required.

> **CHECKPOINT**
>
> Example: Crosswalk sign
>
> Access multimedia content (https://openstax.org/books/introduction-python-programming/pages/4-1-boolean-values)

> **CONCEPTS IN PRACTICE**
>
> Using Boolean variables
>
> Consider the following code:
>
> ```
> is_fruit = "True"
> is_vegetable = 0
> is_dessert = False
> ```
>
> 1. What is the data type of `is_fruit`?
>   a. Boolean
>   b. integer
>   c. string
>
> 2. What is the data type of `is_vegetable`?
>   a. Boolean
>   b. integer
>   c. string
>
> 3. What is the data type of `is_dessert`?
>   a. Boolean
>   b. integer
>   c. string
>
> 4. How many values can a Boolean variable represent?
>   a. 2
>   b. 4
>   c. 8
>
> 5. Which is a valid value for a Boolean variable?
>   a. true
>   b. True
>   c. 1

6. Suppose the following is added to the code above:

   ```
   is_dessert = 0
   print(type(is_dessert))
   ```

   What is the output?
   a. `<class 'bool'>`
   b. `<class 'int'>`
   c. Error

Type conversion with bool()

Deciding whether a value is true or false is helpful when writing programs/statements based on decisions. Converting data types to Booleans can seem unintuitive at first. Ex: Is `"ice cream"` True? But the conversion is actually simple.

bool() converts a value to a Boolean value, True or False.

- True: any non-zero number, any non-empty string
- False: 0, empty string

CHECKPOINT

Converting integers, floats, and strings using bool()

Access multimedia content (https://openstax.org/books/introduction-python-programming/pages/4-1-boolean-values)

CONCEPTS IN PRACTICE

Converting numeric types and strings to Booleans

7. `bool(0.000)`
   a. True
   b. False

8. `bool(-1)`
   a. True
   b. False

9. `bool("")`
   a. True
   b. False

10. `bool("0")`
    a. True
    b. False

11. Given input `False`, what is `bool(input())`?

a. True
   b. False

> **CONCEPTS IN PRACTICE**
>
> Converting Booleans to numeric types and strings
>
> Given `is_on = True`, what is the value of each expression?
>
> 12. `float(is_on)`
>   a. `0.0`
>   b. `1.0`
>
> 13. `str(is_on)`
>   a. `"is_on"`
>   b. `"True"`
>
> 14. `int(is_on)`
>   a. `0`
>   b. `1`

Comparison operators

Programmers often have to answer questions like "Is the current user the admin?" A programmer may want to compare a string variable, user, to the string, "admin". **Comparison operators** are used to compare values, and the result is either true or false. Ex: `is_admin = (user == "admin")`. `user` is compared with `"admin"` using the `==` operator, which tests for equality. The Boolean variable, `is_admin`, is assigned with the Boolean result.

The 6 comparison operators:

- equal to: **==**
- not equal to: **!=**
- greater than: **>**
- less than: **<**
- greater than or equal to: **>=**
- less than or equal to: **<=**

> **CHECKPOINT**
>
> Example: Rolling a d20 in a tabletop game
>
> Access multimedia content (https://openstax.org/books/introduction-python-programming/pages/4-1-boolean-values)

CONCEPTS IN PRACTICE

Comparing values

For each new variable, what is the value of compare_result?

15. x = 14
compare_result = (x <= 13)

   a. True
   b. False

16. w = 0
compare_result = (w != 0.4)

   a. True
   b. False

17. v = 4
compare_result = (v < 4.0)

   a. True
   b. False

18. y = 2
compare_result = (y > "ab")

   a. True
   b. False
   c. Error

19. z = "cilantro"
compare_result = (z == "coriander")

   a. True
   b. False

20. a = "dog"
compare_result = (a < "cat")

   a. True
   b. False

> **= VS ==**
>
> A common mistake is using = for comparison instead of ==. Ex: `is_zero = num=0` will always assign `is_zero` and `num` with `0`, regardless of num's original value. The = operator performs assignment and will modify the variable. The == operator performs comparison, does not modify the variable, and produces `True` or `False`.

> **EXPLORING FURTHER**
>
> - Unicode Basic Latin Chart (https://openstax.org/r/100unicodelatin)

TRY IT

Friday Boolean

"It's Friday, I'm in love" —from "Friday I'm in Love," a song released by the Cure in 1992.

Write a program that reads in the day of the week. Assign the Boolean variable, `in_love`, with the result of whether the day is Friday or not.

Access multimedia content (https://openstax.org/books/introduction-python-programming/pages/4-1-boolean-values)

TRY IT

Even numbers

Write a program that reads in an integer and prints whether the integer is even or not. Remember, a number is even if the number is divisible by 2. To test this use `number % 2 == 0`. Ex: If the input is 6, the output is `"6 is even: True"`.

Access multimedia content (https://openstax.org/books/introduction-python-programming/pages/4-1-boolean-values)

4.2 If-else statements

Learning objectives

By the end of this section you should be able to

- Identify which operations are performed when a program with `if` and `if-else` statements is run.
- Identify the components of an `if` and `if-else` statement and the necessary formatting.
- Create an `if-else` statement to perform an operation when a condition is true and another operation otherwise.

if statement

If the weather is rainy, grab an umbrella! People make decisions based on conditions like if the weather is rainy, and programs perform operations based on conditions like a variable's value. Ex: A program adds two numbers. If the result is negative, the program prints an error.

A **condition** is an expression that evaluates to true or false. An **if statement** is a decision-making structure that contains a condition and a body of statements. If the condition is true, the body is executed. If the condition is false, the body is not executed.

The `if` statement's body must be grouped together and have one level of indentation. The PEP 8 style guide recommends four spaces per indentation level. The Python interpreter will produce an error if the body is empty.

CHECKPOINT

Example: Quantity check

Access multimedia content (https://openstax.org/books/introduction-python-programming/pages/4-2-if-else-statements)

USING BOOLEAN VARIABLES

A Boolean variable already has a value of `True` or `False` and can be used directly in a condition rather than using the equality operator. Ex: `if is_raining == True:` can be simplified to `if is_raining:`.

CONCEPTS IN PRACTICE

Using if statements

1. Given the following, which part is the condition?

   ```
   if age < 12:
      print("Discount for children available")
   ```

   a. age
   b. age < 12
   c. print("Discount for children available")

2. Given the following, which lines execute if the condition is true?

   ```
   1  print("Have a great day.")
   2  if is_raining:
   3     print("Don't forget an umbrella!")
   4  print("See you soon.")
   ```

   a. 1, 2, 3
   b. 1, 2, 4
   c. 1, 2, 3, 4

3. Given the following (same as above), which lines execute if the condition is False?

   ```
   1  print("Have a great day.")
   ```

```
2  if is_raining:
3      print("Don't forget an umbrella!")
4  print("See you soon.")
```

a. 1, 2, 3
b. 1, 2, 4
c. 1, 2, 3, 4

4. Given num = -10, what is the final value of num?

```
if num < 0:
  num = 25
if num < 100:
  num = num + 50
```

a. -10
b. 40
c. 75

5. Given input 10, what is the final value of positive_num?

```
positive_num = int(input("Enter a positive number:"))
if positive_num < 0:
  print("Negative input set to 0")
positive_num = 0
```

a. 10
b. 0
c. Error

if-else statement

An if statement defines actions to be performed when a condition is true. What if an action needs to be performed only when the condition is false? Ex: If the restaurant is less than a mile away, we'll walk. Else, we'll drive.

An **else statement** is used with an if statement and contains a body of statements that is executed when the if statement's condition is false. When an if-else statement is executed, one and only one of the branches is taken. That is, the body of the if or the body of the else is executed. Note: The else statement is at the same level of indentation as the if statement, and the body is indented.

if-else statement template:

```
1  # Statements before
2
3      if condition:
4          # Body
5      else:
6          # Body
7
```

```
8    # Statements after
```

CHECKPOINT

Example: Trivia question

Access multimedia content (https://openstax.org/books/introduction-python-programming/pages/4-2-if-else-statements)

CONCEPTS IN PRACTICE

Exploring if-else statements

6. Given the following code, the `else` branch is taken for which range of x?

   ```
   if x >= 15:
       # Do something
   else:
       # Do something else
   ```

   a. x >= 15
   b. x <= 15
   c. x < 15

7. Given x = 40, what is the final value of y?

   ```
   if x > 30:
       y = x - 10
   else:
       y = x + 10
   ```

   a. 30
   b. 40
   c. 50

8. Given y = 50, which is *not* a possible final value of y?

   ```
   if x < 50:
       y = y / 2
   else:
       y = y * 2
   y = y + 5
   ```

   a. 30
   b. 55
   c. 105

> **TRY IT**
>
> Improved division
>
> The following program divides two integers. Division by 0 produces an error. Modify the program to read in a new denominator (with no prompt) if the denominator is 0.
>
> Access multimedia content (https://openstax.org/books/introduction-python-programming/pages/4-2-if-else-statements)

> **TRY IT**
>
> Converting temperature units
>
> The following program reads in a temperature as a float and the unit as a string: "f" for Fahrenheit or "c" for Celsius.
>
> Calculate new_temp, the result of converting temp from Fahrenheit to Celsius or Celsius to Fahrenheit based on unit. Calculate new_unit: "c" if unit is "f" and "f" if unit is "c".
>
> Conversion formulas:
> - Degrees Celsius = (degrees Fahrenheit - 32) * 5/9
> - Degrees Fahrenheit = (degrees Celsius * 5/9) + 32
>
> Access multimedia content (https://openstax.org/books/introduction-python-programming/pages/4-2-if-else-statements)

4.3 Boolean operations

Learning objectives

By the end of this section you should be able to

- Explain the purpose of logical operators.
- Describe the truth tables for and, or, and not.
- Create expressions with logical operators.
- Interpret if-else statements with conditions using logical operators.

Logical operator: and

Decisions are often based on multiple conditions. Ex: A program printing if a business is open may check that hour >= 9 and hour < 17. A **logical operator** takes condition operand(s) and produces True or False.

Python has three logical operators: *and*, *or*, and *not*. The **and** operator takes two condition operands and returns True if both conditions are true.

p	q	p and q
True	True	True
True	False	False
False	True	False
False	False	False

Table 4.1 Truth table: p and q.

CHECKPOINT

Example: Museum entry

Access multimedia content (https://openstax.org/books/introduction-python-programming/pages/4-3-boolean-operations)

CONCEPTS IN PRACTICE

Using the and operator

1. Consider the example above. Jaden tries to enter when the capacity is 2500 and there are 2 hours before close. Can Jaden enter?
    a. yes
    b. no

2. Consider the example above. Darcy tries to enter when the capacity is 3000. For what values of `hrs_to_close` will Darcy to be able to enter?
    a. `hrs_to_close > 1.0`
    b. no such value

3. Given is_admin = False and is_online = True, what is the value of is_admin and is_online?
    a. True
    b. False

4. Given x = 8 and y = 21, what is the final value of z?

    ```
    if (x < 10) and (y > 20):
      z = 5
    else:
      z = 0
    ```

    a. 0
    b. 5

Logical operator: or

Sometimes a decision only requires one condition to be true. Ex: If a student is in the band or choir, they will perform in the spring concert. The **or** operator takes two condition operands and returns True if either condition is true.

p	q	p or q
True	True	True
True	False	True
False	True	True
False	False	False

Table 4.2 Truth table: p or q.

CHECKPOINT

Example: Streaming prompt

Access multimedia content (https://openstax.org/books/introduction-python-programming/pages/4-3-boolean-operations)

CONCEPTS IN PRACTICE

Using the or operator

5. Given days = 21 and is_damaged is False, is the refund processed?

   ```
   if (days < 30) or is_damaged:
       # Process refund
   ```

   a. yes
   b. no

6. For what values of age is there no discount?

   ```
   if (age < 12) or (age > 65):
       # Apply student/senior discount
   ```

   a. age >= 12
   b. age <= 65
   c. (age >= 12) and (age <= 65)

7. Given a = 9 and b = 10, does the test pass?

   ```
   if (a%2 == 0 and b%2 == 1) or (a%2 == 1 and b%2 == 0):
   ```

```
    # Test passed
else:
    # Test failed
```
a. yes
b. no

Logical operator: not

If the computer is not on, press the power button. The **not** operator takes one condition operand and returns `True` when the operand is false and returns `False` when the operand is true.

not is a useful operator that can make a condition more readable and can be used to toggle a Boolean's value. Ex: `is_on = not is_on`.

p	not p
True	False
False	True

Table 4.3 Truth table: not p.

CHECKPOINT

Example: Diving warning

Access multimedia content (https://openstax.org/books/introduction-python-programming/pages/4-3-boolean-operations)

CONCEPTS IN PRACTICE

Using the not operator

8. Given `x = 13`, what is the value of `not(x < 10)`?
   a. True
   b. False

9. Given `x = 18`, is x in the correct range?

   ```
   if not(x > 15 and x < 20):
       # x in correct range
   ```

   a. yes
   b. no

10. Given `is_turn = False` and `timer = 65`, what is the final value of `is_turn`?

```
if timer > 60:
  is_turn = not is_turn
```

a. True
b. False

TRY IT

Speed limits

Write a program that reads in a car's speed as an integer and checks if the car's speed is within the freeway limits. A car's speed must be at least 45 mph but no greater than 70 mph on the freeway.

If the speed is within the limits, print "Good driving". Else, print "Follow the speed limits".

Access multimedia content (https://openstax.org/books/introduction-python-programming/pages/4-3-boolean-operations)

4.4 Operator precedence

Learning objectives

By the end of this section you should be able to

- Describe how precedence impacts order of operations.
- Describe how associativity impacts order of operations.
- Explain the purpose of using parentheses in expressions with multiple operators.

Precedence

When an expression has multiple operators, which operator is evaluated first? Precedence rules provide the priority level of operators. Operators with the highest precedence execute first. Ex: `1 + 2 * 3` is 7 because multiplication takes precedence over addition. However, `(1 + 2) * 3` is 9 because parentheses take precedence over multiplication.

Operator	Meaning
()	Parentheses
**	Exponentiation (right associative)
*, /, //, %	Multiplication, division, floor division, modulo
+, -	Addition, subtraction
<, <=, >, >=, ==, !=	Comparison operators

Table 4.4 Operator precedence from highest to lowest.

Operator	Meaning
not	Logical not operator
and	Logical and operator
or	Logical or operator

Table 4.4 Operator precedence from highest to lowest.

CHECKPOINT

Operator precedence

Access multimedia content (https://openstax.org/books/introduction-python-programming/pages/4-4-operator-precedence)

CONCEPTS IN PRACTICE

Precedence rules

Which part of each expression is evaluated first?

1. x ** 2 + 6 / 3
   a. 6 / 3
   b. x ** 2
   c. 2 + 6

2. not 3 * 5 > 10
   a. 3 * 5
   b. not 3
   c. 5 > 10

3. z == 5 and x / 8 < 100
   a. 5 and x
   b. x / 8
   c. 8 < 100

Associativity

What if operators beside each other have the same level of precedence? Associativity determines the order of operations when precedence is the same. Ex: 8 / 4 * 3 is evaluated as (8/4) * 3 rather than 8 / (4*3) because multiplication and division are left associative. Most operators are left associative and are evaluated from left to right. Exponentiation is the main exception (noted above) and is right associative: that is, evaluated from right to left. Ex: 2 ** 3 ** 4 is evaluated as 2 ** (3**4).

When comparison operators are chained, the expression is converted into the equivalent combination of comparisons and evaluated from left to right. Ex. `10 < x <= 20` is evaluated as `10 < x and x <= 20`.

CHECKPOINT

Operation precedence

Access multimedia content (https://openstax.org/books/introduction-python-programming/pages/4-4-operator-precedence)

CONCEPTS IN PRACTICE

Associativity

How is each expression evaluated?

4. `10 + 3 * 2 / 4`
   a. `10 + (3 * (2 / 4))`
   b. `10 + ((3 * 2) / 4)`
   c. `(10 + 3) * (2 / 4)`

5. `2 * 2 ** 2 ** 3`
   a. `2 * ((2 ** 2) ** 3)`
   b. `2 * (2 ** (2 ** 3))`
   c. `((2*2) ** 2) ** 3`

6. `100 < x > 150`
   a. `100 < x and x < 150`
   b. `100 < x or x > 150`
   c. `100 < x and x > 150`

Enforcing order and clarity with parentheses

Operator precedence rules can be hard to remember. Parentheses not only assert a different order of operations but also reduce confusion.

CHECKPOINT

Using parentheses

Access multimedia content (https://openstax.org/books/introduction-python-programming/pages/4-4-operator-precedence)

CONCEPTS IN PRACTICE

Using parentheses

7. Consider the example above. Why was the evaluation order different from what the programmer wanted?
   a. Equality has precedence over and.

b. All operators are evaluated right to left.
c. Order is random when parentheses aren't used.

8. Given x = 8 and y = 9, what is the result of the following?
x + 3 * y - 5
   a. 30
   b. 44
   c. 94

9. Given x = 8 and y = 9, what is the result of the following?
(x+3) * (y-5)
   a. 30
   b. 44
   c. 94

PEP 8 RECOMMENDATIONS: SPACING AROUND OPERATORS

The PEP 8 style guide recommends consistent spacing around operators to avoid extraneous and confusing whitespace.

- Avoid multiple spaces and an unequal amount of whitespace around operators with two operands.
  Avoid: x= y * 44
  Better: x = y * 44
- Avoid spaces immediately inside parentheses.
  Avoid: x = (4 * y)
  Better: x = (4 * y)
- Surround the following operators with one space: assignment, augment assignment, comparison, Boolean.
  Avoid: x= y<44
  Better: x = y < 44
- Consider adding whitespace around operators with lower priority.
  Avoid: x = 5 * z+20
  Better: x = 5*z + 20

4.5 Chained decisions

Learning objectives

By the end of this section you should be able to

- Identify the branches taken in an `if-elif` and `if-elif-else` statement.
- Create a chained decision statement to evaluate multiple conditions.

elif

Sometimes, a complicated decision is based on more than a single condition. Ex: A travel planning site reviews the layovers on an itinerary. If a layover is greater than 24 hours, the site should suggest accommodations. *Else if* the layover is less than one hour, the site should alert for a possible missed connection.

Two separate `if` statements do not guarantee that only one branch is taken and might result in both branches being taken. Ex: The program below attempts to add a curve based on the input test score. If the input is `60`, both `if` statements are incorrectly executed, and the resulting score is 75.

```python
score = int(input())
if score < 70:
   score += 10
# Wrong:
if 70 <= score < 85:
   score += 5
```

Chaining decision statements with `elif` allows the programmer to check for multiple conditions. An **elif** (short for else if) statement checks a condition when the prior decision statement's condition is false. An `elif` statement is part of a chain and must follow an `if` (or `elif`) statement.

`if-elif` statement template:

```python
# Statements before

if condition:
   # Body
elif condition:
   # Body

# Statements after
```

CHECKPOINT

Example: Livestream features

Access multimedia content (https://openstax.org/books/introduction-python-programming/pages/4-5-chained-decisions)

CONCEPTS IN PRACTICE

Using elif

1. Fill in the blank to execute Body 2 when `condition_1` is false and `condition_2` is true.

   ```python
   if condition_1:
     # Body 1
   __ condition_2:
     # Body 2
   ```

   a. `if`
   b. `elif`

c. else

2. Given x = 42 and y = 0, what is the final value of y?

   ```
   if x > 44:
       y += 2
   elif x < 50:
       y += 5
   ```

   a. 2
   b. 5
   c. 7

3. Which conditions complete the code such that if x is less than 0, Body 1 executes, else if x equals 0, Body 2 executes.

   ```
   if _____:
       # Body 1
   elif _____:
       # Body 2
   ```

   a. x < 0
      x == 0
   b. x == 0
      x < 0
   c. x <= 0
      [no condition]

4. Which of the following is a valid chained decision statement?
   a. ```
      if condition_1:
          # Body 1
      elif condition_2:
          # Body 2
      ```
   b. ```
      if condition_1:
          # Body 1
          elif condition_2:
              # Body 2
      ```
   c. ```
      elif condition_1:
          # Body 1
      if condition_2:
          # Body 2
      ```

5. Given attendees = 350, what is the final value of rooms?

   ```
   rooms = 1
   if attendees >= 100:
       rooms += 3
   if attendees <= 200:
       rooms += 7
   ```
   ```

```
   elif attendees <= 400:
      rooms += 14
```

a. 4
b. 15
c. 18

if-elif-else statements

Elifs can be chained with an `if-else` statement to create a more complex decision statement. Ex: A program shows possible chess moves depending on the piece type. If the piece is a pawn, show moving forward one (or two) places. Else if the piece is a bishop, show diagonal moves. Else if . . . (finish for the rest of the pieces).

CHECKPOINT

Example: Possible chess moves

Access multimedia content (https://openstax.org/books/introduction-python-programming/pages/4-5-chained-decisions)

CONCEPTS IN PRACTICE

Using elif within if-elif-else statements

6. Given hour = 12, what is printed?

   ```
   if hour < 8:
      print("Too early")
   elif hour < 12:
      print("Good morning")
   elif hour < 13:
      print("Lunchtime")
   elif hour < 17:
      print("Good afternoon")
   else:
      print("Too late")
   ```

   a. Good morning
   b. Lunchtime
   c. Good afternoon
   d. Too late

7. Where can an `elif` statement be added?

   ```
   _1_
   if condition:
      # Body
   ```

```
    _2_
elif condition:
    # Body
    _3_
else:
    # Body
    _4_
```

a. 1
b. 2
c. 3
d. 4

8. Given x = -1 and y = -2, what is the final value of y?

```
if x < 0 and y < 0:
    y = 10
elif x < 0 and y > 0:
    y = 20
else:
    y = 30
```

a. 10
b. 20
c. 30

9. How could the following statements be rewritten as a chained statement?

```
if price < 9.99:
    order = 50
if 9.99 <= price < 19.99:
    order = 30
if price >= 19.99:
    order = 10
```

a.
```
if price < 9.99:
    order = 50
else:
    order = 30
order = 10
```
b.
```
if price < 9.99:
    order = 50
elif price < 19.99:
    order = 30
elif price == 19.99:
    order = 10
```
c.
```
if price < 9.99:
    order = 50
```

```
    elif price < 19.99:
        order = 30
    else:
        order = 10
```

TRY IT

Crochet hook size conversion

Write a program that reads in a crochet hook's US size and computes the metric diameter in millimeters. (A subset of sizes is used.) If the input does not match B-G, the diameter should be assigned with -1.0. Ex: If the input is D, the output is `"3.25 mm"`.

Size conversions for US size: mm

- B : 2.25
- C : 2.75
- D : 3.25
- E : 3.5
- F : 3.75
- G : 4.0

Access multimedia content (https://openstax.org/books/introduction-python-programming/pages/4-5-chained-decisions)

TRY IT

Color wavelengths

Write a program that reads in an integer representing a visible light wavelength in nanometers. Print the corresponding color using the following inclusive ranges:

- Violet: 380–449
- Blue: 450–484
- Cyan: 485–499
- Green: 500–564
- Yellow: 565–589
- Orange: 590–624
- Red: 625–750

Assume the input is within the visible light spectrum, 380-750 inclusive.

Given input:

```
550
```

The output is:

```
Green
```

Access multimedia content (https://openstax.org/books/introduction-python-programming/pages/4-5-chained-decisions)

4.6 Nested decisions

Learning objectives

By the end of this section you should be able to

- Describe the execution paths of programs with nested `if-else` statements.
- Implement a program with nested `if-else` statements.

Nested decision statements

Suppose a programmer is writing a program that reads in a game ID and player count and prints whether the user has the right number of players for the game.

The programmer may start with:

```
if game == 1 and players < 2:
   print("Not enough players")
if game == 1 and players > 4:
   print("Too many players")
if game == 1 and (2 <= players <= 4):
   print("Ready to start")
if game == 2 and players < 3:
   print("Not enough players")
if game == 2 and players > 6:
   print("Too many players")
if game == 2 and (3 <= players <= 6):
   print("Ready to start")
```

The programmer realizes the code is redundant. What if the programmer could decide the game ID first and then make a decision about players? Nesting allows a decision statement to be inside another decision statement, and is indicated by an indentation level.

An improved program:

```
if game == 1:
   if players < 2:
      print("Not enough players")
   elif players > 4:
      print("Too many players")
   else:
      print("Ready to start")
if game == 2:
```

```python
if players < 3:
    print("Not enough players")
elif players > 6:
    print("Too many players")
else:
    print("Ready to start")
# Test game IDs 3-end
```

CHECKPOINT

Example: Poisonous plant identification

Access multimedia content (https://openstax.org/books/introduction-python-programming/pages/4-6-nested-decisions)

CONCEPTS IN PRACTICE

Using nested if-else statements

1. Consider the example above. Given `leaf_count = 9` and `leaf_shape = "teardrop"`, what is the output?
   a. Might be poison ivy
   b. Might be poison oak
   c. Might be poison sumac

2. Given `num_dancers = 49`, what is printed?

   ```
   if num_dancers < 0:
     print("Error: num_dancers is negative")
   else:
     if num_dancers % 2 == 1:
       print("Error: num_dancers is odd")
     print(num_dancers, "dancers")
   ```

   a. Error: num_dancers is odd
   b. 49 dancers
   c. Error: num_dancers is odd
      49 dancers

3. Given `x = 256`, `y = 513`, and `max = 512`, which of the following will execute?

   ```
   if x == y:
     # Body 1
   elif x < y:
     # Body 2
     if y >= max:
       # Body 3
     else:
   ```

```
        # Body 4
    else:
        # Body 5
```

   a. Body 2
   b. Body 2, Body 3
   c. Body 2, Body 5

4. Given x = 118, y = 300, and max = 512, which of the following will execute?

   ```
   if x == y:
       # Body 1
   elif x < y:
       # Body 2
       if y >= max:
           # Body 3
   else:
       # Body 4
   else:
       # Body 5
   ```

   a. Body 2
   b. Body 3
   c. Error

TRY IT

Meal orders

Write a program that reads in a string, `"lunch"` or `"dinner"`, representing the menu choice, and an integer, 1, 2, or 3, representing the user's meal choice. The program then prints the user's meal choice.

Lunch Meal Options

- 1: Caesar salad
- 2: Spicy chicken wrap
- 3: Butternut squash soup

Dinner Meal Options

- 1: Baked salmon
- 2: Turkey burger
- 3: Mushroom risotto

Ex: If the input is:
```
lunch
3
```

The output is:
```
Your order: Butternut squash soup
```

Access multimedia content (https://openstax.org/books/introduction-python-programming/pages/4-6-nested-decisions)

4.7 Conditional expressions

Learning objectives

By the end of this section you should be able to

- Identify the components of a conditional expression.
- Create a conditional expression.

Conditional expressions

A **conditional expression** (also known as a "ternary operator") is a simplified, single-line version of an `if-else` statement.

Conditional expression template:

```
expression_if_true if condition else expression_if_false
```

A conditional expression is evaluated by first checking the condition. If `condition` is true, `expression_if_true` is evaluated, and the result is the resulting value of the conditional expression. Else, `expression_if_false` is evaluated, and the result is the resulting value of the conditional expression.

A variable can be assigned with a conditional expression. Ex: Finding the max of two numbers can be calculated with `max_num = y if x < y else x`

Note: Conditional expressions have the lowest precedence of all Python operations.

CHECKPOINT

Example: Version check

Access multimedia content (https://openstax.org/books/introduction-python-programming/pages/4-7-conditional-expressions)

CONCEPTS IN PRACTICE

Using conditional expressions

1. What is the conditional expression version of the following `if-else` statement?

   ```
   if x%2 == 0:
      response = 'even'
   else:
      response = 'odd'
   ```

   a. `response = if x%2 == 0 "even" else "odd"`
   b. `response = "odd" if x%2 == 0 else "even"`

c. `response = "even" if x%2 == 0 else "odd"`

2. Given `x = 100` and `offset = 10`, what is the value of `result`?

   `result = x + offset if x < 100 else x - offset`

   a. 90
   b. 100
   c. 110

3. Which part of the conditional expression is incorrect?

   `min_num = x if x < y else min_num = y`

   a. `min_num = x`
   b. `x < y`
   c. `min_num = y`

4. Which of the following is an improved version of the following `if-else` statement?

   ```
   if x < 50:
      result = True
   else:
      result = False
   ```

   a. `result = True if x < 50 else False`
   b. `result = x < 50`

5. What are the possible values of `total`?

   `total = fee + 10 if hours > 12 else 2`

   a. 10, 2
   b. `fee + 10`, 2
   c. `fee + 10`, `fee + 2`

TRY IT

Ping values

Write a program that reads in an integer, ping, and prints `ping_report`, a string indicating whether the ping is low to average or too high. ping values under 150 have a `ping_report` of `"low to average"`. ping values of 150 and higher have a `ping_report` of `"too high"`. Use a conditional expression to assign `ping_report`.

Ex: If the input is 30, the output is `"Ping is low to average"`.

Access multimedia content (https://openstax.org/books/introduction-python-programming/pages/4-7-conditional-expressions)

4.8 Chapter summary

Highlights from this chapter include:

- Booleans represent a value of `True` or `False`.
- Comparison operators compare values and produce `True` or `False`.
- Logical operators take condition operand(s) and produce `True` or `False`.
- Operators are evaluated in order according to precedence and associativity.
- Conditions are expressions that evaluate to `True` or `False`.
- Decision statements allow different paths of execution (branches) through code based on conditions.
- Decision statements can be nested inside other decision statements.
- Conditional expressions are single-line versions of `if-else` statements.

At this point, you should be able to write programs that evaluate conditions and execute code statements accordingly with the correct order of operations. The programming practice below ties together most topics presented in the chapter.

Function	Description
`bool(x)`	Converts x to a Boolean value, either `True` or `False`.

Operator	Description
`x == y` (Equality)	Compares the values of x and y and returns True if the values are equal and `False` otherwise. Ex: `10 == 10` is True.
`x != y` (Inequality)	Compares the values of x and y and returns True if the values are inequal and `False` otherwise. Ex: `7 != 4` is True.
`x > y` (Greater than)	Compares the values of x and y and returns True if the x is greater than y and `False` otherwise. Ex: `9 > 3` is True.
`x < y` (Less than)	Compares the values of x and y and returns True if the x is less than y and `False` otherwise. Ex: `9 < 8` is `False`.
`x >= y` (Greater than or equal)	Compares the values of x and y and returns True if the x is greater than or equal to y and `False` otherwise. Ex: `2 >= 2` is True.
`x <= y` (Less than or equal)	Compares the values of x and y and returns True if the x is less than or equal to y and `False` otherwise. Ex: `8 <= 7` is `False`.

Table 4.5 Chapter 4 reference.

Function	Description
x and y (Logical)	Evaluates the Boolean values of x and y and returns True if both are true. Ex: `True and False` is `False`.
x or y (Logical)	Evaluates the Boolean values of x and y and returns True if either is true. Ex: `True or False` is `True`.
not x (Logical)	Evaluates the Boolean value of x and returns True if the value is false and `False` if the value is true. Ex: `not True` is `False`.
Decision statement	**Description**
| if statement | ```
# Statements before

if condition:
    # Body

# Statements after
``` |
| else statement | ```
# Statements before

if condition:
    # Body
else:
    # Body

# Statements after
``` |

Table 4.5 Chapter 4 reference.

Function	Description
| `elif` statement | ```
# Statements before

if condition:
    # Body
elif condition:
    # Body
else:
    # Body

# Statements after
``` |
| Nested `if` statement | ```
# Statements before

if condition:
    if condition:
        # Body
    else:
        # Body
else:
    if condition:
        # Body
    else:
        # Body

# Statements after
``` |
| **Conditional expression** | `expression_if_true if condition else expression_if_false` |

Table 4.5 Chapter 4 reference.

5 Loops

Figure 5.1 credit: modification of work "Quantum Computing", by Kevin Dooley/Flickr, CC BY 2.0

Chapter Outline

- 5.1 While loop
- 5.2 For loop
- 5.3 Nested loops
- 5.4 Break and continue
- 5.5 Loop else
- 5.6 Chapter summary

 ## Introduction

A **loop** is a code block that runs a set of statements while a given condition is true. A loop is often used for performing a repeating task. Ex: The software on a phone repeatedly checks to see if the phone is idle. Once the time set by a user is reached, the phone is locked. Loops can also be used for iterating over lists like student names in a roster, and printing the names one at a time.

In this chapter, two types of loops, `for` loop and `while` loop, are introduced. This chapter also introduces `break` and `continue` statements for controlling a loop's execution.

 ## 5.1 While loop

Learning objectives

By the end of this section you should be able to

- Explain the loop construct in Python.
- Use a `while` loop to implement repeating tasks.

While loop

A **while loop** is a code construct that runs a set of statements, known as the loop body, while a given condition, known as the loop expression, is true. At each iteration, once the loop statement is executed, the loop expression is evaluated again.

- If true, the loop body will execute at least one more time (also called looping or iterating one more time).
- If false, the loop's execution will terminate and the next statement after the loop body will execute.

CHECKPOINT

While loop

Access multimedia content (https://openstax.org/books/introduction-python-programming/pages/5-1-while-loop)

CONCEPTS IN PRACTICE

While loop example

Fibonacci is a series of numbers in which each number is the sum of the two preceding numbers. The Fibonacci sequence starts with two ones: 1, 1, 2, 3, ... Consider the following code that prints all Fibonacci numbers less than 20, and answer the following questions.

```
# Initializing the first two Fibonacci numbers
f = 1
g = 1
print (f, end = ' ')

# Running the loop while the last Fibonacci number is less than 20
while g < 20:
  print(g, end = ' ')
  # Calculating the next Fibonacci number and updating the last two sequence numbers
  temp = f
  f = g
  g = temp + g
```

1. How many times does the loop execute?
    a. 5
    b. 6
    c. 7

2. What is the variable g's value when the while loop condition evaluates to `False`?
    a. 13
    b. 20
    c. 21

3. What are the printed values in the output?
    a. 1 1 2 3 5 8 13
    b. 1 2 3 5 8 13
    c. 1 1 2 3 5 8 13 21

Counting with a while loop

A while loop can be used to count up or down. A counter variable can be used in the loop expression to determine the number of iterations executed. Ex: A programmer may want to print all even numbers between 1 and 20. The task can be done by using a counter initialized with 1. In each iteration, the counter's value is increased by one, and a condition can check whether the counter's value is an even number or not. The change in the counter's value in each iteration is called the **step size**. The step size can be any positive or negative value. If the step size is a positive number, the counter counts in ascending order, and if the step size is a negative number, the counter counts in descending order.

EXAMPLE 5.1

A program printing all odd numbers between 1 and 10

```python
# Initialization
counter = 1

# While loop condition
while counter <= 10:
  if counter % 2 == 1:
    print(counter)
  # Counting up and increasing counter's value by 1 in each iteration
  counter += 1
```

CHECKPOINT

Counting with while loop

Access multimedia content (https://openstax.org/books/introduction-python-programming/pages/5-1-while-loop)

CONCEPTS IN PRACTICE

while loop counting examples

Given the code, answer the following questions.

```python
n = 4
while n > 0:
  print(n)
  n = n - 1

print("value of n after the loop is", n)
```

4. How many times does the loop execute?
   a. 3
   b. 4
   c. 5

5. Which line is printed as the last line of output?
   a. `value of n after the loop is -1`.
   b. `value of n after the loop is 0`.
   c. `value of n after the loop is 1`.

6. What happens if the code is changed as follows?

   ```
   n = 4
   while n > 0:
       print(n)
       # Modified line
       n = n + 1

   print("value of n after the loop is", n)
   ```

   a. The code will not run.
   b. The code will run for one additional iteration.
   c. The code will never terminate.

TRY IT

Reading inputs in a while loop

Write a program that takes user inputs in a `while` loop until the user enters `"begin"`. Test the code with the given input values to check that the loop does not terminate until the input is `"begin"`. Once the input `"begin"` is received, print `"The while loop condition has been met."`.

Enter different input words to see when the `while` loop condition is met.

Access multimedia content (https://openstax.org/books/introduction-python-programming/pages/5-1-while-loop)

TRY IT

Sum of odd numbers

Write a program that reads two integer values, n1 and n2. Use a `while` loop to calculate the sum of odd numbers between n1 and n2 (inclusive of n1 and n2). Remember, a number is odd if `number % 2 != 0`.

Access multimedia content (https://openstax.org/books/introduction-python-programming/pages/5-1-while-loop)

5.2 For loop

Learning objectives

By the end of this section you should be able to

- Explain the `for` loop construct.
- Use a `for` loop to implement repeating tasks.

For loop

In Python, a **container** can be a range of numbers, a string of characters, or a list of values. To access objects within a container, an iterative loop can be designed to retrieve objects one at a time. A **for loop** iterates over all elements in a container. Ex: Iterating over a class roster and printing students' names.

> **CHECKPOINT**
>
> For loop example for iterating over a container object
>
> Access multimedia content (https://openstax.org/books/introduction-python-programming/pages/5-2-for-loop)

> **CONCEPTS IN PRACTICE**
>
> For loop over a string container
>
> A string variable can be considered a container of multiple characters, and hence can be iterated on. Given the following code, answer the questions.
>
> ```
> str_var = "A string"
>
> count = 0
> for c in str_var:
>     count += 1
>
> print(count)
> ```
>
> 1. What is the program's output?
>   a. 7
>   b. 8
>   c. 9
>
> 2. What's the code's output if the line `count += 1` is replaced with `count *= 2`?
>   a. 0
>   b. 16
>   c. 2^8
>
> 3. What is printed if the code is changed as follows?

```
str_var = "A string"

count = 0
for c in str_var:
  count += 1
  # New line
  print(c, end = '*')

print(count)
```

   a. A string*
   b. A*s*t*r*i*n*g*
   c. A* *s*t*r*i*n*g*

Range() function in for loop

A for loop can be used for iteration and counting. The range() function is a common approach for implementing counting in a for loop. A **range()** function generates a sequence of integers between the two numbers given a step size. This integer sequence is inclusive of the start and exclusive of the end of the sequence. The range() function can take up to three input values. Examples are provided in the table below.

Range function	Description	Example	Output
range(end)	• Generates a sequence beginning at 0 until end. • Step size: 1	range(4)	0, 1, 2, 3
range(start, end)	• Generates a sequence beginning at start until end. • Step size: 1	range(0, 3)	0, 1, 2
		range(2, 6)	2, 3, 4, 5
		range(-13, -9)	-13, -12, -11, -10
range(start, end, step)	• Generates a sequence beginning at start until end. • Step size: step	range(0, 4, 1)	0, 1, 2, 3
		range(1, 7, 2)	1, 3, 5

Table 5.1 Using the range() function.

Range function	Description	Example	Output
		range(3, -2, -1)	3, 2, 1, 0, -1
		range(10, 0, -4)	10, 6, 2

Table 5.1 Using the range() function.

EXAMPLE 5.2

Two programs printing all integer multiples of 5 less than 50 (Notice the compactness of the `for` construction compared to the `while`)

```
# For loop condition using
# range() function to print
# all multiples of 5 less than 50
for i in range(0, 50, 5):
    print(i)
```

```
# While loop implementation of printing
# multiples of 5 less than 50

# Initialization
i = 0
# Limiting the range to be less than 50
while i < 50:
    print(i)
    i+=5
```

Table 5.2

CONCEPTS IN PRACTICE

For loop using a range() function

4. What are the arguments to the `range()` function for the increasing sequence of every 3rd integer from 10 to 22 (inclusive of both ends)?
   a. range(10, 23, 3)
   b. range(10, 22, 3)
   c. range(22, 10, -3)

5. What are the arguments to the `range()` function for the decreasing sequence of every integer from 5 to 1 (inclusive of both ends)?
   a. range(5, 1, 1)
   b. range(5, 1, -1)
   c. range(5, 0, -1)

6. What is the sequence generated from `range(-1, -2, -1)`?
   a. 1
   b. -1, -2
   c. -2

7. What is the output of the `range(1, 2, -1)`?
   a. 1
   b. 1, 2
   c. empty sequence

8. What is the output of `range(5, 2)`?
   a. 0, 2, 4
   b. 2, 3, 4
   c. empty sequence

TRY IT

Counting spaces

Write a program using a `for` loop that takes in a string as input and counts the number of spaces in the provided string. The program must print the number of spaces counted. Ex: If the input is `"Hi everyone"`, the program outputs 1.

Access multimedia content (https://openstax.org/books/introduction-python-programming/pages/5-2-for-loop)

TRY IT

Sequences

Write a program that reads two integer values, n1 and n2, with n1 < n2, and performs the following tasks:

1. Prints all even numbers between the two provided numbers (inclusive of both), in ascending order.
2. Prints all odd numbers between the two provided numbers (exclusive of both), in descending order.

```
Input: 2 8


prints
2 4 6 8
7 5 3
```

Note: the program should return an error message if the second number is smaller than the first.

Access multimedia content (https://openstax.org/books/introduction-python-programming/pages/5-2-for-loop)

5.3 Nested loops

Learning objectives

By the end of this section you should be able to

- Implement nested `while` loops.
- Implement nested `for` loops.

Nested loops

A **nested loop** has one or more loops within the body of another loop. The two loops are referred to as **outer loop** and **inner loop**. The outer loop controls the number of the inner loop's full execution. More than one inner loop can exist in a nested loop.

> **CHECKPOINT**
>
> **Nested while loops**
>
> Access multimedia content (https://openstax.org/books/introduction-python-programming/pages/5-3-nested-loops)

> **EXAMPLE 5.3**
>
> **Available appointments**
>
> Consider a doctor's office schedule. Each appointment is 30 minutes long. A program to print available appointments can use a nested `for` loop where the outer loop iterates over the hours, and the inner loop iterates over the minutes. This example prints time in hours and minutes in the range between 8:00am and 10:00am. In this example, the outer loop iterates over the time's hour portion between 8 and 9, and the inner loop iterates over the time's minute portion between 0 and 59.

```python
hour = 8
minute = 0
while hour <= 9:
   while minute <= 59:
      print(hour, ":", minute)
      minute += 30
   hour += 1
   minute = 0
```

The above code's output is:

```
8 : 0
8 : 30
9 : 0
9 : 30
```

CONCEPTS IN PRACTICE

Nested while loop question set

1. Given the following code, how many times does the print statement execute?

   ```
   i = 1
   while i <= 5:
     j = 1
     while i + j <= 5:
       print(i, j)
       j += 1
     i += 1
   ```

   a. 5
   b. 10
   c. 25

2. What is the output of the following code?

   ```
   i = 1

   while i <= 2:
     j = 1
     while j <= 3:
       print('*', end = '')
       j += 1
     print()
     i += 1
   ```

   a. ******
   b. ***
      ***
   c. **
      **
      **

3. Which program prints the following output?

   ```
   1 2 3 4
   2 4 6 8
   3 6 9 12
   4 8 12 16
   ```

   a. ```
      i = 1
      while i <= 4:
        while j <= 4:
          print(i * j, end = ' ')
          j += 1
        print()
      ```
      ```

```
        i += 1
  b. i = 1
     while i <= 4:
        j = 1
        while j <= 4:
           print(i * j, end = ' ')
           j += 1
        print()
        i += 1
  c. i = 1
     while i <= 4:
        j = 1
        while j <= 4:
           print(i * j, end = ' ')
           j += 1
        i += 1
```

Nested for loops

A nested `for` loop can be implemented and used in the same way as a nested `while` loop. A `for` loop is a preferable option in cases where a loop is used for counting purposes using a `range()` function, or when iterating over a container object, including nested situations. Ex: Iterating over multiple course rosters. The outer loop iterates over different courses, and the inner loop iterates over the names in each course roster.

CHECKPOINT

Nested for loops

Access multimedia content (https://openstax.org/books/introduction-python-programming/pages/5-3-nested-loops)

CONCEPTS IN PRACTICE

Nested loop practices

4. Given the following code, how many times does the outer loop execute?

   ```
   for i in range(3):
      for j in range(4):
         print(i, ' ', j)
   ```

   a. 3
   b. 4
   c. 12

5. Given the following code, how many times does the inner loop execute?

   ```
   for i in range(3):
   ```

```
   for j in range(4):
     print(i, ' ', j)
```

a. 4
b. 12
c. 20

6. Which program prints the following output?

```
0 1 2 3
0 2 4 6
0 3 6 9
```

a.
```
for i in range(4):
   for j in range(4):
      print(i * j, end = ' ')
   print()
```
b.
```
for i in range(1, 4):
   for j in range(4):
      print(i * j)
```
c.
```
for i in range(1, 4):
   for j in range(4):
      print(i * j, end = ' ')
   print()
```

MIXED LOOPS

The two for and while loop constructs can also be mixed in a nested loop construct. Ex: Printing even numbers less than a given number in a list. The outer loop can be implemented using a for loop iterating over the provided list, and the inner loop iterates over all even numbers less than a given number from the list using a while loop.

```
numbers = [12, 5, 3]

i = 0
for n in numbers:
   while i < n:
      print (i, end = " ")
      i += 2
   i = 0
   print()
```

TRY IT

Printing a triangle of numbers

Write a program that prints the following output:

```
1 2 3 4 5 6 7 8 9
1 2 3 4 5 6 7 8
1 2 3 4 5 6 7
1 2 3 4 5 6
1 2 3 4 5
1 2 3 4
1 2 3
1 2
1
```

Finish!

Access multimedia content (https://openstax.org/books/introduction-python-programming/pages/5-3-nested-loops)

TRY IT

Printing two triangles

Write a program that prints the following output using nested `while` and `for` loops:

```
****
***
**
*
++++
+++
++
+
```

Access multimedia content (https://openstax.org/books/introduction-python-programming/pages/5-3-nested-loops)

5.4 Break and continue

Learning objectives

By the end of this section you should be able to

- Analyze a loop's execution with `break` and `continue` statements.
- Use `break` and `continue` control statements in `while` and `for` loops.

Break

A **break** statement is used within a `for` or a `while` loop to allow the program execution to exit the loop once a given condition is triggered. A `break` statement can be used to improve runtime efficiency when further loop execution is not required.

Ex: A loop that looks for the character "a" in a given string called `user_string`. The loop below is a regular `for` loop for going through all the characters of `user_string`. If the character is found, the break statement takes execution out of the `for` loop. Since the task has been accomplished, the rest of the `for` loop execution is bypassed.

```python
user_string = "This is a string."
for i in range(len(user_string)):
    if user_string[i] == 'a':
        print("Found at index:", i)
        break
```

CHECKPOINT

Break statement in a while loop

Access multimedia content (https://openstax.org/books/introduction-python-programming/pages/5-4-break-and-continue)

INFINITE LOOP

A `break` statement is an essential part of a loop that does not have a termination condition. A loop without a termination condition is known as an **infinite loop**. Ex: An infinite loop that counts up starting from 1 and prints the counter's value while the counter's value is less than 10. A `break` condition is triggered when the counter's value is equal to 10, and hence the program execution exits.

```python
counter = 1
while True:
    if counter >= 10:
        break
    print(counter)
    counter += 1
```

CONCEPTS IN PRACTICE

Using a break statement

1. What is the following code's output?

```
string_val = "Hello World"
for c in string_val:
   if c == " ":
      break
   print(c)
```

a. Hello
b. Hello World
c. H
   e
   l
   l
   o

2. Given the following code, how many times does the print statement get executed?

```
i = 1
while True:
   if i%3 == 0 and i%5 == 0:
      print(i)
      break
   i += 1
```

a. 0
b. 1
c. 15

3. What is the final value of i?

```
i = 1
count = 0
while True:
   if i%2 == 0 or i%3 == 0:
      count += 1
   if count >= 5:
      print(i)
      break
   i += 1
```

a. 5
b. 8
c. 30

Continue

A **continue** statement allows for skipping the execution of the remainder of the loop without exiting the loop entirely. A continue statement can be used in a for or a while loop. After the continue statement's execution, the loop expression will be evaluated again and the loop will continue from the loop's expression. A continue statement facilitates the loop's control and readability.

CHECKPOINT

Continue statement in a while loop

Access multimedia content (https://openstax.org/books/introduction-python-programming/pages/5-4-break-and-continue)

CONCEPTS IN PRACTICE

Using a continue statement

4. Given the following code, how many times does the print statement get executed?

   ```
   i = 10
   while i >= 0:
     i -= 1
     if i%3 != 0:
        continue
     print(i)
   ```

   a. 3
   b. 4
   c. 11

5. What is the following code's output?

   ```
   for c in "hi Ali":
     if c == " ":
        continue
     print(c)
   ```

   a. h
      i

      A
      l
      i
   b. h
      i
      A
      l
      i
   c. hi
      Ali

TRY IT

Using break control statement in a loop

Write a program that reads a string value and prints `"Found"` if the string contains a space character. Else, prints `"Not found"`.

Access multimedia content (https://openstax.org/books/introduction-python-programming/pages/5-4-break-and-continue)

TRY IT

Using a continue statement in a loop

Complete the following code so that the program calculates the sum of all the numbers in list `my_list` that are greater than or equal to 5.

Access multimedia content (https://openstax.org/books/introduction-python-programming/pages/5-4-break-and-continue)

5.5 Loop else

Learning objectives

By the end of this section you should be able to

- Use loop `else` statement to identify when the loop execution is interrupted using a `break` statement.
- Implement a loop `else` statement with a `for` or a `while` loop.

Loop else

A **loop else** statement runs after the loop's execution is completed without being interrupted by a break statement. A loop `else` is used to identify if the loop is terminated normally or the execution is interrupted by a `break` statement.

Ex: A `for` loop that iterates over a list of numbers to find if the value `10` is in the list. In each iteration, if `10` is observed, the statement `"Found 10!"` is printed and the execution can terminate using a break statement. If `10` is not in the list, the loop terminates when all integers in the list are evaluated, and hence the `else` statement will run and print `"10 is not in the list."` Alternatively, a Boolean variable can be used to track whether number `10` is found after loop's execution terminates.

EXAMPLE 5.4

Finding the number 10 in a list

In the code examples below, the code on the left prints `"Found 10!"` if the variable i's value is `10`. If the value `10` is not in the list, the code prints `"10 is not in the list."`. The code on the right uses the seen Boolean variable to track if the value `10` is in the list. After loop's execution, if seen's value is still false, the code prints `"10 is not in the list."`.

```
numbers = [2, 5, 7, 11, 12]
for i in numbers:
  if i == 10:
    print("Found 10!")
    break
else:
  print("10 is not in the list.")
```

```
numbers = [2, 5, 7, 11, 12]
seen = False
for i in numbers:
  if i == 10:
    print("Found 10!")
    seen = True
if seen == False:
  print("10 is not in the list.")
```

Table 5.3

CHECKPOINT

Loop else template

Access multimedia content (https://openstax.org/books/introduction-python-programming/pages/5-5-loop-else)

CONCEPTS IN PRACTICE

Loop else practices

1. What is the output?

   ```
   n = 16
   exp = 0
   i = n
   while i > 1:
     if n%2 == 0:
       i = i/2
       exp += 1
     else:
       break
   else:
     print(n,"is 2 to the", exp)
   ```

   a. 16 is 2 to the 3
   b. 16 is 2 to the 4
   c. no output

2. What is the output?

```
n = 7
exp = 0
i = n
while i > 1:
  if n%2 == 0:
    i = i//2
    exp += 1
  else:
    break
else:
  print(n,"is 2 to the", exp)
```

a. no output
b. 7 is 2 to the 3
c. 7 is 2 to the 2

3. What is the output?

```
numbers = [1, 2, 2, 6]
for i in numbers:
  if i >= 5:
    print("Not all numbers are less than 5.")
    break
  else:
    print(i)
    continue
else:
  print("all numbers are less than 5.")
```

a. 1
   2
   2
   6
   Not all numbers are less than 5.
b. 1
   2
   2
   Not all numbers are less than 5.
c. 1
   2
   2
   6
   all numbers are less than 5.

TRY IT

Sum of values less than 10

Write a program that, given a list, calculates the sum of all integer values less than 10. If a value greater than or equal to 10 is in the list, no output should be printed. Test the code for different values in the list.

Access multimedia content (https://openstax.org/books/introduction-python-programming/pages/5-5-loop-else)

5.6 Chapter summary

Highlights from this chapter include:

- A `while` loop runs a set of statements, known as the loop body, while a given condition, known as the loop expression, is true.
- A `for` loop can be used to iterate over elements of a container object.
- A `range()` function generates a sequence of integers between the two numbers given a step size.
- A nested loop has one or more loops within the body of another loop.
- A `break` statement is used within a `for` or a `while` loop to allow the program execution to exit the loop once a given condition is triggered.
- A `continue` statement allows for skipping the execution of the remainder of the loop without exiting the loop entirely.
- A loop `else` statement runs after the loop's execution is completed without being interrupted by a `break` statement.

At this point, you should be able to write programs with loop constructs. The programming practice below ties together most topics presented in the chapter.

Function	Description
`range(end)`	Generates a sequence beginning at 0 until end with step size of 1.
`range(start, end)`	Generates a sequence beginning at `start` until end with step size of 1.
`range(start, end, s)`	Generates a sequence beginning at `start` until end with the step size of s.
Loop constructs	**Description**

Table 5.4 Chapter 5 reference.

Function	Description
| while loop | ```
# initialization
while expression:
    # loop body

# statements after the loop
``` |
| for loop | ```
# initialization
for loop_variable in container:
    # loop body

# statements after the loop
``` |
| Nested while loop | ```
while outer_loop_expression:
    # outer loop body (1)
    while inner_loop_expression:
        # inner loop body
    # outer loop body (2)

# statements after the loop
``` |
| break statement | ```
# initialization
while loop_expression:
    # loop body
    if break_condition:
        break
    # remaining body of loop

# statements after the loop
``` |

Table 5.4 Chapter 5 reference.

Function	Description
| continue statement | ```
# initialization
while loop_expression:
    # loop body
    if continue_condition:
       continue
    # remaining body of loop

# statements after the loop
``` |
| Loop else statement | ```
# initialization
for loop_expression:
    # loop body
    if break_condition:
       break
    # remaining body of loop
else:
    # loop else statement

# statements after the loop
``` |

Table 5.4 Chapter 5 reference.

TRY IT

Prime numbers

Write a program that takes in a positive integer number (N) and prints out the first N prime numbers on separate lines.

Note: A prime number is a number that is not divisible by any positive number larger than 1. To check whether a number is prime, the condition of `number % i != 0` can be checked for `i` greater than `1` and less than `number`.

Ex: if N = 6, the output is:

```
2
3
5
7
```

11
13

[Access multimedia content](https://openstax.org/books/introduction-python-programming/pages/5-6-chapter-summary)

6 Functions

Figure 6.1 credit: modification of work "IMG_3037", by Jay Roc/Flickr, Public Domain

Chapter Outline

- 6.1 Defining functions
- 6.2 Control flow
- 6.3 Variable scope
- 6.4 Parameters
- 6.5 Return values
- 6.6 Keyword arguments
- 6.7 Chapter summary

 ## Introduction

Functions are the next step toward creating optimized code as a software developer. If the same block of code is reused repeatedly, a function allows the programmer to write the block of code once, name the block, and use the code as many times as needed by calling the block by name. Functions can read in values and return values to perform tasks, including complex calculations.

Like branching statements discussed in the Decisions chapter, functions allow different paths of execution through a program, and this chapter discusses control flow and the scope of variables in more detail.

 ## 6.1 Defining functions

Learning objectives

By the end of this section you should be able to

- Identify function calls in a program.
- Define a parameterless function that outputs strings.
- Describe benefits of using functions.

Calling a function

Throughout the book, functions have been called to perform tasks. Ex: `print()` prints values, and `sqrt()` calculates the square root. A **function** is a named, reusable block of code that performs a task when called.

CHECKPOINT

Example: Simple math program

Access multimedia content (https://openstax.org/books/introduction-python-programming/pages/6-1-defining-functions)

CONCEPTS IN PRACTICE

Identifying function calls

1. Which line has a function call?

   ```
   1  input_num = 14
   2  offset_num = input_num - 10
   3  print(offset_num)
   ```

   a. line 1
   b. line 2
   c. line 3

2. How many times is print() called?

   ```
   print("Please log in")
   username = input("Username:")
   password = input("Password:")
   print("Login successful")
   print("Welcome,", username)
   ```

   a. 1
   b. 3
   c. 5

3. How many function calls are there?

   ```
   # Use float() to convert input for area calculation
   width = float(input("Enter width:"))
   height = float(input("Enter height:"))
   print("Area is", width*height)
   ```

   a. 3
   b. 5
   c. 6

Defining a function

A function is defined using the **def** keyword. The first line contains `def` followed by the function name (in snake case), parentheses (with any parameters—discussed later), and a colon. The indented body begins with a documentation string describing the function's task and contains the function statements. A function must be defined before the function is called.

CHECKPOINT

Example: Welcome message function

Access multimedia content (https://openstax.org/books/introduction-python-programming/pages/6-1-defining-functions)

CONCEPTS IN PRACTICE

Defining functions

4. What's wrong with the first line of the function definition?

   ```
   def water_plant:
   ```

   a. A docstring should go after the colon.
   b. Parentheses should go after `water_plant`.
   c. `def` should be `define` before `water_plant`.

5. What is the output?

   ```
   def print_phone_num():
      print("Phone: (", 864, ")", 555, "-", 0199)

   print("User info:")
   print_phone_num()
   ```

   a. Phone: (864) 555 - 1000
      User info:
      Phone: (864) 555 - 1000
   b. User info:
   c. User info:
      Phone: (864) 555 - 1000

6. Which statement calls a function named `print_pc_specs()`?
   a. `print_pc_specs`
   b. `print_pc_specs()`
   c. `print_pc_specs():`

7. Which is an appropriate name for a function that calculates a user's taxes?
   a. `calc_tax`
   b. `calculate user tax`
   c. `c_t`

Benefits of functions

A function promotes modularity by putting code statements related to a single task in a separate group. The body of a function can be executed repeatedly with multiple function calls, so a function promotes reusability. Modular, reusable code is easier to modify and is shareable among programmers to avoid reinventing the wheel.

CHECKPOINT

Improving a program with a function

Access multimedia content (https://openstax.org/books/introduction-python-programming/pages/6-1-defining-functions)

CONCEPTS IN PRACTICE

Improving programs with functions

Consider the code above.

8. If the points were changed from floats to integers, how many statements would need to be changed in the original and revised programs respectively?
   a. 3, 1
   b. 4, 4
   c. 12, 4

9. How many times can `calc_distance()` be called?
   a. 1
   b. 3
   c. many

TRY IT

Cinema concession stand

Write a function, `concessions()`, that prints the food and drink options at a cinema.

Given:

```
concessions()
```

The output is:

```
Food/Drink Options:
Popcorn: $8-10
Candy: $3-5
Soft drink: $5-7
```

Access multimedia content (https://openstax.org/books/introduction-python-programming/pages/6-1-defining-functions)

TRY IT

Terms and conditions prompt

Write a function, `terms()`, that asks the user to accept the terms and conditions, reads in Y/N, and outputs a response. In the main program, read in the number of users and call `terms()` for each user.

Given inputs `1` and `"Y"`, the output is:

```
Do you accept the terms and conditions?
Y
Thank you for accepting.
```

Given inputs `2`, `"N"`, and `"Y"`, the output is:

```
Do you accept the terms and conditions?
N
Have a good day.
Do you accept the terms and conditions?
Y
Thank you for accepting.
```

Access multimedia content (https://openstax.org/books/introduction-python-programming/pages/6-1-defining-functions)

6.2 Control flow

Learning objectives

By the end of this section you should be able to

- Identify the control flow of a program.
- Describe how control flow moves between statements and function calls.

Control flow and functions

Control flow is the sequence of program execution. A program's control flow begins at the main program but rarely follows a strict sequence. Ex: Control flow skips over lines when a conditional statement isn't executed.

When execution reaches a function call, control flow moves to where the function is defined and executes the function statements. Then, control flow moves back to where the function was called and continues the sequence.

CHECKPOINT

Calling a brunch menu function

Access multimedia content (https://openstax.org/books/introduction-python-programming/pages/6-2-control-flow)

CONCEPTS IN PRACTICE

Following the control flow

1. Which line is executed first?

   ```
   1  def park_greet():
   2      """Output greeting."""
   3      print("Welcome. Open sunrise to sunset.")
   4
   5  car_count = 1
   6  park_greet()
   7  if car_count > 50:
   8      # Direct to extra parking lot
   ```

   a. 1
   b. 3
   c. 5

2. Control flow moves to line 9, and `park_greet()` is called. Which line does control flow move to next?

   ```
   1   def extra_lot():
   2       # Function definition
   3
   4   def park_greet():
   5       """Output greeting."""
   6       print("Welcome. Open sunrise to sunset.")
   7
   8   car_count = 1
   9   park_greet()
   10  if car_count > 50:
   11      extra_lot()
   ```

   a. 1
   b. 4
   c. 10

3. Control flow moves to line 12, and `extra_lot()` is called. Which line does control flow move to after line 3 is executed?

   ```
   1  def extra_lot():
   2      """Output extra parking lot info."""
   ```

```
 3      print("Take the second right to park.")
 4
 5   def park_greet():
 6       """Output greeting."""
 7       print("Welcome. Open sunrise to sunset.")
 8
 9   car_count = 1
10   park_greet()
11   if car_count > 50:
12       extra_lot()
```

a. 5
b. 8
c. 12

4. What is the output?

   ```
   def park_greet():
      """Output greeting."""
      print("Welcome to the park")
   print("Open sunrise to sunset")

   park_greet()
   ```

   a. Welcome to the park
   b. Welcome to the park
      Open sunrise to sunset
   c. Open sunrise to sunset
      Welcome to the park

Functions calling functions

Functions frequently call other functions to keep the modularity of each function performing one task. Ex: A function that calculates an order total may call a function that calculates sales tax. When a function called from another function finishes execution, control flow returns to the calling function.

CHECKPOINT

Example: Book club email messages

Access multimedia content (https://openstax.org/books/introduction-python-programming/pages/6-2-control-flow)

CONCEPTS IN PRACTICE

Functions calling functions

Consider the book club example above.

5. How many function calls occur during the execution of the program?
   a. 2
   b. 3
   c. 6

6. When line 3 is reached and executed, which line does control flow return to?
   a. 1
   b. 11
   c. 16

TRY IT

Updated terms and conditions prompt

Write an updated function, `terms()`, that asks the user to accept the terms and conditions, reads in Y/N, and outputs a response by calling `accepted()` or `rejected()`. `accepted()` prints "Thank you for accepting the terms." and `rejected()` prints "You have rejected the terms. Thank you.".

Given inputs 2, "Y" and "N", the output is:

```
Do you accept the terms and conditions?
Y
Thank you for accepting the terms.
```

Given a function call to `terms()` and input "N", the output is:

```
Do you accept the terms and conditions?
N
You have rejected the terms. Thank you.
```

Access multimedia content (https://openstax.org/books/introduction-python-programming/pages/6-2-control-flow)

TRY IT

Laundromat information

Write a program that uses three functions to print information about a laundromat, Liam's Laundry:

- `laundromat_info()`: Prints the name, Liam's Laundry, and hours of operation, 7a - 11p, and calls `washers_open()` and `dryers_open()`
- `washers_open()`: Reads an integer, assigns `washer_count` with the value, and prints `washer_count`
- `dryers_open()`: Reads an integer, assigns `dryer_count` with the value, and prints `dryer_count`

The main program should just call `laundromat_info()`.

Given inputs `50` and `40`, the output is:

```
Liam's Laundry
7a - 11p
 Open washers: 50
 Open dryers: 40
```

Access multimedia content (https://openstax.org/books/introduction-python-programming/pages/6-2-control-flow)

6.3 Variable scope

Learning objectives

By the end of this section you should be able to

- Identify the scope of a program's variables.
- Discuss the impact of a variable's scope.

Global scope

A variable's **scope** is the part of a program where the variable can be accessed. A variable created outside of a function has **global scope** and can be accessed anywhere in the program. A Python program begins in global scope, and the global scope lasts for the entire program execution.

CHECKPOINT

Global variables in a program with a function

Access multimedia content (https://openstax.org/books/introduction-python-programming/pages/6-3-variable-scope)

CONCEPTS IN PRACTICE

Global variables

1. Which variables are global?

   ```
   num = float(input())
   num_sq = num * num
   print(num, "squared is", num_sq)
   ```

   a. num only
   b. num_sq only
   c. num and num_sq

2. Which variables have global scope?

   ```
   def print_square():
   ```

```
    num_sq = num * num
    print(num, "squared is", num_sq)

num = float(input())
print_square()
```

a. num only
b. num_sq only
c. num and num_sq

3. Which functions can access num?

```
def print_double():
    num_d = num * 2
    print(num, "doubled is", num_d)

def print_square():
    num_sq = num * num
    print(num, "squared is", num_sq)

num = float(input())
print_double()
print_square()
```

a. print_double()
b. print_square()
c. print_double() and print_square()

Local scope

A variable created within a function has **local scope** and only exists within the function. A local variable cannot be accessed outside of the function in which the variable was created. After a function finishes executing, the function's local variables no longer exist.

CHECKPOINT

Global and local variables in a program with a function

Access multimedia content (https://openstax.org/books/introduction-python-programming/pages/6-3-variable-scope)

CONCEPTS IN PRACTICE

Local variables

4. Which variables are local?

```
def print_time():
   out_str = "Time is " + str(hour) + ":" + str(min)
   print(out_str)

hour = int(input())
min = int(input())
print_time()
```

a. hour and min
b. out_str
c. hour, min, and out_str

5. Which variables are local?

```
def print_greeting():
   print(out_str)

hour = int(input())
min = int(input())
if hour < 12:
   out_str = "Good morning"
else:
   out_str = "Good day"
print_greeting()
```

a. hour and min
b. out_str
c. none

6. Which functions directly access out_str?

```
def print_greeting():
   print("Good day,")
   print_time()

def print_time():
   out_str = "Time is " + str(hour) + ":" + str(min)
   print(out_str)

hour = int(input())
min = int(input())
print_greeting()
```

a. print_greeting()
b. print_time()
c. print_greeting() and print_time()

Using local and global variables together

Python allows global and local variables to have the same name, which can lead to unexpected program behavior. A function treats a variable edited within the function as a local variable unless told otherwise. To edit a global variable inside a function, the variable must be declared with the `global` keyword.

CHECKPOINT

Editing global variables in a program with a function

Access multimedia content (https://openstax.org/books/introduction-python-programming/pages/6-3-variable-scope)

CONCEPTS IN PRACTICE

Using both local and global variables

Consider the following variations on the example program with the input 9.

7. What is the output?

    ```python
    def update_hour():
        tmp = hour
        if is_dst:
            tmp += 1
        else:
            tmp -= 1

    is_dst = True
    hour = int(input("Enter hour: "))
    update_hour()
    print("New hour:", hour)
    ```

    a. New hour: 9
    b. New hour: 10
    c. Error

8. What is the output?

    ```python
    def update_hour():
        new_hour = hour
        if is_dst:
            new_hour += 1
        else:
            new_hour -= 1

    is_dst = True
    hour = int(input("Enter hour: "))
    update_hour()
    print("New hour:", new_hour)
    ```

a. New hour: 9
   b. New hour: 10
   c. Error

9. What is the output?

   ```
   Enter hour: "))
   update_hour()
   print("New hour:", new_hour)
   def update_hour():
      global new_hour
      new_hour = hour
      if is_dst:
         new_hour += 1
      else:
         new_hour -= 1

   is_dst = True
   hour = int(input("Enter hour: "))
   update_hour()
   print("New hour:", new_hour)
   ```

   a. New hour: 9
   b. New hour: 10
   c. Error

BENEFITS OF LIMITING SCOPE

A programmer might ask, "Why not just make all variables global variables to avoid access errors?" Making every variable global can make a program messy. Ex: A programmer debugging a large program discovers a variable has the wrong value. If the whole program can modify the variable, then the bug could be anywhere in the large program. Limiting a variable's scope to only what's necessary and restricting global variable use make a program easier to debug, maintain, and update.

TRY IT

Battle royale game launch

Write a program that reads in a selected game mode and calls one of two functions to launch the game. If the input is "br", call battle_royale(). Otherwise, call practice().

battle_royale():

- Reads in the number of players.
- Computes the number of teammates still needed. A full team is 3 players.
- Calls the function find_teammates() with the calculated number.
- Prints "Match starting . . .".

```
practice():
```
- Reads in a string representing the desired map.
- Prints `"Launching practice on [desired map]"`.

Note: `find_teammates()` is provided and does not need to be edited.

Given input:

```
br
1
```

The output is:

```
Finding 2 players...
Match starting...
```

Given input:

```
p
Queen's Canyon
```

The output is:

```
Launching practice on Queen's Canyon
```

Access multimedia content (https://openstax.org/books/introduction-python-programming/pages/6-3-variable-scope)

6.4 Parameters

Learning objectives

By the end of this section you should be able to

- Identify a function's arguments and parameters.
- Describe how mutability affects how a function can modify arguments.

Arguments and parameters

What if a programmer wants to write a function that prints the contents of a list? Good practice is to pass values directly to a function rather than relying on global variables. A function **argument** is a value passed as input during a function call. A function **parameter** is a variable representing the input in the function definition. Note: The terms "argument" and "parameter" are sometimes used interchangeably in conversation and documentation.

CHECKPOINT

Global and local variables in a program with a function

Access multimedia content (https://openstax.org/books/introduction-python-programming/pages/6-4-parameters)

CONCEPTS IN PRACTICE

Arguments and parameters

Consider the following:

```
1  def print_welcome(name):
2      print(f"Welcome {name}!")
3
4  username = int(input("Enter new username: "))
5  print_welcome(username)
```

1. Which is an argument?
   a. name
   b. username
   c. name and username

2. Which is a parameter?
   a. name
   b. username
   c. name and username

3. What is the scope of name?
   a. print_welcome() only
   b. whole program

4. What would happen if username was changed to name on lines 4 and 5?
   a. same output
   b. error/wrong output

Multiple arguments and parameters

Functions can have multiple parameters. Ex: A function uses two parameters, length and width, to compute the square footage of a room. Function calls must use the correct order and number of arguments to avoid undesired behavior and errors (unless using optional or keyword arguments as discussed later).

EXAMPLE 6.1

Using multiple arguments in a function call

```python
def print_div(op_1, op_2):
    """ Prints division operation """
    print(f"{op_1}/{op_2} = {op_1/op_2}")

num_1 = 6
num_2 = 3
print_div(num_1, num_2)  # Prints "6/3 = 2.0"
print_div(num_2, num_1)  # Prints "3/6 = 0.5"
print_div(num_1)         # Error: Missing argument: op_2
```

CONCEPTS IN PRACTICE

Multiple arguments and parameters

Consider the following:

```python
def calc_distance(x1, y1, x2, y2):
    dist = math.sqrt((x2-x1)**2 + (y2-y1)**2)
    print(dist)

p1_x =int(input("Enter point 1's x: "))
p1_y =int(input("Enter point 1's y: "))
p2_x =int(input("Enter point 2's x: "))
p2_y =int(input("Enter point 2's y: "))
calc_distance(p1_x, p1_y, p2_x, p2_y)
```

5. Which is an argument?
   a. p1_x
   b. x1

6. Which is a parameter?
   a. p1_y
   b. y1

7. What would be the value of x2 for the function call, calc_distance(2, 4, 3, 6)?
   a. 2
   b. 4
   c. 3
   d. 6
   e. Error

Modifying arguments and mutability

In Python, a variable is a name that refers to an object stored in memory, aka an object reference, so Python uses a **pass-by-object-reference** system. If an argument is changed in a function, the changes are kept or lost depending on the object's mutability. A **mutable** object can be modified after creation. A function's changes to the object then appear outside the function. An **immutable** object cannot be modified after creation. So a function must make a local copy to modify, and the local copy's changes don't appear outside the function.

Programmers should be cautious of modifying function arguments as these side effects can make programs difficult to debug and maintain.

EXAMPLE 6.2

Converting temperatures

What are the values of weekend_temps and type after convert_temps() finishes?

```python
def convert_temps(temps, unit):
   if unit == "F":
      for i in range(len(temps)):
         temps[i] = (temps[i]-32) * 5/9
      unit = "C"
   else:
      for i in range(len(temps)):
         temps[i] = (temps[i]*9/5) + 32
      unit = "F"

# Weekend temperatures in Fahrenheit.
wknd_temps = [49.0, 51.0, 44.0]
deg_sign = u"\N{DEGREE SIGN}" # Unicode
metric = "F"

# Convert from Fahrenheit to Celsius.
convert_temps(wknd_temps, metric)
for temp in wknd_temps:
   print(f"{temp:.2f}{deg_sign}{metric}", end=" ")
```

The output is 9.44°F 10.56°F 6.67°F. type was changed to "C" in the function but didn't keep the change outside of the function. Why is the list argument change kept and not the string argument change? (Hint: A list is mutable. A string is immutable.)

CHECKPOINT

Exploring a faulty function

Access multimedia content (https://openstax.org/books/introduction-python-programming/pages/6-4-parameters)

CONCEPTS IN PRACTICE

Mutability and function arguments

8. In `convert_temps()`, `wknd_temps` and `temps` refer to _____ in memory.
   a. the same object
   b. different objects

9. After `unit` is assigned with `"C"`, `metric` and `unit` refer to _____ in memory.
   a. the same object
   b. different objects

10. `deg_sign` is a string whose value cannot change once created. `deg_sign` is _____.
    a. immutable
    b. mutable

11. On line 16, `unit` _____.
    a. refers to an object with the value `"C"`
    b. does not exist

TRY IT

Printing right triangle area

Write a function, `print_area()`, that takes in the base and height of a right triangle and prints the triangle's area. The area of a right triangle is $\frac{bh}{2}$, where b is the base and h is the height.

Given input:

```
3
4
```

The output is:

```
Triangle area: 6.0
```

Access multimedia content (https://openstax.org/books/introduction-python-programming/pages/6-4-parameters)

TRY IT

Curving scores

Write a function, `print_scores()`, that takes in a list of test scores and a number representing how many points to add. For each score, print the original score and the sum of the score and bonus. Make sure not to change the list.

Given function call:

```
print_scores([67, 68, 72, 71, 69], 10)
```

The output is:

```
67 would be updated to 77
68 would be updated to 78
72 would be updated to 82
71 would be updated to 81
69 would be updated to 79
```

Access multimedia content (https://openstax.org/books/introduction-python-programming/pages/6-4-parameters)

6.5 Return values

Learning objectives

By the end of this section you should be able to

- Identify a function's return value.
- Employ return statements in functions to return values.

Returning from a function

When a function finishes, the function returns and provides a result to the calling code. A **return statement** finishes the function execution and can specify a value to return to the function's caller. Functions introduced so far have not had a `return` statement, which is the same as returning None, representing no value.

CHECKPOINT

Returning a value from a function

Access multimedia content (https://openstax.org/books/introduction-python-programming/pages/6-5-return-values)

CONCEPTS IN PRACTICE

Using return statements

1. What is returned by calc_mpg(miles, gallons)?

   ```
   def calc_mpg(miles, gallons):
   ```

```
    mpg = miles/gallons
    return mpg
```

a. mpg
b. None
c. Error

2. What is returned by calc_sqft()?

```
def calc_sqft(length, width):
   sqft = length * width
   return
```

a. sqft
b. None
c. Error

3. What is the difference between hw_1() and hw_2()?

```
def hw_1():
   print("Hello world!")
   return

def hw_2():
   print("Hello world!")
```

a. hw_1() returns a string, hw_2() does not
b. hw_1() returns None, hw_2() does not
c. no difference

Using multiple return statements

Functions that have multiple execution paths may use multiple `return` statements. Ex: A function with an `if-else` statement may have two `return` statements for each branch. Return statements always end the function and return control flow to the calling code.

In the table below, `calc_mpg()` takes in miles driven and gallons of gas used and calculates a car's miles per gallon. `calc_mpg()` checks if gallons is 0 (to avoid division by 0), and if so, returns -1, a value often used to indicate a problem.

```
def calc_mpg(miles, gallons):
  if gallons > 0:
    mpg = miles/gallons
    return mpg
  else:
    print("Gallons can't be 0")
    return -1

car_1_mpg = calc_mpg(448, 16)
print("Car 1's mpg is", car_1_mpg)
car_2_mpg = calc_mpg(300, 0)
print("Car 2's mpg is", car_2_mpg)
```

```
Car 1's mpg is 28.0
Gallons can't be 0
Car 2's mpg is -1
```

Table 6.1 Calculating miles-per-gallon and checking for division by zero.

CONCEPTS IN PRACTICE

Multiple return statements

4. What does yarn_weight(3) return?

   ```
   def yarn_weight(num):
     if num == 0:
       return "lace"
     elif num == 1:
       return "sock"
     elif num == 2:
       return "sport"
     elif num == 3:
       return "dk"
     elif num == 4:
       return "worsted"
     elif num == 5:
       return "bulky"
     else:
       return "super bulky"
   ```

   a. "lace"
   b. "dk"
   c. "super bulky"

5. What is the output?

   ```
   def inc_volume(level, max):
   ```

```
    if level < max:
      return level
      level += 1
    else:
      return level

vol1 = inc_volume(9, 10)
print(vol1)
vol2 = inc_volume(10, 10)
print(vol2)
```

   a. 9
      10
   b. 10
      10
   c. 10
      11

Using functions as values

Functions are objects that evaluate to values, so function calls can be used in expressions. A function call can be combined with other function calls, variables, and literals as long as the return value is compatible with the operation.

CHECKPOINT

Using function calls in expressions

Access multimedia content (https://openstax.org/books/introduction-python-programming/pages/6-5-return-values)

CONCEPTS IN PRACTICE

Using function values

6. What is the updated value of bill?

```
def tax(total):
  return .06 * total

def auto_tip(total):
  return .2 * total

bill = 100.0
bill += tax(bill) + auto_tip(bill)
```

   a. 26.0

b. 126.0

7. What is the value of val2?

   ```
   def sq(num):
       return num * num

   def offset(num):
       return num - 2

   val = 5
   val2 = sq(offset(val))
   ```

   a. 9
   b. 23

TRY IT

Estimated days alive

Write a function, `days_alive()`, that takes in an age in years and outputs the estimated days the user has been alive as an integer. Assume each year has 365.24 days. Use `round()`, which takes a number and returns the nearest whole number.

Then write a main program that reads in a user's age and outputs the result of `days_alive()`.

Given input:

```
21
```

The output is:

```
You have been alive about 7670 days.
```

Access multimedia content (https://openstax.org/books/introduction-python-programming/pages/6-5-return-values)

TRY IT

Averaging lists

Write a function, `avg_list()`, that takes in a list and returns the average of the list values.

Access multimedia content (https://openstax.org/books/introduction-python-programming/pages/6-5-return-values)

6.6 Keyword arguments

Learning objectives

By the end of this section you should be able to

- Describe the difference between positional and keyword arguments.
- Create functions that use positional and keyword arguments and default parameter values.

Keyword arguments

So far, functions have been called using **positional arguments**, which are arguments that are assigned to parameters in order. Python also allows **keyword arguments**, which are arguments that use parameter names to assign values rather than order. When mixing positional and keyword arguments, positional arguments must come first in the correct order, before any keyword arguments.

CHECKPOINT

Using keyword arguments

Access multimedia content (https://openstax.org/books/introduction-python-programming/pages/6-6-keyword-arguments)

CONCEPTS IN PRACTICE

Using keyword and positional arguments

Consider the following function:

```
def greeting(msg, name, count):
   i = 0
   for i in range(0, count):
      print(msg, name)
```

1. Which is the positional argument in greeting(count=1, name="Ash", msg="Hiya")?
   a. count=1
   b. name="Ash"
   c. msg="Hiya"
   d. None

2. What is the output of greeting(count=2, name="Ash", msg="Hiya")?
   a. Ash Hiya
      Ash Hiya
   b. Hiya Ash
      Hiya Ash

3. Which is the positional argument in greeting("Welcome", count=1, name="Anita")?
   a. "Welcome"
   b. count=1

c. `name="Anita"`

4. Which function call would produce an error?
   a. `greeting("Morning", "Morgan", count=3)`
   b. `greeting(count=1,"Hi", "Bea")`
   c. `greeting("Cheers", "Colleagues", 10)`

Default parameter values

Functions can define default parameter values to use if a positional or keyword argument is not provided for the parameter. Ex: `def season(m, d, hemi="N"):` defines a default value of "N" for the hemi parameter. Note: Default parameter values are only defined once to be used by the function, so mutable objects (such as lists) should not be used as default values.

The physics example below calculates weight as a force in newtons given mass in kilograms and acceleration in $\frac{m}{s^2}$. Gravity on Earth is 9.8 $\frac{m}{s^2}$, and gravity on Mars is 3.7 $\frac{m}{s^2}$.

CHECKPOINT

Using default parameter values

Access multimedia content (https://openstax.org/books/introduction-python-programming/pages/6-6-keyword-arguments)

CONCEPTS IN PRACTICE

Using default parameter values

Consider the following updated version of `greeting()`:

```
def greeting(msg, name="Friend", count=1):
   i = 0
   for i in range(0, count):
      print(msg, name)
```

5. Which parameters have default values?
   a. `msg`
   b. `name` and `count`
   c. all

6. Which function call is correct?
   a. `greeting()`
   b. `greeting(name="Gina")`
   c. `greeting("Greetings")`

7. What is the output of `greeting(count=0, msg="Hello")`?

a. `Hello Friend`
b. `nothing`
c. `Error`

> **PEP 8 RECOMMENDATIONS: SPACING**
>
> The PEP 8 style guide recommends no spaces around = when indicating keyword arguments and default parameter values.

TRY IT

Stream donations

Write a function, `donate()`, that lets an online viewer send a donation to a streamer. `donate()` has three parameters:

- `amount`: amount to donate, default value: 5
- `name`: donor's name, default value: "Anonymous"
- `msg`: donor's message, default value: ""

Given:

```
donate(10, "gg")
```

The output is:

```
Anonymous donated 10 credits: gg
```

Write function calls that use the default values along with positional and keyword arguments.

Access multimedia content (https://openstax.org/books/introduction-python-programming/pages/6-6-keyword-arguments)

6.7 Chapter summary

Highlights from this chapter include:

- Functions are named blocks of code that perform tasks when called and make programs more organized and optimized.
- Control flow is the sequence of program execution. Control flow moves between calling code and function code when a function is called.
- Variable scope refers to where a variable can be accessed. Global variables can be accessed anywhere in a program. Local variables are limited in scope, such as to a function.
- Parameters are function inputs defined with the function. Arguments are values passed to the function as

input by the calling code. Parameters are assigned with the arguments' values.
- Function calls can use positional arguments to map values to parameters in order.
- Function calls can use keyword arguments to map values using parameter names in any order.
- Functions can define default parameter values to allow for optional arguments in function calls.
- Python uses a pass-by-object-reference system to assign parameters with the object values referenced by the arguments.
- Functions can use `return` statements to return values back to the calling code.

At this point, you should be able to write functions that have any number of parameters and return a value, and programs that call functions using keyword arguments and optional arguments.

Construct	Description

Function definition	```def function_name():```
	``` """Docstring"""```
	``` # Function body```

Parameter	```def function_name(parameter_1):``` ``` # Function body```

Argument	```def function_name(parameter_1):```
	``` # Function body```
	
	```function_name(argument_1)```

Return statement	```def function_name():```
	``` # Function body```
	``` return result # Returns the value of result to the caller```

Variables (scope)	```def function_name(parameter_1):```
	``` # Function body```
	``` local_var = parameter_1 * 5```
	``` return local_var```
	
	```global_var = function_name(arg_1)```

Table 6.2 Chapter 6 reference.

Construct	Description

Keyword arguments	```def function_name(parameter_1, parameter_2):```
	  `# Function body`
	
	`function_name(parameter_2 = 5, parameter_1 = 2)`

Default parameter value	`def function_name(parameter_1 = 100):` `# Function body`

Table 6.2 Chapter 6 reference.

7 Modules

Figure 7.1 credit: modification of work "Lone Pine Sunset", by Romain Guy/Flickr, Public Domain

Chapter Outline

7.1 Module basics
7.2 Importing names
7.3 Top-level code
7.4 The help function
7.5 Finding modules
7.6 Chapter summary

 Introduction

As programs get longer and more complex, organizing the code into modules is helpful. This chapter shows how to define, import, and find new modules. Python's standard library (https://openstax.org/r/100pythlibrary) provides over 200 built-in modules (https://openstax.org/r/100200modules). Hundreds of thousands of other modules (https://openstax.org/r/100pypi) are available online.

A **module** is a *.py* file containing function definitions and other statements. The module's name is the file's name without the *.py* extension at the end. Ex: The following code, written in a file named *greetings.py*, defines a module named `greetings`.

```
"""Functions that print standard greetings."""

def hello():
   print("Hello!")

def bye():
   print("Goodbye!")
```

Technically, every program in this book is a module. But not every module is designed to run like a program. Running *greetings.py* as a program would accomplish very little. Two functions would be defined, but the functions would never be called. These functions are intended to be called in other modules.

7.1 Module basics

Learning objectives

By the end of this section you should be able to

- Write a module that consists only of function definitions.
- Import the module and use the functions in a program.

Defining a module

Modules are defined by putting code in a *.py* file. The `area` module below is in a file named area.py. This module provides functions for calculating area.

EXAMPLE 7.1

The area module

```python
"""Functions to calculate the area of geometric shapes."""

import math

# 2D shapes

def square(side):
    """Gets the area of a square."""
    return side**2

def rectangle(length, width):
    """Gets the area of a rectangle."""
    return length * width

def triangle(base, height):
    """Gets the area of a triangle."""
    return 0.5 * base * height

def trapezoid(base1, base2, height):
    """Gets the area of a trapezoid."""
    return 0.5 * (base1 + base2) * height

def circle(radius):
    """Gets the area of a circle."""
    return math.pi * radius**2

def ellipse(major, minor):
```

```
        """Gets the area of an ellipse."""
        return math.pi * major * minor

    # 3D shapes

    def cube(side):
        """Gets the surface area of a cube."""
        return 6 * side**2

    def cylinder(radius, height):
        """Gets the surface area of a cylinder."""
        return 2 * math.pi * radius * (radius + height)

    def cone(radius, height):
        """Gets the surface area of a cone."""
        return math.pi * radius * (radius + math.hypot(height, radius))

    def sphere(radius):
        """Gets the surface area of a sphere."""
        return 4 * math.pi * radius**2
```

CONCEPTS IN PRACTICE

Defining a module

1. How many functions are defined in the area module?
   a. 6
   b. 10
   c. 49

2. What would be the result of running *area.py* as a program?
   a. Functions would be defined and ready to be called.
   b. Nothing; the module has no statements to be run.
   c. SyntaxError

3. What is the return value of cube(5)?
   a. 60
   b. 125
   c. 150

Importing a module

The module defined in *area.py* can be used in other programs. When importing the area module, the suffix .py is removed:

```
import area

print("Area of a basketball court:", area.rectangle(94, 50))
print("Area of a circus ring:", area.circle(21))
```

The output is:

```
Area of a basketball court: 4700
Area of a circus ring: 1385.4423602330987
```

CHECKPOINT

Importing area in a Python shell

Access multimedia content (https://openstax.org/books/introduction-python-programming/pages/7-1-module-basics)

CONCEPTS IN PRACTICE

Importing a module

4. What statement would import a module from a file named *secret.py*?
   a. `import secret`
   b. `import secret.py`
   c. `import "secret.py"`

5. What code would return the area of a circle with a radius of 3 meters?
   a. `circle(3)`
   b. `area.circle(3)`
   c. `circle.area(3)`

6. A programmer would like to write a function that calculates the area of a hexagon. Where should the function be written?
   a. the main program
   b. the area module
   c. the secret module

TRY IT

Conversion module

Write a module that defines the following functions:

1. `cel2fah(c)` –
   Converts a temperature in Celsius to Fahrenheit.

The formula is `9/5 * c + 32`.
2. `fah2cel(f)` –
Converts a temperature in Fahrenheit to Celsius.
The formula is `5/9 * (f - 32)`.
3. `km2mi(km)` –
Converts a distance in kilometers to miles.
The formula is `km / 1.60934`.
4. `mi2km(mi)` –
Converts a distance in miles to kilometers.
The formula is `mi * 1.60934`.

Each function should include a docstring as the first line. A docstring for the module has been provided for you.

The module should not do anything except define functions. When you click the "Run" button, the module should run without error. No output should be displayed.

Access multimedia content (https://openstax.org/books/introduction-python-programming/pages/7-1-module-basics)

TRY IT

European vacation

Write a program that uses the `conversion` module from the previous exercise to complete a short story. The program's output should match the following example (input in bold):

```
How fast were you driving? 180
Woah, that's like 112 mph!
What was the temperature? 35
That's 95 degrees Fahrenheit!
```

Notice this exercise requires two files:

1. *european.py*, the main program. Input and output statements are provided as a starting point. Edit the lines with TODO comments to use the conversion module.
2. *conversion.py*, the other module. Copy and paste your code from the previous exercise. Import this module in *european.py* after the docstring.

Access multimedia content (https://openstax.org/books/introduction-python-programming/pages/7-1-module-basics)

7.2 Importing names

Learning objectives

By the end of this section you should be able to

- Import functions from a module using the `from` keyword.
- Explain how to avoid a name collision when importing a module.

The from keyword

Specific functions in a module can be imported using the `from` keyword:

```
from area import triangle, cylinder
```

These functions can be called directly, without referring to the module:

```
print(triangle(1, 2))
print(cylinder(3, 4))
```

EXPLORING FURTHER

As shown below, the `from` keyword can lead to confusing names.

CHECKPOINT

Importing functions

Access multimedia content (https://openstax.org/books/introduction-python-programming/pages/7-2-importing-names)

CONCEPTS IN PRACTICE

The from keyword

1. Which import statement would be needed before running `print(sqrt(25))`?
    a. `from math import sqrt`
    b. `import sqrt from math`
    c. `import math`

2. How many variables are defined by the statement `from math import sin, cos, tan`?
    a. 0
    b. 3
    c. 4

3. What error would occur if attempting to call a function that was not imported?
    a. `ImportError`
    b. `NameError`
    c. `SyntaxError`

Name collisions

Modules written by different programmers might use the same name for a function. A **name collision** occurs when a function is defined multiple times. If a function is defined more than once, the most recent definition is used:

```
from area import cube

def cube(x):    # Name collision (replaces the imported function)
   return x ** 3

print(cube(2)) # Calls the local cube() function, not area.cube()
```

A programmer might not realize the cube function is defined twice because no error occurs when running the program. Name collisions are not considered errors and often lead to unexpected behavior.

Care should be taken to avoid name collisions. Selecting specific functions from a module to import reduces the memory footprint; however, importing a complete module can help to avoid collisions because a *module.name* format would be used. This is a tradeoff the programmer must consider.

CHECKPOINT

Module and function names

Access multimedia content (https://openstax.org/books/introduction-python-programming/pages/7-2-importing-names)

CONCEPTS IN PRACTICE

Name collisions

4. A program begins with `from area import square, circle`. What code causes a name collision?
   a. `def area(phone):`
        `"""Gets the area code of a phone number."""`
   b. `def circle(x, y, size):`
        `"""Draws a circle centered at (x, y)."""`
   c. `def is_square(length, width):`
        `"""Returns True if length and width are equal."""`

5. A program begins with `import area`. What code causes a name collision?
   a. `area = 51`
   b. `import cylinder from volume`
   c. `def cube(size):`
        `"""Generates a "size X size" rubik's cube."""`

6. Which line will cause an error?

```
1  def hello():
2     print("Hello!")
3
4  def hello(name):
5     print("Hello,", name)
```

```
6
7  hello()
8  hello("Chris")
```

a. line 4
b. line 7
c. line 8

EXPLORING FURTHER

If a name is defined, imported, or assigned multiple times, Python uses the most recent definition. Other languages allow multiple functions to have the same name if the parameters are different. This feature, known as **function overloading**, is not part of the Python language.

TRY IT

Missing imports

Add the missing import statements to the top of the file. Do not make any changes to the rest of the code. In the end, the program should run without errors.

Access multimedia content (https://openstax.org/books/introduction-python-programming/pages/7-2-importing-names)

TRY IT

Party favors

The following program does not run correctly because of name collisions. Fix the program by modifying import statements, function calls, and variable assignments. The output should be:

```
Bouncy ball area: 13
Bouncy ball volume: 4
Cone hat area: 227
Cone hat volume: 209
```

Access multimedia content (https://openstax.org/books/introduction-python-programming/pages/7-2-importing-names)

7.3 Top-level code

Learning objectives

By the end of this section you should be able to

- Identify code that will run as a side effect of importing.
- Explain the purpose of if __name__ == "__main__".

Side effects

Modules define functions and constants to be used in other programs. When importing a module, *all* code in the module is run from top to bottom. If a module is not designed carefully, unintended code might run as a side effect. The unintended code is generally at the top level, outside of function definitions.

CHECKPOINT

Sphere test code

Access multimedia content (https://openstax.org/books/introduction-python-programming/pages/7-3-top-level-code)

CONCEPTS IN PRACTICE

Side effects

1. Which line would cause a side effect when imported?

   ```
   1  import math
   2
   3  print("Defining sphere function")
   4
   5  def sphere(radius):
   6      """Gets the volume of a sphere."""
   7      return 4/3 * math.pi * radius**3
   ```

   a. line 1
   b. line 3
   c. line 5

2. The following *volume.py* module causes a side effect.

   ```
   import math

   def sphere(radius):
       """Gets the volume of a sphere."""
       return 4/3 * math.pi * radius**3

   for r in range(10000000):
       volume = sphere(r)
   ```

   a. true
   b. false

3. The following *greeting.py* module causes a side effect.

   ```
   name = input("What is your name? ")
   ```

```
print(f"Nice to meet you, {name}!")
live = input("Where do you live? ")
print(f"{live} is a great place.")
```

a. true
b. false

Using __name__

Python modules often include the statement if __name__ == "__main__" to prevent side effects. This statement is true when the module is run as a program and false when the module is imported.

CHECKPOINT

The main module

Access multimedia content (https://openstax.org/books/introduction-python-programming/pages/7-3-top-level-code)

CONCEPTS IN PRACTICE

Using __name__

4. What is the output when **running** the following *test.py* module?

   ```
   import math

   print(math.__name__)
   print(__name__)
   ```

   a. >math
      test
   b. __main__
      test
   c. math
      __main__

5. What is the output when **importing** the following *test.py* module?

   ```
   import math

   print(math.__name__)
   print(__name__)
   ```

   a. math
      test
   b. __main__
      test

c. math
   __main__

6. What line is useful for preventing side effects when importing?
   a. if __name__ == "main":
   b. if __name__ == __main__:
   c. if __name__ == "__main__":

EXPLORING FURTHER

Variables that begin and end with double underscores have special meaning in Python. Double underscores are informally called "dunder" or "magic" variables. Other examples include __doc__ (the module's docstring) and __file__ (the module's filename).

TRY IT

Side effects

This exercise is a continuation of the "Missing imports" exercise. Previously, you added missing import statements to the top of the program. Now, modify the program to prevent side effects when importing the program as a module:

1. Add if __name__ == "__main__" at the end.
2. Move all test code under that if statement.

The program should run without errors and produce the same output as before.

Access multimedia content (https://openstax.org/books/introduction-python-programming/pages/7-3-top-level-code)

TRY IT

Conversion test

This exercise is a continuation of the "Conversion module" exercise. Previously, you wrote the functions cel2fah, fah2cel, km2mi, and mi2km. Write test code at the end of *conversion.py* (the original file) for each of these functions. The test code must not run as a side effect when conversion is imported by other programs. When running *conversion.py* as the main program, the test output should be:

```
0 C is 32 F
5 C is 41 F
10 C is 50 F
15 C is 59 F
20 C is 68 F
```

```
20 F is -7 C
25 F is -4 C
30 F is -1 C
35 F is 2 C
40 F is 4 C

1 km is 0.6 mi
2 km is 1.2 mi
3 km is 1.9 mi
4 km is 2.5 mi
5 km is 3.1 mi

5 mi is 8.0 km
6 mi is 9.7 km
7 mi is 11.3 km
8 mi is 12.9 km
9 mi is 14.5 km
```

Access multimedia content (https://openstax.org/books/introduction-python-programming/pages/7-3-top-level-code)

7.4 The help function

Learning objectives

By the end of this section you should be able to

- Use the `help()` function to explore a module's contents.
- Identify portions of code included in the documentation.

Colors on websites

This section introduces an example module for working with HTML colors (https://openstax.org/r/100htmlcolors). HyperText Markup Language (HTML) is used to design websites and graphical applications. Web browsers like Chrome and Safari read HTML and display the corresponding contents. Ex: The HTML code `<p style="color: Red">Look out!</p>` represents a paragraph with red text.

HTML defines 140 standard color names (https://openstax.org/r/100colornames). Additional colors can be specified using a hexadecimal format: *#RRGGBB*. The digits RR, GG, and BB represent the red, green, and blue components of the color. Ex: *#DC143C* is 220 red + 20 green + 60 blue, which is the color `Crimson`.

Red, green, and blue values range from 0 to 255 (or 00 to FF in hexadecimal). Lower values specify darker colors, and higher values specify lighter colors. Ex: *#008000* is the color `Green`, and *#00FF00* is the color `Lime`.

CHECKPOINT

HTML color codes

Access multimedia content (https://openstax.org/books/introduction-python-programming/pages/7-4-the-help-function)

> **CONCEPTS IN PRACTICE**
>
> HTML color codes
>
> 1. What color is *#000080*?
>   a. maroon red
>   b. navy blue
>   c. olive green
>
> 2. What is 255 in hexadecimal?
>   a. 00
>   b. 80
>   c. FF
>
> 3. Which color is lighter?
>   a. *#FFA500 (orange)*
>   b. *#008000 (green)*

Example colors module

A module for working with HTML color codes would be helpful to graphic designers and web developers. The following Python code is in a file named *colors.py*.

- Line 1 is the docstring for the module.
- Lines 3–16 assign variables for frequently used colors.
- Lines 18–24 define a function to be used *within* the module.
- Lines 26–45 define functions to be used in other modules.

Note: The `tohex()` and `torgb()` functions use Python features (string formatting and slicing) described later in the book. For now, the documentation and comments are more important than the implementation details.

```python
"""Functions for working with color names and hex/rgb values."""

# Primary colors
RED = "#FF0000"
YELLOW = "#FFFF00"
BLUE = "#0000FF"

# Secondary colors
ORANGE = "#FFA500"
GREEN = "#008000"
VIOLET = "#EE82EE"

# Neutral colors
BLACK = "#000000"
GRAY = "#808080"
WHITE = "#FFFFFF"

def _tohex(value):
```

```python
    """Converts an integer to an 8-bit (2-digit) hexadecimal string."""
    if value <= 0:
      return "00"
    if value >= 255:
      return "FF"
    return format(value, "02X")

def tohex(r, g, b):
    """Formats red, green, and blue integers as a color in hexadecimal."""
    return "#" + _tohex(r) + _tohex(g) + _tohex(b)

def torgb(color):
    """Converts a color in hexadecimal to red, green, and blue integers."""
    r = int(color[1:3], 16)  # First 2 digits
    g = int(color[3:5], 16)  # Middle 2 digits
    b = int(color[5:7], 16)  # Last 2 digits
    return r, g, b

def lighten(color):
    """Increases the red, green, and blue values of a color by 32 each."""
    r, g, b = torgb(color)
    return tohex(r+32, g+32, b+32)

def darken(color):
    """Decreases the red, green, and blue values of a color by 32 each."""
    r, g, b = torgb(color)
    return tohex(r-32, g-32, b-32)
```

CONCEPTS IN PRACTICE

The colors module

4. What are the components of the color YELLOW?
    a. red=0, green=255, blue=255
    b. red=255, green=255, blue=0
    c. red=255, green=0, blue=255

5. What code would return a darker shade of blue?
    a. darken(BLUE)
    b. colors.darken(BLUE)
    c. colors.darken(colors.BLUE)

6. What symbol indicates that a function is not intended to be called by other modules?
    a. underscore (_)
    b. number sign (#)
    c. colon (:)

Module documentation

The built-in `help()` function provides a summary of a module's functions and data. Calling `help(module_name)` in a shell is a convenient way to learn about a module.

EXAMPLE 7.2

Output of help(colors) in a shell

The documentation below is automatically generated from the docstrings in *colors.py*.

help(colors)

```
Help on module colors:

NAME
    colors - Functions for working with color names and hex/rgb values.

FUNCTIONS
    darken(color)
        Decreases the red, green, and blue values of a color by 32 each.

    lighten(color)
        Increases the red, green, and blue values of a color by 32 each.

    tohex(r, g, b)
        Formats red, green, and blue integers as a color in hexadecimal.

    torgb(color)
        Converts a color in hexadecimal to red, green, and blue integers.

DATA
    BLACK = '#000000'
    BLUE = '#0000FF'
    GRAY = '#808080'
    GREEN = '#008000'
    ORANGE = '#FFA500'
    RED = '#FF0000'
    VIOLET = '#EE82EE'
    WHITE = '#FFFFFF'
    YELLOW = '#FFFF00'

FILE
    /home/student/Desktop/colors.py

>>> help(colors)

Help on module colors:

NAME
```

```
colors - Functions for working with color names and hex/rgb values.

FUNCTIONS
    darken(color)
        Decreases the red, green, and blue values of a color by 32 each.

    lighten(color)
        Increases the red, green, and blue values of a color by 32 each.

    tohex(r, g, b)
        Formats red, green, and blue integers as a color in hexadecimal.

    torgb(color)
        Converts a color in hexadecimal to red, green, and blue integers.

DATA
    BLACK = '#000000'
    BLUE = '#0000FF'
    GRAY = '#808080'
    GREEN = '#008000'
    ORANGE = '#FFA500'
    RED = '#FF0000'
    VIOLET = '#EE82EE'
    WHITE = '#FFFFFF'
    YELLOW = '#FFFF00'

FILE
    /home/student/Desktop/colors.py
```

CONCEPTS IN PRACTICE

The help() function

7. The documentation includes comments from the source code.
    a. true
    b. false

8. In what order are the functions listed in the documentation?
    a. alphabetical order
    b. definition order
    c. random order

9. Which function defined in *colors.py* is not included in the documentation?
    a. _tohex
    b. tohex

c. `torgb`

TRY IT

Help on modules

The random and `statistics` modules are useful for running scientific experiments. You can become familiar with these two modules by skimming their documentation.

Open a Python shell on your computer, or use the one at python.org/shell (https://openstax.org/r/100pythonshell). Type the following lines, one at a time, into the shell.

- `import random`
- `help(random)`
- `import statistics`
- `help(statistics)`

Many shell environments, including the one on python.org, display the output of `help()` one page at a time. Use the navigation keys on the keyboard (up/down arrows, page up/down, home/end) to read the documentation. When you are finished reading, press the Q key ("quit") to return to the Python shell.

TRY IT

Help on functions

The `help()` function can be called on specific functions in a module. Open a Python shell on your computer, or use the one at python.org/shell (https://openstax.org/r/100pythonshell). Type the following lines, one at a time, into the shell.

- `import random`
- `help(random.randint)`
- `help(random.choice)`
- `import statistics`
- `help(statistics.median)`
- `help(statistics.mode)`

Remember to use the navigation keys on the keyboard, and press the Q key ("quit") to return to the Python shell.

7.5 Finding modules

Learning objectives

By the end of this section you should be able to

- Explain differences between the standard library and PyPI.
- Search python.org and pypi.org for modules of interest.

Built-in modules

The **Python Standard Library** is a collection of built-in functions and modules that support common programming tasks. Ex: The `math` module provides functions like `sqrt()` and constants like `pi`. Python's official documentation includes a library reference (https://openstax.org/r/100pythlibrary) and a module index (https://openstax.org/r/100200modules) for becoming familiar with the standard library.

For decades, Python has maintained a "batteries included (https://openstax.org/r/100batteries)" philosophy. This philosophy means that the standard library should come with everything most programmers need. In fact, the standard library includes over 200 built-in modules!

Module	Description
`calendar`	General calendar-related functions.
`datetime`	Basic date and time types and functions.
`email`	Generate and process email messages.
`math`	Mathematical functions and constants.
`os`	Interact with the operating system.
`random`	Generate pseudo-random numbers.
`statistics`	Mathematical statistics functions.
`sys`	System-specific parameters and functions.
`turtle`	Educational framework for simple graphics.
`zipfile`	Read and write ZIP-format archive files.

Table 7.1 Example built-in modules in the standard library.

CONCEPTS IN PRACTICE

Built-in modules

Use the library reference, module index, and documentation links above to answer the questions.

1. Which page provides a list of built-in modules sorted by category?
    a. library reference
    b. module index
    c. PEP 2

2. What is the value of `calendar.SUNDAY`?
   a. 1
   b. 6
   c. 7

3. Which built-in module enables the development of graphical user interfaces?
   a. `tkinter`
   b. `turtle`
   c. `webbrowser`

Third-party modules

The **Python Package Index** (PyPI), available at pypi.org (https://openstax.org/r/100pypi), is the official third-party software library for Python. The abbreviation "PyPI" is pronounced like *pie pea eye* (in contrast to PyPy (https://openstax.org/r/100pypy), a different project).

PyPI allows anyone to develop and share modules with the Python community. Module authors include individuals, large companies, and non-profit organizations. PyPI helps programmers install modules and receive updates.

Most software available on PyPI is free and open source. PyPI is supported by the Python Software Foundation (https://openstax.org/r/100foundation) and is maintained by an independent group of developers.

Module	Description
`arrow`	Convert and format dates, times, and timestamps.
`BeautifulSoup`	Extract data from HTML and XML documents.
`bokeh`	Interactive plots and applications in the browser.
`matplotlib`	Static, animated, and interactive visualizations.
`moviepy`	Video editing, compositing, and processing.
`nltk`	Natural language toolkit for human languages.
`numpy`	Fundamental package for numerical computing.
`pandas`	Data analysis, time series, and statistics library.
`pillow`	Image processing for jpg, png, and other formats.

Table 7.2 Example third-party modules available from PyPI.

Module	Description
pytest	Full-featured testing tool and unit test framework.
requests	Elegant HTTP library for connecting to web servers.
scikit-learn	Simple, efficient tools for predictive data analysis.
scipy	Fundamental algorithms for scientific computing.
scrapy	Crawl websites and scrape data from web pages.
tensorflow	End-to-end machine learning platform for everyone.

Table 7.2 Example third-party modules available from PyPI.

CONCEPTS IN PRACTICE

Third-party modules

Use pypi.org and the links in the table above to answer the questions.

4. Which modules can be used to edit pictures and videos?
    a. BeautifulSoup and Scrapy
    b. Bokeh and Matplotlib
    c. MoviePy and Pillow

5. Which third-party module is a replacement for the built-in datetime module?
    a. arrow
    b. calendar
    c. time

6. Search for the webcolors module on PyPI. What function provided by webcolors looks up the color name for a hex code?
    a. hex_to_name
    b. name_to_hex
    c. normalize_hex

EXPLORING FURTHER

Programming blogs often highlight PyPI modules to demonstrate the usefulness of Python. The following examples provide more background information about the modules listed above.

- Top 20 Python Libraries for Data Science for 2023 (https://openstax.org/r/100simplelearn)
- 24 Best Python Libraries You Should Check in 2022 (https://openstax.org/r/100library2022)

- [Most Popular Python Packages in 2021 (https://openstax.org/r/100packages2021)](https://openstax.org/r/100packages2021)

TRY IT

Happy birthday

Module documentation pages often include examples to help programmers become familiar with the module. For this exercise, refer to the following examples from the `datetime` module documentation:

- [Examples of Usage: date (https://openstax.org/r/100dateexamples)](https://openstax.org/r/100dateexamples)
- [Examples of Usage: timedelta (https://openstax.org/r/100timedeltaex)](https://openstax.org/r/100timedeltaex)

Write a program that creates a `date` object representing your birthday. Then get a `date` object representing today's date (the date the program is run). Calculate the difference between the two dates, and output the results in the following format:

```
Your birth date: 2005-03-14
Today's date is: 2023-06-01

You were born 6653 days ago
(that is 574819200 seconds)

You are about 18 years old
```

[Access multimedia content (https://openstax.org/books/introduction-python-programming/pages/7-5-finding-modules)](https://openstax.org/books/introduction-python-programming/pages/7-5-finding-modules)

TRY IT

More exact age

The `datetime` module does not provide a built-in way to display a person's exact age. Ex: The following program calculates an exact age (in years and days) using floor division and modulo. The output is: You are 15 years and 4 days old.

```python
from datetime import date

birth = date(2005, 3, 14)
today = date(2020, 3, 14) # 15 years later
delta = today - birth

years = delta.days // 365
days = delta.days % 365
print("You are", years, "years and", days, "days old")
```

Notice how leap years are included in the calculation. February 29th occurs four times between `birth` and `today`. Therefore, the user is not only 15 years old, but 15 years and 4 days old.

Many commonly used modules from PyPI, including `arrow`, are installed in the Python shell at python.org/shell (https://openstax.org/r/100pythonshell). Open the Python shell and type the following lines:

```
import arrow
birth = arrow.get(2005, 3, 14)
birth.humanize()
```

Refer to the humanize() (https://openstax.org/r/100humanize) examples from the `arrow` module documentation. In the Python shell, figure out how to display the number of years and days since `birth` using *one line of code*. Then display the number of years, months, and days since `birth`. Finally, use the `print()` function to output the results in this format: `You are 18 years 4 months and 7 days old`.

As time permits, experiment with other functions provided by the `arrow` module.

7.6 Chapter summary

Highlights from this chapter include:

- Programs can be organized into multiple *.py* files (modules). The `import` keyword allows a program to use functions defined in another *.py* file.
- The `from` keyword can be used to import specific functions from a module. However, programs should avoid importing (or defining) multiple functions with the same name.
- Modules often include the line `if __name__ == "__main__"` to prevent code from running as a side effect when the module is imported by other programs.
- When working in a shell, the `help()` function can be used to look up the documentation for a module. The documentation is generated from the docstrings.
- Python comes with over 200 built-in modules and hundreds of thousands of third-party modules. Programmers can search for modules on docs.python.org (https://openstax.org/r/100docstrings) and pypi.org (https://openstax.org/r/100pypi).

Statement	Description
`import module`	Imports a module for use in another program.
`from module import function`	Imports a specific function from a module.
`if __name__ == "__main__":`	A line of code found at the end of many modules. This statement indicates what code to run if the module is executed as a program (in other words, what code *not* to run if this module is imported by another program).

Table 7.3 Chapter 7 reference.

Statement	Description
`help(module_name)`	Shows the documentation for the given module. The documentation includes the module's docstring, followed by a list of functions defined in the module, followed by a list of global variables assigned in the module, followed by the module's file name.
`help(function_name)`	Shows the docstring for the given function.
`date(2023, 2, 14)`	Creates a date object representing February 14, 2023. Requires: `from datetime import date`.

Table 7.3 Chapter 7 reference.

8 Strings

Figure 8.1 credit: modification of work "Project 366 #65: 050316 A Night On The Tiles", by Pete/Flickr, CC BY 2.0

Chapter Outline

- 8.1 String operations
- 8.2 String slicing
- 8.3 Searching/testing strings
- 8.4 String formatting
- 8.5 Splitting/joining strings
- 8.6 Chapter summary

Introduction

A **string** is a sequence of characters. Python provides useful methods for processing string values. In this chapter, string methods will be demonstrated including comparing string values, string slicing, searching, testing, formatting, and modifying.

8.1 String operations

Learning objectives

By the end of this section you should be able to

- Compare strings using logical and membership operators.
- Use `lower()` and `upper()` string methods to convert string values to lowercase and uppercase characters.

String comparison

String values can be compared using logical operators (<, <=, >, >=, ==, !=) and membership operators (in and not in). When comparing two string values, the matching characters in two string values are compared sequentially until a decision is reached. For comparing two characters, ASCII values are used to apply logical operators.

Operator	Description	Example	Output	Explanation
> or >=	Checks whether the first string value is greater than (or greater than or equal to) the second string value.	"c" > "d"	False	When comparing "c" operand to "d" operand, the ASCII value for "c" is smaller than the ASCII value for "d". Therefore, "c" < "d". The expression "c" > "d" evaluates to False.
< or <=	Checks whether the first string value is less than (or less than or equal to) the second string value.	"ab" < "ac"	True	When comparing "ab" operand to "ac" operand, the first characters are the same, but the second character of "ab" is less than the second character in "ac" and as such "ab" < "ac".
==	Checks whether two string values are equal.	"aa" == "aa"	True	Since all characters in the first operand and the second operand are the same, the two string values are equal.
!=	Checks whether two string values are not equal.	"a" != "b"	True	The two operands contain different string values ("a" vs. "b"), and the result of checking whether the two are not the same evaluates to True.
in	Checks whether the second operand contains the first operand.	"a" in "bc"	False	Since string "bc" does not contain string "a", the output of "a" in "bc" evaluates to False.
not in	Checks whether the second operand does not contain the first operand.	"a" not in "bc"	True	Since string "bc" does not contain string "a", the output of "a" not in "bc" evaluates to True.

Table 8.1 Comparing string values.

CONCEPTS IN PRACTICE

Using logical and membership operators to compare string values

1. What is the output of ("aaa" < "aab")?
   a. True
   b. False

2. What is the output of ("aa" < "a")?
   a. True
   b. False

3. What is the output of ("aples" in "apples")?
   a. undefined
   b. True
   c. False

lower() and upper()

Python has many useful methods for modifying strings, two of which are lower() and upper() methods. The **lower()** method returns the converted alphabetical characters to lowercase, and the **upper()** method returns the converted alphabetical characters to uppercase. Both the lower() and upper() methods do *not* modify the string.

EXAMPLE 8.1

Converting characters in a string

In the example below, the lower() and upper() string methods are called on the string variable x to convert all characters to lowercase and uppercase, respectively.

```
x = "Apples"

# The lower() method converts a string to all lowercase characters
print(x.lower())

# The upper() method converts a string to all uppercase characters
print(x.upper())
```

The above code's output is:

```
apples
APPLES
```

CONCEPTS IN PRACTICE

Using lower() and upper()

4. What is the output of "aBbA".lower()?
   a. abba
   b. ABBA
   c. abbA

5. What is the output of "aBbA".upper()?
   a. abba

b. ABBA
c. ABbA
d. aBBA

6. What is the output of `("a".upper() == "A")`?
   a. True
   b. False

TRY IT

Number of characters in the string

A string variable, `s_input`, is defined. Use `lower()` and `upper()` to convert the string to lowercase and uppercase, and print the results in the output. Also, print the number of characters in the string, including space characters.

Access multimedia content (https://openstax.org/books/introduction-python-programming/pages/8-1-string-operations)

TRY IT

What is my character?

Given the string, `s_input`, which is a one-character string object, if the character is between "a" and "t" or "A" and "T", print True. Otherwise, print False.
Hint: You can convert `s_input` to lowercase and check if `s_input` is between "a" and "t".

Access multimedia content (https://openstax.org/books/introduction-python-programming/pages/8-1-string-operations)

8.2 String slicing

Learning objectives

By the end of this section you should be able to

- Use string indexing to access characters in the string.
- Use string slicing to get a substring from a string.
- Identify immutability characteristics of strings.

String indexing

A string is a type of sequence. A string is made up of a sequence of characters indexed from left to right, starting at 0. For a string variable s, the left-most character is indexed 0 and the right-most character is indexed `len(s)` - 1. Ex: The length of the string "Cloud" is 5, so the last index is 4.

Negative indexing can also be used to refer to characters from right to left starting at -1. For a string variable s, the left-most character is indexed -`len(s)` and the right-most character is indexed -1. Ex: The length of the string "flower" is 6, so the index of the first character with negative indexing is -6.

CHECKPOINT

String indexing

Access multimedia content (https://openstax.org/books/introduction-python-programming/pages/8-2-string-slicing)

CONCEPTS IN PRACTICE

Accessing characters in a string using indexing

1. Which character is at index 1 in the string `"hello"`?
   a. `"h"`
   b. `"e"`
   c. `"o"`

2. What is the character at index -2 in the string `"Blue"`?
   a. `"e"`
   b. `"u"`
   c. `"l"`

3. What is the output of the following code?

   ```
   word = "chance"
   print(word[-1] == word[5])
   ```

   a. True
   b. False

String slicing

String slicing is used when a programmer must get access to a sequence of characters. Here, a string slicing operator can be used. When `[a:b]` is used with the name of a string variable, a sequence of characters starting from index a (inclusive) up to index b (exclusive) is returned. Both a and b are optional. If a or b are not provided, the default values are 0 and `len(string)`, respectively.

EXAMPLE 8.2

Getting the minutes

Consider a time value is given as `"hh:mm"` with `"hh"` representing the hour and `"mm"` representing the minutes. To retrieve only the string's minutes portion, the following code can be used:

```
time_string = "13:46"
minutes = time_string[3:5]
print(minutes)
```

The above code's output is:

46

EXAMPLE 8.3

Getting the hour

Consider a time value is given as `"hh:mm"` with `"hh"` representing the hour and `"mm"` representing the minutes. To retrieve only the string's hour portion, the following code can be used:

```
time_string = "14:50"
hour = time_string[:2]
print(hour)
```

The above code's output is:

14

CONCEPTS IN PRACTICE

Getting a substring using string slicing

4. What is the output of the following code?

   ```
   a_string = "Hello world"
   print(a_string[2:4])
   ```

   a. `"el"`
   b. `"ll"`
   c. `"llo"`

5. What is the output of the following code?

   ```
   location = "classroom"
   print(location[-3:-1])
   ```

   a. `"ro"`
   b. `"oo"`
   c. `"oom"`

6. What is the output of the following code?

```
greeting = "hi Leila"
name = greeting[3:]
```

a. " Leila"
b. "Leila"
c. "ila"

String immutability

String objects are **immutable** meaning that string objects cannot be modified or changed once created. Once a string object is created, the string's contents cannot be altered by directly modifying individual characters or elements within the string. Instead, to make changes to a string, a new string object with the desired changes is created, leaving the original string unchanged.

CHECKPOINT

Strings are immutable

Access multimedia content (https://openstax.org/books/introduction-python-programming/pages/8-2-string-slicing)

CONCEPTS IN PRACTICE

Modifying string content

7. What is the correct way of replacing the first character in a string to character "*" in a new string?

   a. ```
      x = "string"
      x[0] = "*"
      ```
   b. ```
      x = "string"
      x = "*" + x[1:]
      ```
   c. ```
      x = "string"
      x = "*" + x
      ```

8. What type of error will result from the following code?

   ```
   string_variable = "example"
   string_variable[-1] = ""
   ```

   a. TypeError
   b. IndexError
   c. NameError

9. What is the output of the following code?

   ```
   str = "morning"
   str = str[1]
   print(str)
   ```
   ```

a. TypeError
b. m
c. o

TRY IT

Changing the greeting message

Given the string "Hello my fellow classmates" containing a greeting message, print the first word by getting the beginning of the string up to (and including) the 5th character. Change the first word in the string to "Hi" instead of "hello" and print the greeting message again.

Access multimedia content (https://openstax.org/books/introduction-python-programming/pages/8-2-string-slicing)

TRY IT

Editing the string at specified locations

Given a string variable, `string_variable`, and a list of indexes, remove characters at the specified indexes and print the resulting string.

```
Input:
string_variable = "great"
indices = [0, 1]


prints eat
```

Access multimedia content (https://openstax.org/books/introduction-python-programming/pages/8-2-string-slicing)

8.3 | Searching/testing strings

Learning objectives

By the end of this section you should be able to

- Use the `in` operator to identify whether a given string contains a substring.
- Call the `count()` method to count the number of substrings in a given string.
- Search a string to find a substring using the `find()` method.
- Use the `index()` method to find the index of the first occurrence of a substring in a given string.
- Write a for loop on strings using in operator.

in operator

The **in** Boolean operator can be used to check if a string contains another string. `in` returns `True` if the first string exists in the second string, `False` otherwise.

CHECKPOINT

What is in the phrase?

Access multimedia content (https://openstax.org/books/introduction-python-programming/pages/8-3-searchingtesting-strings)

CONCEPTS IN PRACTICE

Using in operator to find substrings

1. What is the output of (`"a" in "an umbrella"`)?
   a. 2
   b. False
   c. True
   d. 1

2. What is the output of (`"ab" in "arbitrary"`)?
   a. True
   b. False

3. What is the output of (`"" in "string"`)?
   a. True
   b. False

For loop using in operator

The `in` operator can be used to iterate over characters in a string using a `for` loop. In each `for` loop iteration, one character is read and will be the loop variable for that iteration.

CHECKPOINT

for loop using in operator

Access multimedia content (https://openstax.org/books/introduction-python-programming/pages/8-3-searchingtesting-strings)

CONCEPTS IN PRACTICE

Using in operator within for loop

4. What is the output of the following code?

```
for c in "string":
    print(c, end = "")
```

a. string
b. s
   t
   r
   i
   n
   g
c. s t r i n g

5. What is the output of the following code?

```
count = 0
for c in "abca":
    if c == "a":
        count += 1
print(count)
```

a. 0
b. 1
c. 2

6. What is the output of the following code?

```
word = "cab"
for i in word:
    if i == "a":
        print("A", end = "")
    if i == "b":
        print("B", end = "")
    if i == "c":
        print("C", end = "")
```

a. cab
b. abc
c. CAB
d. ABC

count()

The **count()** method counts the number of occurrences of a substring in a given string. If the given substring does not exist in the given string, the value 0 is returned.

CHECKPOINT

Counting the number of occurrences of a substring

Access multimedia content (https://openstax.org/books/introduction-python-programming/pages/8-3-searchingtesting-strings)

CONCEPTS IN PRACTICE

Using count() to count the number of substrings

7. What is the output of (aaa".count("a"))?
   a. True
   b. 1
   c. 3

8. What is the output of ("weather".count("b"))?
   a. 0
   b. -1
   c. False

9. What is the output of ("aaa".count("aa"))?
   a. 1
   b. 2
   c. 3

find()

The **find()** method returns the index of the first occurrence of a substring in a given string. If the substring does not exist in the given string, the value of -1 is returned.

CHECKPOINT

Finding the first index of a substring

Access multimedia content (https://openstax.org/books/introduction-python-programming/pages/8-3-searchingtesting-strings)

CONCEPTS IN PRACTICE

Using find() to locate a substring

10. What is the output of "banana".find("a")?
    a. 1
    b. 3
    c. 5

11. What is the output of "banana".find("c")?

a. `0`
   b. `-1`
   c. `ValueError`

12. What is the output of `"b".find("banana")`?
    a. `-1`
    b. `0`
    c. `ValueError`

index()

The **index()** method performs similarly to the `find()` method in which the method returns the index of the first occurrence of a substring in a given string. The `index()` method assumes that the substring exists in the given string; otherwise, throws a `ValueError`.

EXAMPLE 8.4

Getting the time's minute portion

Consider a time value is given as part of a string using the format of `"hh:mm"` with `"hh"` representing the hour and `"mm"` representing the minutes. To retrieve only the string's minute portion, the following code can be used:

```
time_string = "The time is 12:50"
index = time_string.index(":")
print(time_string[index+1:index+3])
```

The above code's output is:

```
50
```

CONCEPTS IN PRACTICE

Using index() to locate a substring

13. What is the output of `"school".index("o")`?
    a. `3`
    b. `4`
    c. `-3`

14. What is the output of `"school".index("ooo")`?
    a. `3`
    b. `4`

c. `ValueError`

15. What is the output of the following code?

    ```
    sentence = "This is a sentence"
    index = sentence.index(" ")
    print(sentence[:index])
    ```

    a. `"This"`
    b. `"This "`
    c. `"sentence"`

TRY IT

Finding all spaces

Write a program that, given a string, counts the number of space characters in the string. Also, print the given string with all spaces removed.

    Input: "This is great"

    prints:
    2
    Thisisgreat

Access multimedia content (https://openstax.org/books/introduction-python-programming/pages/8-3-searchingtesting-strings)

8.4 String formatting

Learning objectives

By the end of this section you should be able to

- Format a string template using input arguments.
- Use `format()` to generate numerical formats based on a given template.

String format specification

Python provides string substitutions syntax for formatting strings with input arguments. **Formatting string** includes specifying string pattern rules and modifying the string according to the formatting specification. Examples of formatting strings include using patterns for building different string values and specifying modification rules for the string's length and alignment.

String formatting with replacement fields

Replacement fields are used to define a pattern for creating multiple string values that comply with a given format. The example below shows two string values that use the same template for making requests to different individuals for taking different courses.

EXAMPLE 8.5

String values from the same template

```
Dear John, I'd like to take a programming course with Prof. Potter.

Dear Kishwar, I'd like to take a math course with Prof. Robinson.
```

In the example above, replacement fields are 1) the name of the individual the request is being made to, 2) title of the course, and 3) the name of the instructor. To create a template, replacement fields can be added with {} to show a placeholder for user input. The **format()** method is used to pass inputs for replacement fields in a string template.

EXAMPLE 8.6

String template formatting for course enrollment requests

A string template with replacement fields is defined below to create string values with different input arguments. The `format()` method is used to pass inputs to the template in the same order.

```
s = "Dear {}, I'd like to take a {} course with Prof. {}."

print(s)
print(s.format("John", "programming", "Potter"))
print(s.format("Kishwar", "math", "Robinson"))
```

The above code's output is:

```
Dear {}, I'd like to take a {} course with Prof. {}.
Dear John, I'd like to take a programming course with Prof. Potter.
Dear Kishwar, I'd like to take a math course with Prof. Robinson.
```

CONCEPTS IN PRACTICE

String template and formatting

1. What is the output of `print("Hello {}!".format("Ana"))`?
    a. Ana

b. `Hello Ana`
  c. `Hello Ana!`

2. What is the output of `print("{}:{}".format("One", "1"))`?
   a. `One1`
   b. `One:1`
   c. `1:One`

3. What is the output of `print("{}".format("one", "two", "three"))`?
   a. `one`
   b. `two`
   c. `onetwothree`

Named replacement fields

Replacement fields can be tagged with a label, called **named replacement fields**, for ease of access and code readability. The example below illustrates how named replacement fields can be used in string templates.

EXAMPLE 8.7

Season weather template using named replacement fields

A named replacement argument is a convenient way of assigning name tags to replacement fields and passing values associated with replacement fields using corresponding names (instead of passing values in order).

```
s = "Weather in {season} is {temperature}."

print(s)
print(s.format(season = "summer", temperature = "hot"))
print(s.format(season = "winter", temperature = "cold"))
```

The above code's output is:

```
Weather in {season} is {temperature}.
Weather in summer is hot.
Weather in winter is cold.
```

MULTIPLE USE OF A NAMED ARGUMENT

Since named replacement fields are referred to using a name key, a named replacement field can appear and be used more than once in the template. Also, positional ordering is not necessary when named replacement fields are used.

```
s = "Weather in {season} is {temperature}; very very {temperature}."

print(s)
print(s.format(season = "summer", temperature = "hot"))
print(s.format(temperature = "cold", season = "winter"))
```

The above code's output is:

```
Weather in {season} is {temperature}; very very {temperature}.
Weather in summer is hot; very very hot.
Weather in winter is cold; very very cold.
```

CONCEPTS IN PRACTICE

Named replacement field examples

4. What is the output of `print("Hey {name}!".format(name = "Bengio"))`?
   a. Hey name!
   b. Hey Bengio
   c. Hey Bengio!

5. What is the output of `print("Hey {name}!".format("Bengio"))`?
   a. Hey name!
   b. KeyError
   c. Hey Bengio!

6. What is the output of the following code?

   ```
   greeting = "Hi"
   name = "Jess"
   print("{greeting} {name}".format(greeting = greeting, name = name))
   ```

   a. greeting name
   b. Hi Jess
   c. Jess Hi

Numbered replacement fields

Python's string `format()` method can use positional ordering to match the numbered arguments. The replacement fields that use the positional ordering of arguments are called **numbered replacement fields**. The indexing of the arguments starts from 0. Ex: `print("{1}{0}".format("Home", "Welcome"))` outputs the string value `"Welcome Home"` as the first argument. `"Home"` is at index 0, and the second argument, `"Welcome"`, is at index 1. Replacing these arguments in the order of `"{1}{0}"` creates the string `"Welcome`

Home".

Numbered replacement fields can use argument's values for multiple replacement fields by using the same argument index. The example below illustrates how an argument is used for more than one numbered replacement field.

EXAMPLE 8.8

Numbered replacement field to build a phrase

Numbered replacement fields are used in this example to build phrases like "very very cold" or "very hot".

```
template1 = "{0} {0} {1}"
template2 = "{0} {1}"

print(template1.format("very", "cold"))
print(template2.format("very", "hot"))
```

The above code's output is:

```
very very cold
very hot
```

String length and alignment formatting

Formatting the string length may be needed for standardizing the output style when multiple string values of the same context are being created and printed. The example below shows a use case of string formatting in printing a table with minimum-length columns and specific alignment.

EXAMPLE 8.9

A formatted table of a class roster

A formatted table of a class roster

```
Student Name         Major            Grade
-------------------------------------------
Manoj Sara        Computer Science      A-
Gabriel Wang    Electrical Engineering   A
Alex Narayanan     Social Sciences      A+
```

In the example above, the table is formatted into three columns. The first column takes up 15 characters and is left-aligned. The second column uses 25 characters and is center-aligned, and the last column uses two characters and is right aligned. Alignment and length format specifications controls are used to create the formatted table.

The field width in string format specification is used to specify the minimum length of the given string. If the string is shorter than the given minimum length, the string will be padded by space characters. A **field width** is included in the format specification field using an integer after a colon. Ex: {name:15} specifies that the minimum length of the string values that are passed to the name field is 15.

Since the field width can be used to specify the minimum length of a string, the string can be padded with space characters from right, left, or both to be left-aligned, right-aligned, and centered, respectively. The **string alignment type** is specified using <, >, or ^characters after the colon when field length is specified. Ex: {name:^20} specifies a named replacement field with the minimum length of 20 characters that is center-aligned.

Alignment Type	Symbol	Example	Output
Left-aligned	<	`template = "{hex:<7}{name:<10}"` `print(template.format(hex = "#FF0000", name = "Red")) print(template.format(hex = "#00FF00", name = "green"))`	#FF0000Red #00FF00green
Right-aligned	>	`template = "{hex:>7}{name:>10}"` `print(template.format(hex = "#FF0000", name = "Red")) print(template.format(hex = "#00FF00", name = "green"))`	#FF0000 Red #00FF00 green
Centered	^	`template = "{hex:^7}{name:^10}"` `print(template.format(hex = "#FF0000", name = "Red")) print(template.format(hex = "#00FF00", name = "green"))`	#FF0000 Red #00FF00 green

Table 8.2 String alignment formatting.

> **CONCEPTS IN PRACTICE**
>
> Specifying field width and alignment
>
> 7. What is the output of the following code?
>
>    ```
>    template = "{name:12}"
>    formatted_name = template.format(name = "Alice")
>    print(len(formatted_name))
>    ```
>
>   a. 5
>   b. 12
>   c. "Alice"
>
> 8. What is the output of the following code?

```
template = "{greeting:>6}"
formatted_greeting = template.format(greeting = "Hello")
print(formatted_greeting[0])
```

a. H
b. " Hello"
c. Space character

9. What is the output of the following code?

```
template = "{:5}"
print(template.format("123456789"))
```

a. 56789
b. 123456
c. 123456789

Formatting numbers

The `format()` method can be used to format numerical values. Numerical values can be padded to have a given minimum length, precision, and sign character. The syntax for modifying numeric values follows the `{[index]:[width][.precision][type]}` structure. In the given syntax,

- The `index` field refers to the index of the argument.
- The `width` field refers to the minimum length of the string.
- The `precision` field refers to the floating-point precision of the given number.
- The `type` field shows the type of the input that is passed to the `format()` method. Floating-point and decimal inputs are identified by `"f"` and `"d"`, respectively. String values are also identified by `"s"`.

The table below summarizes formatting options for modifying numeric values.

Example	Output	Explanation
`print("{:.7f}".format(0.9795))`	0.9795000	The format specification .7 shows the output must have seven decimal places. The f specification is an identifier of floating-point formatting.
`print("{:.3f}".format(12))`	12.000	The format specification .3 shows the output must have three decimal places. The f specification is an identifier of floating-point formatting.

Table 8.3 Numerical formatting options.

Example	Output	Explanation
`print("{:+.2f}".format(4))`	+4.00	The format specification .2 shows the output must have two decimal places. The f specification is an identifier of floating-point formatting. The + sign before the precision specification adds a sign character to the output.
`print("{:0>5d}".format(5))`	00005	The format specification 0>5 defines the width field as 5, and thus the output must have a minimum length of 5. And, if the number has fewer than five digits, the number must be padded with 0's from the left side. The d specification is an identifier of a decimal number formatting.
`print("{:.3s}".format("12.50"))`	12.	The format specification .3 shows the output will have three characters. The s specification is an identifier of string formatting.

Table 8.3 Numerical formatting options.

CONCEPTS IN PRACTICE

Numeric value formatting examples

10. What is the output of `print('{0:.3f}'.format(3.141592))`?
    a. 3.141592
    b. 3.1
    c. 3.142

11. What is the output of `print('{:1>3d}'.format(3))`?
    a. 113
    b. 311
    c. 3.000

12. What is the output of `print('{:+d}'.format(123))`?
    a. 123
    b. +123
    c. :+123

TRY IT

Formatting a list of numbers

Given a list of numbers (floating-point or integer), print numbers with two decimal place precision and at least six characters.

    Input: [12.5, 2]

    Prints: 012.50

    002:00

Access multimedia content (https://openstax.org/books/introduction-python-programming/pages/8-4-string-formatting)

8.5 Splitting/joining strings

Learning objectives

By the end of this section you should be able to

- Use the `split()` method to split a string into substrings.
- Combine objects in a list into a string using `join()` method.

split()

A string in Python can be broken into substrings given a **delimiter**. A delimiter is also referred to as a separator. The **split()** method, when applied to a string, splits the string into substrings by using the given argument as a delimiter. Ex: `"1-2".split('-')` returns a list of substrings `["1", "2"]`. When no arguments are given to the `split()` method, blank space characters are used as delimiters. Ex: `"1\t2\n3 4".split()` returns `["1", "2", "3", "4"]`.

CHECKPOINT

split() for breaking down the string into tokens

Access multimedia content (https://openstax.org/books/introduction-python-programming/pages/8-5-splittingjoining-strings)

CONCEPTS IN PRACTICE

Examples of string delimiters and split() method

1. What is the output of `print("1*2*3*".split('*'))`?
   a. `["1", "*", "2", "*", "3", "*"]`

b. `["1", "2', "3"]`
   c. `[1, 2, 3]`

2. What is the output of `print("a year includes 12 months".split())`?
   a. `["a year includes 12 months"]`
   b. `["a", "year", "includes", 12, "months"]`
   c. `["a", "year", "includes", "12", "months"]`

3. What is the output of the following code?

   ```
   s = """This is a test"""

   out = s.split()
   print(out)
   ```

   a. Error
   b. `['This', 'is', 'a', 'test']`
   c. `>['This', 'is a', 'test']`

join()

The **join()** method is the inverse of the `split()` method: a list of string values are concatenated together to form one output string. When joining string elements in the list, the delimiter is added in-between elements. Ex: `','.join(["this", "is", "great"])` returns `"this,is,great"`.

CHECKPOINT

join() for combining tokens into one string

Access multimedia content (https://openstax.org/books/introduction-python-programming/pages/8-5-splittingjoining-strings)

CONCEPTS IN PRACTICE

Applying join() method on list of string values

4. What is the output of the following code?

   ```
   elements = ['A', 'beautiful', 'day', 'for', 'learning']

   print(",".join(elements))
   ```

   a. `'A beautiful day for learning'`
   b. `['A, beautiful, day, for, learning']`
   c. `'A,beautiful,day,for,learning'`

5. What is the length of the string `"sss".join(["1","2"])`?
   a. 2

b. 5
c. 8

6. What is the value stored in the variable out?

   ```
   s = ["1", "2"]
   out = "".join(s)
   ```

   a. 12
   b. "12"
   c. "1 2"

TRY IT

Unique and comma-separated words

Write a program that accepts a comma-separated sequence of words as input, and prints words in separate lines. Ex: Given the string "happy,smiling,face", the output would be:

```
happy
smiling
face
```

Access multimedia content (https://openstax.org/books/introduction-python-programming/pages/8-5-splittingjoining-strings)

TRY IT

Lunch order

Use the join() method to repeat back a user's order at a restaurant, separated by commas. The user will input each food item on a separate line. When finished ordering, the user will enter a blank line. The output depends on how many items the user orders:

- If the user inputs nothing, the program outputs:
  You ordered nothing.
- If the user inputs one item (Ex: eggs), the program outputs:
  You ordered eggs.
- If the user inputs two items (Ex: eggs, ham), the program outputs:
  You ordered eggs and ham.
- If the user inputs three or more items (Ex: eggs, ham, toast), the program outputs:
  You ordered eggs, ham, and toast.

In the general case with three or more items, each item should be separated by a comma and a space. The word "and" should be added before the last item.

Access multimedia content (https://openstax.org/books/introduction-python-programming/pages/

8-5-splittingjoining-strings)

8.6 Chapter summary

Highlights from this chapter include:

- A string is a sequence of characters.
- Logical operators can be used to compare two string values. String comparison is done by comparing corresponding ASCII values of characters in the order of appearance in the string.
- String indexing is used to access a character or a sequence of characters in the string.
- String objects are immutable.
- String splicing.

At this point, you should be able to write programs dealing with string values.

Method	Description
`len()`	Returns the string length.
`upper()`	Returns uppercase characters.
`lower()`	Returns lowercase characters.
`count()`	Returns the number of a given substring in a string.
`find()`	Returns the index of the first occurrence of a given substring in a string. If the substring does not exist in the string, -1 is returned.
`index()`	Returns the index of the first occurrence of a given substring in a string. If the substring does not exist in the string, a `ValueError` is returned.
`format()`	Used to create strings with specified patterns using arguments.
`join()`	Takes a list of string values and combines string values into one string by placing a given separator between values.
`split()`	Separates a string into tokens based on a given separator string. If no separator string is provided, blank space characters are used as separators.
Operator	**Description**

Table 8.4 Chapter 8 reference.

Method	Description
`in`	Checks if a substring exists in a string.
| `in` operator in a `for` loop | ```
for character in string:
    # loop body
``` |

Table 8.4 Chapter 8 reference.
```

9 Lists

Figure 9.1 credit: modification of work "Budget and Bills" by Alabama Extension/Flickr, Public Domain

Chapter Outline

- 9.1 Modifying and iterating lists
- 9.2 Sorting and reversing lists
- 9.3 Common list operations
- 9.4 Nested lists
- 9.5 List comprehensions
- 9.6 Chapter summary

Introduction

Programmers often work on collections of data. Lists are a useful way of collecting data elements. Python lists are extremely flexible, and, unlike strings, a list's contents can be changed.

The Objects chapter introduced lists. This chapter explores operations that can be performed on lists.

 ## 9.1 Modifying and iterating lists

Learning objectives

By the end of this section you should be able to

- Modify a list using `append()`, `remove()`, and `pop()` list operations.
- Search a list using a `for` loop.

Using list operations to modify a list

An `append()` operation is used to add an element to the end of a list. In programming, **append** means add to the end. A `remove()` operation removes the specified element from a list. A `pop()` operation removes the last item of a list.

EXAMPLE 9.1

Simple operations to modify a list

The code below demonstrates simple operations for modifying a list.

Line 8 shows the append() operation, line 12 shows the remove() operation, and line 17 shows the pop() operation. Since the pop() operation removes the last element, no parameter is needed.

```
1  """Operations for adding and removing elements from a list."""
2
3      # Create a list of students working on a project
4      student_list = ["Jamie", "Vicky", "DeShawn", "Tae"]
5      print(student_list)
6
7      # Another student joins the project. The student must be added to the list.
8      student_list.append("Ming")
9      print(student_list)
10
11     # "Jamie" withdraws from the project. Jamie must be removed from the list.
12     student_list.remove("Jamie")
13     print(student_list)
14
15     # Suppose "Ming" had to be removed from the list.
16     # A pop() operation can be used since Ming is last in the list.
17     student_list.pop()
18     print(student_list)
```

The above code's output is:

```
['Jamie', 'Vicky', 'DeShawn', 'Tae']
['Jamie', 'Vicky', 'DeShawn', 'Tae', 'Ming']
['Vicky', 'DeShawn', 'Tae', 'Ming']
['Vicky', 'DeShawn', 'Tae']
```

CONCEPTS IN PRACTICE

Modifying lists

1. Which operation can be used to add an element to the end of a list?
    a. add()
    b. append()
    c. pop()

2. What is the correct syntax to remove the element 23 from a list called `number_list`?
   a. `remove()`
   b. `number_list.remove()`
   c. `number_list.remove(23)`

3. Which operation can be used to remove an element from the end of a list?
   a. only `pop()`
   b. only `remove()`
   c. either `pop()` or `remove()`

Iterating lists

An iterative for loop can be used to iterate through a list. Alternatively, lists can be iterated using list indexes with a counting for loop. The animation below shows both ways of iterating a list.

CHECKPOINT

Using len() to get the length of a list

Access multimedia content (https://openstax.org/books/introduction-python-programming/pages/9-1-modifying-and-iterating-lists)

CONCEPTS IN PRACTICE

Iterating lists

For the following questions, consider the list:

`my_list = [2, 3, 5, 7, 9]`

4. How many times will the following `for` loop execute?
   ```
   for element in my_list:
   ```
   a. 5
   b. 4

5. What is the final value of i for the following counting `for` loop?
   ```
   for i in range(0, len(my_list)):
   ```
   a. 9
   b. 4
   c. 5

6. What is the output of the code below?
   ```
   for i in range(0, len(my_list), 2):
       print(my_list[i], end=' ')
   ```
   a. 2 5 9
   b. 2 3 5 7 9

c. 2
   5
   9

TRY IT

Sports list

Create a list of sports played on a college campus. The sports to be included are baseball, football, tennis, and table tennis.

Next, add volleyball to the list.

Next, remove `"football"` from the list and add `"soccer"` to the list.

Show the list contents after each modification.

Access multimedia content (https://openstax.org/books/introduction-python-programming/pages/9-1-modifying-and-iterating-lists)

TRY IT

Simple Searching

Write a program that prints `"found!"` if `"soccer"` is found in the given list.

Access multimedia content (https://openstax.org/books/introduction-python-programming/pages/9-1-modifying-and-iterating-lists)

9.2 Sorting and reversing lists

Learning objectives

By the end of this section you should be able to

- Understand the concept of sorting.
- Use built-in `sort()` and `reverse()` methods.

Sorting

Ordering elements in a sequence is often useful. **Sorting** is the task of arranging elements in a sequence in ascending or descending order.

Sorting can work on numerical or non-numerical data. When ordering text, dictionary order is used. Ex: "bat" comes before "cat" because "b" comes before "c".

CHECKPOINT

Sorting

Access multimedia content (https://openstax.org/books/introduction-python-programming/pages/

9-2-sorting-and-reversing-lists)

CONCEPTS IN PRACTICE

Sorting

1. What would be the last element of the following list if it is sorted in descending order?
   `[12, 3, 19, 25, 16, -3, 5]`
   a. 25
   b. -3
   c. 5

2. Arrange the following list in ascending order.
   `["cat", "bat", "dog", "coyote", "wolf"]`
   a. `["bat", "cat", "coyote", "dog", "wolf"]`
   b. `["wolf", "coyote", "dog", "cat", "bat"]`

3. How are the words `"flask"` and `"flash"` related in Python?
   a. `"flask" < "flash"`
   b. `"flask" == "flash"`
   c. `"flask" > "flash"`

Using sort() and reverse()

Python provides methods for arranging elements in a list.

- The `sort()` method arranges the elements of a list in ascending order. For strings, ASCII values are used and uppercase characters come before lowercase characters, leading to unexpected results. Ex: `"A"` is ordered before `"a"` in ascending order but so is `"G"`; thus, `"Gail"` comes before `"apple"`.
- The `reverse()` method reverses the elements in a list.

EXAMPLE 9.2

Sorting and reversing lists

```
# Setup a list of numbers
num_list = [38, 92, 23, 16]
print(num_list)

# Sort the list
num_list.sort()
print(num_list)

# Setup a list of words
dance_list = ["Stepping", "Ballet", "Salsa", "Kathak", "Hopak", "Flamenco", "Dabke"]
```

```
# Reverse the list
dance_list.reverse()
print(dance_list)

# Sort the list
dance_list.sort()
print(dance_list)
```

The above code's output is:

```
[38, 92, 23, 16]
[16, 23, 38, 92]
["Dabke", "Flamenco", "Hopak", "Kathak", "Salsa", "Ballet", "Stepping"]
["Ballet", "Dabke", "Flamenco", "Hopak", "Kathak", "Salsa", "Stepping"]
```

CONCEPTS IN PRACTICE

sort() and reverse() methods

Use the following list for the questions below.

`board_games = ["go", "chess", "scrabble", "checkers"]`

4. What is the correct way to sort the list `board_games` in ascending order?
    a. `sort(board_games)`
    b. `board_games.sort()`
    c. `board_games.sort('ascending')`

5. What is the correct way to reverse the list `board_games`?
    a. `board_games.reverse()`
    b. `reverse(board_games)`

6. What would be the last element of `board_games` after the `reverse()` method has been applied?
    a. `'go'`
    b. `'checkers'`
    c. `'scrabble'`

TRY IT

Sorting and reversing

Complete the program below to arrange and print the numbers in ascending and descending order.

Access multimedia content (https://openstax.org/books/introduction-python-programming/pages/9-2-sorting-and-reversing-lists)

9.3 Common list operations

Learning objectives
By the end of this section you should be able to
- Use built-in functions `max()`, `min()`, and `sum()`.
- Demonstrate how to copy a list.

Using built-in operations
The `max()` function called on a list returns the largest element in the list. The `min()` function called on a list returns the smallest element in the list. The `max()` and `min()` functions work for lists as long as elements within the list are comparable.

The `sum()` function called on a list of numbers returns the sum of all elements in the list.

EXAMPLE 9.3

Common list operations

```
"""Common list operations."""

# Set up a list of number
snum_list = [28, 92, 17, 3, -5, 999, 1]

# Set up a list of words
city_list = ["New York", "Missoula", "Chicago", "Bozeman",
"Birmingham", "Austin", "Sacramento"]

# Usage of the max() funtion
print(max(num_list))

# max() function works for strings as well
print(max(city_list))

# Usage of the min() funtion which also works for strings
print(min(num_list))

print(min(city_list))

# sum() only works for a list of numbers
print(sum(num_list))
```

The above code's output is:

```
999
Sacramento
-5
Austin
1135
```

CONCEPTS IN PRACTICE

List operations

1. What is the correct way to get the minimum of a list named nums_list?
   a. `min(nums_list)`
   b. `nums_list.min()`
   c. `minimum(nums_list)`

2. What is the minimum of the following list?
   `["Lollapalooza", "Coachella", "Newport Jazz festival", "Hardly Strictly Bluegrass", "Austin City Limits"]`
   a. Coachella
   b. Austin City Limits
   c. The minimum doesn't exist.

3. What value does the function call return?
   `sum([1.2, 2.1, 3.2, 5.9])`
   a. `sum()` only works for integers.
   b. 11
   c. 12.4

Copying a list

The `copy()` method is used to create a copy of a list.

CHECKPOINT

Copying a list

Access multimedia content (https://openstax.org/books/introduction-python-programming/pages/9-3-common-list-operations)

CONCEPTS IN PRACTICE

Copying a list

4. What is the output of the following code?

```
my_list = [1, 2, 3]
list2 = my_list
list2[0] = 13
print(sum(my_list))
```

a. 6
b. 13
c. 18

5. What is the output of the following code?

```
my_list = [1, 2, 3]
list2 = my_list.copy()
list2[0] = 13
print(max(my_list))
```

a. 3
b. 13
c. 18

6. What is the output of the following code?

```
my_list = ["Cat", "Dog", "Hamster"]
list2 = my_list
list2[2] = "Pigeon"
print(sum(my_list))
```

a. CatDogPigeon
b. Error

TRY IT

Copy

Make a copy of `word_list` called wisdom. Sort the list called wisdom. Create a sentence using the words in each list and print those sentences (no need to add periods at the end of the sentences).

Access multimedia content (https://openstax.org/books/introduction-python-programming/pages/9-3-common-list-operations)

9.4 Nested lists

Learning objectives

By the end of this section you should be able to

- Demonstrate the use of a list-of-lists to structure data.
- Demonstrate individual element addressing using multi-dimensional indexing.
- Use nested loops to iterate a list-of-lists.

List-of-lists

Lists can be made of any type of element. A list element can also be a list. Ex: [2, [3, 5], 17] is a valid list with the list [3, 5] being the element at index 1.

When a list is an element inside a larger list, it is called a **nested list**. Nested lists are useful for expressing multidimensional data. When each of the elements of a larger list is a smaller list, the larger list is called a **list-of-lists**.

Ex: A table can be stored as a two-dimensional list-of-lists, where each row of data is a list in the list-of-lists.

CHECKPOINT

List-of-lists

Access multimedia content (https://openstax.org/books/introduction-python-programming/pages/9-4-nested-lists)

CONCEPTS IN PRACTICE

Lists

For each of the questions below, consider the following matrix:

$$\text{mat A} = \begin{bmatrix} 7 & 4 & 5 \\ 3 & 9 & 6 \\ 1 & 2 & 8 \end{bmatrix}$$

1. What would be the correct way to represent matA in Python?
   a. [[7, 4, 5], [3, 9, 6], [1, 2, 8]]
   b. [7, 4, 5
      3, 9, 6
      1, 2, 8]
   c. [[7, 3, 1], [4, 9, 2], [1, 2, 8]

2. What would be the correct index for the number 6 in the above list?
   a. [5]
   b. [2][1]
   c. [1][2]

3. What would be the result of the following code:

   ```
   print(matA[0])
   ```

   a. Error
   b. 7
   c. [7, 4, 5]

Using nested loops to iterate nested lists

A nested loop structure can be used to iterate a list-of-lists. For a two-dimensional list-of-lists, an outer `for` loop can be used for rows, and an inner `for` loop can be used for columns.

EXAMPLE 9.4

Iterating a list-of-lists

The code below demonstrates how to iterate a list-of-lists.

The outer loop on line 9 goes element by element for the larger list. Each element in the larger list is a list. The inner loop on line 10 iterates through each element in each nested list.

```
1  """Iterating a list-of-lists."""
2
3      # Create a list of numbers
4      list1 = [[1, 2, 3],
5               [1, 4, 9],
6               [1, 8, 27]]
7
8      # Iterating the list-of-lists
9      for row in list1:
10         for num in row:
11             print(num, end=" ")
12         print()
```

The above code's output is:

```
1 2 3
1 4 9
1 8 27
```

CONCEPTS IN PRACTICE

Iterating a list-of-lists

For each question below, consider the following list:

```
my_list = [[7, 4, 5, 12],
           [24, 3, 9, 16],
           [12, 8, 91, -5]]
```

4. Which code prints each number in my_list starting from 7, then 4, and so on ending with -5?
   a. ```
      for row in my_list:
          for elem in row:
              print(elem)
      ```
   b. ```
      for elem in my_list:
          print(elem)
      ```

5. The range() function can also be used to iterate a list-of-lists. Which code prints each number in my_list starting from 7, then 4, and so on, ending with -5, using counting for loops?

```
a. for column_index in range(0, len(my_list[0])):
       for row_index in range (0, len(my_list)):
           print(my_list[row_index][column_index])
b. for row_index in range(0, len(my_list)):
       for column_index in range (0, len(my_list)):
           print(my_list[row_index][column_index])
       print()
c. for row_index in range(0, len(my_list)):
       for column_index in range (0, len(my_list[0])):
           print(my_list[row_index][column_index])
```

TRY IT

Matrix multiplication

Write a program that calculates the matrix multiplication product of the matrices matW and matZ below and prints the result. The expected result is shown.

$$\text{mat } W = \begin{bmatrix} 13 & 4 & 5 \\ 2 & -9 & 7 \\ 7 & 3 & 19 \end{bmatrix} \text{mat } Z = \begin{bmatrix} 2 & 1 & 5 \\ 3 & 7 & 9 \\ -1 & 13 & 19 \end{bmatrix}$$

$$\text{result} = \begin{bmatrix} 33 & 106 & 196 \\ -30 & 30 & 62 \\ 4 & 275 & 423 \end{bmatrix}$$

In the result matrix, each element is calculated according to the position of the element. The result at position [i][j] is calculated using row i from the first matrix, W, and column j from the second matrix, Z.

Ex:

result[1][2] = (row 1 in W) times (column 2 in Z)

$$\text{result}[1][2] = \begin{bmatrix} 2 & -9 & 7 \end{bmatrix} * \begin{bmatrix} 5 \\ 9 \\ 19 \end{bmatrix}$$

result[1][2] = 2 * 5 + (−9) * 9 + 7 * 19 = 10 − 81 + 133 = 62

Access multimedia content (https://openstax.org/books/introduction-python-programming/pages/9-4-nested-lists)

9.5 List comprehensions

Learning objectives

By the end of this section you should be able to

- Identify the different components of a list comprehension statement.
- Implement filtering using list comprehension.

List comprehensions

A **list comprehension** is a Python statement to compactly create a new list using a pattern.

The general form of a list comprehension statement is shown below.

list_name = [expression for loop_variable in iterable]

list_name refers to the name of a new list, which can be anything, and the for is the for loop keyword. An expression defines what will become part of the new list. loop_variable is an iterator, and iterable is an object that can be iterated, such as a list or string.

EXAMPLE 9.5

Creating a new list with a list comprehension

A list comprehension shown below in the second code has the same effect as the regular for loop shown in the first code. The resultant list is [0, 1, 4, 9, 16, 25, 36, 49, 64, 81] in both cases.

Creating a list of squares using a for loop.

```python
# Create an empty List.
squares_list = []

# Add items to a list, as squares of numbers starting at 0 and ending at 9.
for i in range(10):
    squares_list.append(i*i)
```

Creating a list of squares using the list comprehension.

```python
square_list = [i*i for i in range(10)]
```

The expression i*i is applied for each value of the loop_variable i.

EXAMPLE 9.6

A Dr. Seuss poem

A list comprehension can be used to create a list based on another list. In line 6, the for loop is written on the list poem_lines.

```
1  # Create a list of words
2      words_list = ["one", "two", "red", "blue"]
3
4      # Use a list comprehension to create a new list called
   poem_lines
5      # Inserting the word "fish" attached to each word in words_list
6      poem_lines = [w + " fish" for w in words_list]
```

```
7        for line in poem_lines:
8            print(line)
```

The above code's output is:

```
one fish
two fish
red fish
blue fish
```

CONCEPTS IN PRACTICE

List comprehensions

1. The component of a list comprehension defining an element of the new list is the _____.
   a. expression
   b. loop_variable
   c. container

2. What would be the contents of b_list after executing the code below?

   ```
   a_list = [1, 2, 3, 4, 5]
   b_list = [i+2 for i in a_list]
   ```

   a. [1, 2, 3, 4, 5]
   b. [0, 1, 2, 3, 4]
   c. [3, 4, 5, 6, 7]

3. What does new_list contain after executing the statement below?

   ```
   new_list = [i//3 for i in range(1, 15, 3)]
   ```

   a. [0.3333333333333333, 1.3333333333333333, 2.3333333333333335, 3.3333333333333335, 4.333333333333333]
   b. [0, 1, 2, 3, 4]
   c. [1, 2, 3, 4, 5, 6, 7, 8, 9, 10, 11, 12, 13, 14]

Filtering using list comprehensions

List comprehensions can be used to filter items from a given list. A *condition* is added to the list comprehension.

```
list_name = [expression for loop_variable in container if condition]
```

In a filter list comprehension, an element is added into list_name only if the condition is met.

CHECKPOINT

Filtering a list

Access multimedia content (https://openstax.org/books/introduction-python-programming/pages/9-5-list-comprehensions)

CONCEPTS IN PRACTICE

Filtering using list comprehensions

For each code using list comprehension, select the correct resultant list in new_list.

4. ```
   my_list = [21, -1, 50, -9, 300, -50, 2]

   new_list = [m for m in my_list if m < 0]
   ```
   a. [21, 50, 300, 2]
   b. [21, -1, 50, -9, 300, -50, 2]
   c. [-1, -9, -50]

5. ```
   my_string = "This is a home."

   new_list = [i for i in my_string if i in 'aeiou']
   ```
   a. [i, i, a, o, e]
   b. ['i', 'i'', 'a', 'o', 'e']
   c. Error

6. ```
   new_list = [r for r in range (0, 21, 2) if r%2 != 0]
   ```
   a. []
   b. [21]
   c. [1, 3, 5, 7, 9, 11, 13, 15, 17, 19]

TRY IT

Selecting five-letter words

Write a program that creates a list of only five-letter words from the given list and prints the new list.

Access multimedia content (https://openstax.org/books/introduction-python-programming/pages/9-5-list-comprehensions)
   ```

TRY IT

Books starting with "A"

Write a program that selects words that begin with an "A" in the given list. Make sure the new list is then sorted in dictionary order. Finally, print the new sorted list.

Access multimedia content (https://openstax.org/books/introduction-python-programming/pages/9-5-list-comprehensions)

9.6 Chapter summary

Highlights from this chapter include:

- Lists are mutable and can be easily modified by using `append()`, `remove()`, and `pop()` operations.
- Lists are iterable and can be iterated using an iterator or element indexes.
- The `sort()` operation arranges the elements of a list in ascending order if all elements of the list are of the same type.
- The `reverse()` operation reverses a list.
- The `copy()` method is used to create a copy of a list.
- Lists have built-in functions for finding the maximum, minimum, and summation of a list for lists with only numeric values.
- Lists can be nested to represent multidimensional data.
- A list comprehension is a compact way of creating a new list, which can be used to filter items from an existing list.

At this point, you should be able to write programs using lists.

Function	Description
`append(element)`	Adds the specified element to the end of a list.
`remove(element)`	Removes the specified element from the list if the element exists.
`pop()`	Removes the last element of a list.
`max(list)`	Returns the maximum element of the list specified.
`min(list)`	Returns the maximum element of the list specified.
`sum(list)`	Returns the summation of a list composed of numbers.
`sort()`	Sorts a list on which the method is called in ascending order.

Table 9.1 Chapter 9 reference.

Function	Description
`reverse()`	Reverses the order of elements in a list.
`copy()`	Makes a complete copy of a list.

Table 9.1 Chapter 9 reference.

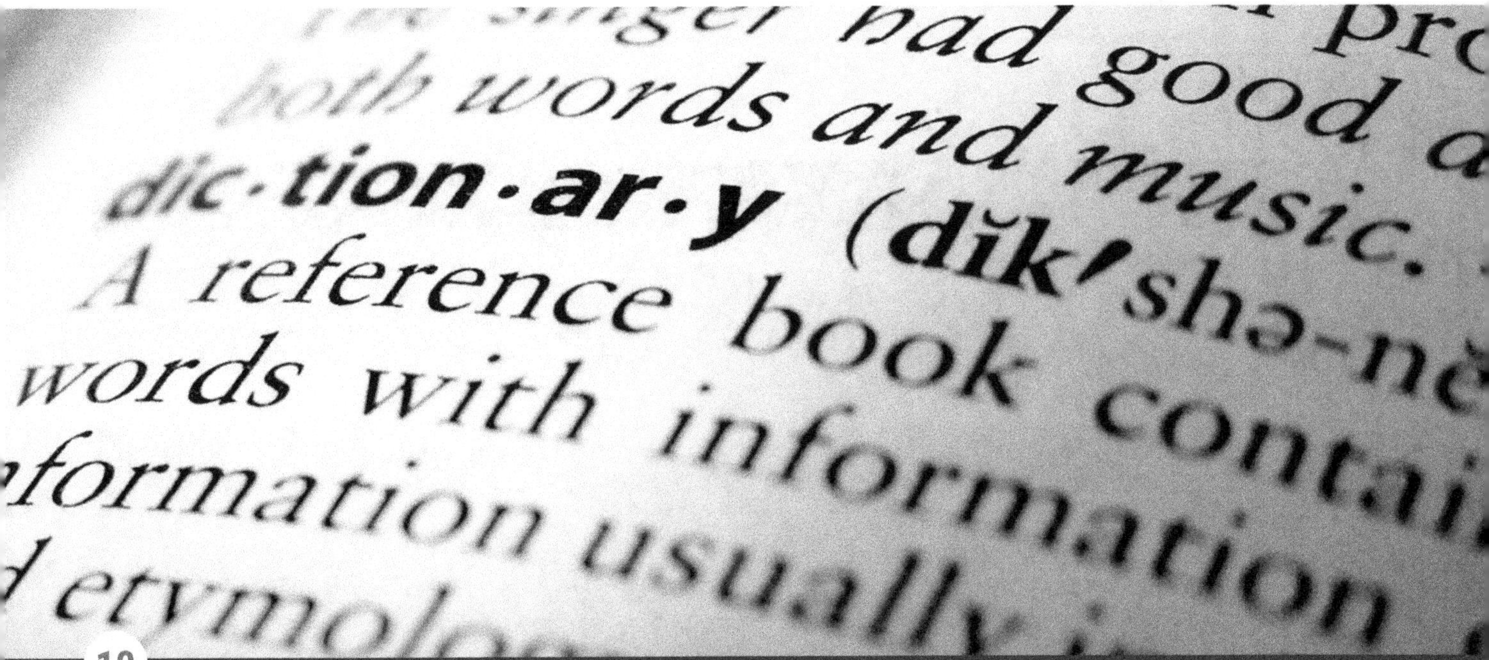

10 Dictionaries

Figure 10.1 credit: modification of work "Dictionary", by Caleb Roenigk/Flickr, CC BY 2.0

Chapter Outline

- 10.1 Dictionary basics
- 10.2 Dictionary creation
- 10.3 Dictionary operations
- 10.4 Conditionals and looping in dictionaries
- 10.5 Nested dictionaries and dictionary comprehension
- 10.6 Chapter summary

 Introduction

A Python **dictionary** is a data type for storing the data in a key-value pair format. In this chapter, the dictionary data type is introduced. This chapter also introduces ways to use dictionaries, including looping over dictionary items and performing conditional statements on a dictionary.

10.1 Dictionary basics

Learning objectives

By the end of this section you should be able to

- Describe the structure of a dictionary object.
- Use `type()` to identify the type of a dictionary object.
- Explain why a dictionary object does not have duplicate key values.

Dictionaries

A **dictionary** in Python is a container object including key-value pairs. An example of a **key-value** item is a word in an English dictionary with its corresponding definition.

CHECKPOINT

Dictionaries

Access multimedia content (https://openstax.org/books/introduction-python-programming/pages/10-1-dictionary-basics)

CONCEPTS IN PRACTICE

Dictionary basics

Given the dictionary object `days = {"Sunday": 1, "Monday": 2, "Tuesday": 3}`, answer the following questions.

1. What are the keys in the days dictionary object?
   a. `"Sunday", "Monday", "Tuesday"`
   b. `1, 2, 3`
   c. `0, 1, 2`

2. What are the values in the days dictionary object?
   a. `0, 1, 2`
   b. `1, 2, 3`
   c. `"Sunday", "Monday", "Tuesday"`

3. What is the value associated with key `"Sunday"`?
   a. `"Sunday"`
   b. `1`
   c. `0`

Dictionary type and properties

The **dict** type implements a dictionary in Python. Since a dictionary object is used to look up values using keys, a dictionary object cannot hold duplicate key values.

CHECKPOINT

Dictionary properties

Access multimedia content (https://openstax.org/books/introduction-python-programming/pages/10-1-dictionary-basics)

CONCEPTS IN PRACTICE

Dictionary type and properties

Given the dictionary object `encoding = {"a": 97, "b": 98, "A": 65, "B": 66}`, answer the following questions.

4. What does `type(encoding)` return?

a. `dictionary`
b. `dict`
c. `str`

5. The encoding dictionary contains duplicate keys since it has both "a" and "A" as keys.
   a. true
   b. false

6. A dictionary can have duplicate values.
   a. true
   b. false

TRY IT

Investigate variable types

Given the variables in the code below, examine the variables' types.

Access multimedia content (https://openstax.org/books/introduction-python-programming/pages/10-1-dictionary-basics)

10.2 Dictionary creation

Learning objectives

By the end of this section you should be able to

- Create a dictionary object with given key/value pairs.

Dictionary creation

Two methods exist for creating an empty dictionary:

- Using curly braces `{}`. Ex: `dict_1 = {}`.
- Using the `dict()` function. Ex: `dict_2 = dict()`.

A dictionary object can also be created with initial key-value pairs enclosed in curly braces. Ex: `my_dict = {"pizza": 2, "pasta": 3, "drink": 4}` creates a dictionary object `my_dict`. A key and associated value are separated by a colon, and key-value pairs are separated by commas.

CHECKPOINT

Creating a dictionary object

Access multimedia content (https://openstax.org/books/introduction-python-programming/pages/10-2-dictionary-creation)

CONCEPTS IN PRACTICE

Creating dictionary exercises

1. What is the correct syntax to create an empty dictionary in Python?
   a. `my_dict = ()`
   b. `my_dict = {}`
   c. `my_dict = []`

2. What is the correct syntax to create a dictionary with one item `"one": 1`?
   a. `my_dict = ("one": 1)`
   b. `my_dict = ("one", 1)`
   c. `my_dict = {"one": 1}`

3. How many items does the `my_dict` object contain?

   `my_dict = {"a": 1, "b": 2}`
   a. 1
   b. 2
   c. 4

dict() for dictionary creation

A dictionary object can be created with initial key-value pairs using the `dict()` function.

- Creating a dictionary from a list of tuples.

    ```
    my_list = [("apple", 2), ("banana", 3), ("orange", 4)]
    my_dict = dict(my_list)
    ```

- Creating a dictionary using keyword arguments.

    ```
    my_dict = dict(apple=2, banana=3, orange=4)
    ```

- Creating a dictionary from another dictionary.

    ```
    old_dict = {"apple": 2, "banana": 3, "orange": 4}
    new_dict = dict(old_dict)
    ```

CHECKPOINT

dict() for dictionary initialization

Access multimedia content (https://openstax.org/books/introduction-python-programming/pages/10-2-dictionary-creation)

CONCEPTS IN PRACTICE

dict() function for dictionary creation

4. What is the correct syntax to create a dictionary with initial values in Python?
   a. `my_dict = [key1:value1, key2:value2]`
   b. `my_dict = dict(key1=value1, key2=value2)`
   c. `my_dict = {key1=value1, key2=value2}`

5. What is the output of the following code?

   ```
   my_dict = dict({"a": 1})
   print(my_dict)
   ```

   a. `{"a": 1}`
   b. `<class, 'dict'>`
   c. `"a"`
      `1`

6. Which option creates a dictionary with two key-value pairs, "a": "A" and "b": "B"?
   a. `dict(a: A, b: B)`
   b. `dict([("a", "A"), ("b", "B")])`
   c. `dict({"a" = "A", "b" = "B"})`

TRY IT

Personal information dictionary

Create a dictionary, `my_info`, with three key-value pairs. The keys should be `"first name"`, `"last name"`, and `"age"` with the values being corresponding information about yourself. Then, print `my_info`.

Access multimedia content (https://openstax.org/books/introduction-python-programming/pages/10-2-dictionary-creation)

10.3 Dictionary operations

Learning objectives

By the end of this section you should be able to

- Recognize that a dictionary object is mutable.
- Evaluate dictionary items, keys, and values.
- Demonstrate the ability to access, evaluate, and modify dictionary items.
- Modify a dictionary by adding items.
- Modify a dictionary by removing items.

Accessing dictionary items

In Python, values associated with keys in a dictionary can be accessed using the keys as indexes. Here are two ways to access dictionary items in Python:

- Square bracket notation: Square brackets [] with the key inside access the value associated with that key. If the key is not found, an exception will be thrown.
- get() method: The get() method is called with the key as an argument to access the value associated with that key. If the key is not found, the method returns None by default, or a default value specified as the second argument.

Ex: In the code below, a dictionary object my_dict is initialized with items {"apple": 2, "banana": 3, "orange": 4}. The square bracket notation and get() method are used to access values associated with the keys "banana" and "apple", respectively. When accessing the dictionary to obtain the key "pineapple", -1 is returned since the key does not exist in the dictionary.

```
my_dict = {"apple": 2, "banana": 3, "orange": 4}
print(my_dict["banana"]) # Prints: 3
print(my_dict.get("apple")) # Prints: 2
print(my_dict.get("pineapple", -1)) # Prints: -1
```

CHECKPOINT

Accessing dictionary items

Access multimedia content (https://openstax.org/books/introduction-python-programming/pages/10-3-dictionary-operations)

CONCEPTS IN PRACTICE

Dictionary items

Given the dictionary members = {"Jaya": "Student", "John": "TA", "Ksenia": "Staff"}, answer the following questions.

1. What is the output of members["Jaya"]?
   a. 0
   b. None
   c. "Student"

2. What is the output of members.get("jaya")?
   a. 0
   b. None
   c. "Student"

3. What is the output of members.get("jaya", "does not exist")?
   a. "Student"
   b. "does not exist"
   c. None

Obtaining dictionary keys and values

Dictionary keys, values, and both keys and values can be obtained using keys(), values(), and items()

function calls, respectively. The return type of keys(), values(), and items() are dict_keys, dict_values, and dict_items, which can be converted to a list object using the list constructor list().

EXAMPLE 10.1

String template formatting for course enrollment requests

A dictionary object with items {"a": 97, "b": 98, "c": 99} is created. Functions keys(), values(), and items() are called to obtain keys, values, and items in the dictionary, respectively. list() is also used to convert the output to a list object.

```
dictionary_object = {"a": 97, "b": 98, "c": 99}

print(dictionary_object.keys())
print(list(dictionary_object.keys()))
print(dictionary_object.values())
print(dictionary_object.items())
```

The above code's output is:

```
dict_keys(["a", "b", "c"])
["a", "b", "c"]
dict_values([97, 98, 99])
dict_items([("a", 97), ("b", 98), ("c", 99)])
```

CONCEPTS IN PRACTICE

Dictionary keys and values

Given the dictionary numbers = {"one": 1, "two": 2, "three": 3}, answer the following questions.

4. What is the output type of numbers.keys()?
    a. dict_keys
    b. dict_values
    c. list

5. What is the output of print(numbers.values())?
    a. [1, 2, 3]
    b. dict_keys([1, 2, 3])
    c. dict_values([1, 2, 3])

6. What is the output of print(list(numbers.keys()))?
    a. ["three", "two", "one"]
    b. ["one", "two", "three"]
    c. dict_keys(["one", "two", "three"])

Dictionary mutability

In Python, a dictionary is a mutable data type, which means that a dictionary's content can be modified after creation. Dictionary items can be added, updated, or deleted from a dictionary after a dictionary object is created.

To add an item to a dictionary, either the square bracket notation or update() function can be used.

- Square bracket notation: When using square brackets to create a new key object and assign a value to the key, the new key-value pair will be added to the dictionary.

    ```
    my_dict = {"apple": 2, "banana": 3, "orange": 4}
    my_dict["pineapple"] = 1
    print(my_dict) # Prints: {"apple": 2, "banana": 3, "orange": 4, "pineapple": 1}
    ```

- update() method: the update() method can be called with additional key-value pairs to update the dictionary content.

    ```
    my_dict = {"apple": 2, "banana": 3, "orange": 4}
    my_dict.update({"pineapple": 1, "cherry": 0})
    print(my_dict) # Prints: {"apple": 2, "banana": 3, "orange": 4, "pineapple": 1, "cherry": 0}
    ```

To modify a dictionary item, the two approaches above can be used on an existing dictionary key along with the updated value. Ex:

- Square bracket notation:

    ```
    my_dict = {"apple": 2, "banana": 3, "orange": 4}
    my_dict["apple"] = 1
    print(my_dict) # Prints: {"apple": 1, "banana": 3, "orange": 4}
    ```

- update() method:

    ```
    my_dict = {"apple": 2, "banana": 3, "orange": 4}
    my_dict.update({"apple": 1})
    print(my_dict) # Prints: {"apple": 1, "banana": 3, "orange": 4}
    ```

Items can be deleted from a dictionary using the del keyword or the pop() method.

- del keyword:

    ```
    my_dict = {"apple": 2, "banana": 3, "orange": 4}
    del my_dict["orange"]
    print(my_dict) # Prints: {"apple": 2, "banana": 3}
    ```

- pop() method:

    ```
    my_dict = {"apple": 2, "banana": 3, "orange": 4}
    deleted_value = my_dict.pop("banana")
    print(deleted_value) # Prints: 3
    ```

```
print(my_dict) # Output: {"apple": 2, "orange": 4}}
```

> **CHECKPOINT**
>
> **Modifying dictionary items**
>
> Access multimedia content (https://openstax.org/books/introduction-python-programming/pages/10-3-dictionary-operations)

> **CONCEPTS IN PRACTICE**
>
> **Modifying a dictionary**
>
> Given the dictionary food = {"Coconut soup": "$15", "Butter Chicken": "$18", "Kabob": "$20"}, answer the following questions.
>
> 7. Which option modifies the value for the key "Coconut soup" to "$11" while keeping other items the same?
>   a. food = {""Coconut soup": "$15""}
>   b. food["Coconut soup"] = 11
>   c. food["Coconut soup"] = "$11"
>
> 8. Which option removes the item "Butter Chicken": "$18" from the food dictionary?
>   a. food.remove("Butter Chicken")
>   b. del food["Butter Chicken"]
>   c. del food.del("Butter Chicken")
>
> 9. What is the content of the food dictionary after calling food.update({"Kabob": "$22", "Sushi": "$16"})?
>   a. {"Coconut soup": "$15", "Butter Chicken": "$18", "Kabob": "$22", "Sushi": "$16"}
>   b. {"Coconut soup": "$15", "Butter Chicken": "$18", "Kabob": "$20", "Sushi": "$16"}
>   c. { "Sushi": "$16", "Coconut soup": "$15", "Butter Chicken": "$18", "Kabob": "$20"}

> **TRY IT**
>
> **Create a dictionary of cars step-by-step**
>
> Follow the steps below to create a dictionary of cars and modify it step-by-step.
>
> 1. Create an empty dictionary.
> 2. Add a key-value pair of "Mustang": 10.
> 3. Add another key-value pair of "Volt": 3.
> 4. Print the dictionary.
> 5. Modify the value associated with key "Mustang" to be equal to 2.

6. Delete key `"Volt"` and the associated value.
7. Print the dictionary content.

```
Prints {"Mustang": 2}
```

Access multimedia content (https://openstax.org/books/introduction-python-programming/pages/10-3-dictionary-operations)

TRY IT

The number of unique characters

Given a string value, calculate and print the number of unique characters using a dictionary.

```
Input:
string_value = "This is a string"
```

```
Prints 10
```

Access multimedia content (https://openstax.org/books/introduction-python-programming/pages/10-3-dictionary-operations)

10.4 Conditionals and looping in dictionaries

Learning objectives

By the end of this section you should be able to

- Write a conditional statement to check for a key/value.
- Write a `for` loop to iterate over elements of a dictionary.

Conditionals for dictionary

Conditional statements can be used with dictionaries to check if certain keys, values, or dictionary items exist in the dictionary or if a value satisfies a particular condition.

10.4 • Conditionals and looping in dictionaries

EXAMPLE 10.2

Templates and examples of a conditional statement on a dictionary

dict.items()

`# (key, value) in dictionary.items()`
 	
`movies = {"The godfather": 1974, "Interstellar": 2014}`
 	
`print(("Interstellar", 2014) in movies.items())`

True

Table 10.1

Conditionals on values or keys

`# dictionary[key] operand test_value`
 	
`movies = {"The godfather": 1974, "Interstellar": 2014}`
 	
`print(movies["The godfather"] < 2000)`

True

Table 10.2

dict.keys()

`# key in dictionary.keys()`
 	
`movies = {"The godfather": 1974, "Interstellar": 2014}`
 	
`print("Interstellar" in movies.keys())`

True

Table 10.3

dict.values()

`# value in dictionary.values()`
 	
`movies = {"The godfather": 1974, "Interstellar": 2014}`
 	
`print(2014 in movies.values())`

True

Table 10.4

CONCEPTS IN PRACTICE

Conditionals on dictionaries

Given the dictionary `fruit_count = {"apple": 2, "orange": 5, "pomegranate": 1}`, answer the following questions.

1. What is the output of `"apple"` in `fruit_count.keys()`?
    a. True
    b. False

2. What is the output of `("orange", 5)` in `fruit_count.items()`?
    a. SyntaxError
    b. True
    c. False

3. Which conditional statement checks if the value associated with the key "pomegranate" is greater than 0?
   a. fruit_count("pomegranate") > 0
   b. fruit_count["pomegranate"] > 0
   c. fruit_count.get("pomegranate" > 0)

Looping on a dictionary

Looping over a Python dictionary is a way to iterate through key-value pairs in the dictionary. Looping in a dictionary can be done by iterating over keys or items. When looping using keys, keys are obtained using the keys() function and are passed to the loop variable one at a time. When looping over items using the items() function, both the key and value for each item are passed to the loop variable.

A FOR LOOP OVER A DICTIONARY RETRIEVES EACH KEY IN THE DICTIONARY

```
for key in dictionary:   # Loop expression
    # Statements to execute in the loop

# Statements to execute after the loop
```

EXAMPLE 10.3

Iterating over a dictionary

dict.items()
| ```
zip_codes = {"Berkeley": 94709, "Santa Cruz": 95064, "Mountain View": 94030}

for key, value in zip_codes.items():
    print(key, value)
``` |
| ```
Berkeley 94709
Santa Cruz 95064
Mountain View 94030
``` |

Table 10.5

dict.keys()
| ```
zip_codes = {"Berkeley": 94709, "Santa Cruz": 95064, "Mountain View": 94030}

for key in zip_codes.keys():
    print(key)
``` |
| ```
Berkeley
Santa Cruz
Mountain View
``` |

Table 10.6

dict.values()
| ```
zip_codes = {"Berkeley": 94709, "Santa Cruz": 95064, "Mountain View": 94030}

for value in zip_codes.values():
    print(value)
``` |
| ```
94709
95064
94030
``` |

Table 10.7

CONCEPTS IN PRACTICE

Loops on dictionaries

4. Which method is used to loop over the values in a Python dictionary?
    a. keys()
    b. values()
    c. items()

5. What is the output of the following code?

```
fruit_count = {"apple": 2, "orange": 5, "banana": 1}
for key in fruit_count.keys():
  print(key, end = " ")
```

a. apple orange banana
b. 2 5 1
c. ("apple", 2) ("orange", 5) ("banana", 1)

6. What is the output of the following code?

```
fruit_count = {"apple": 2, "orange": 5, "banana": 1}
for value in fruit_count.values():
  print(value * 2, end = " ")
```

a. apple orange banana
b. 2 5 1
c. 4 10 2

TRY IT

Character count in a string

Given a string value, calculate and print the number of occurrences of all characters using a dictionary.

```
Input:
string_value = "This is a string"
```

```
Prints {"T": 1, "h": 1, "i": 3, "s": 3, " ": 3, "a": 1, "t": 1, "r": 1, "n": 1, "g": 1}
```

Access multimedia content (https://openstax.org/books/introduction-python-programming/pages/10-4-conditionals-and-looping-in-dictionaries)

TRY IT

Calculate the total number of fruits

Given a `fruit_count` dictionary that contains information about fruits and the count of each fruit, calculate the total number of fruits across all fruit types.

```
Input:
fruit_count = {"banana": 2, "orange": 5, "peach": 5}
```

```
Prints 12
```

Access multimedia content (https://openstax.org/books/introduction-python-programming/pages/10-4-conditionals-and-looping-in-dictionaries)

10.5 Nested dictionaries and dictionary comprehension

Learning objectives

By the end of this section you should be able to

- Explain the structure of nested dictionaries.
- Use dictionary comprehension to create a dictionary object.

Nested dictionaries

As described before, Python dictionaries are a type of data structure that allows for storing data in key-value pairs. **Nested dictionaries** are dictionaries that are stored as values within another dictionary. Ex: An organizational chart with keys being different departments and values being dictionaries of employees in a given department. For storing employee information in a department, a dictionary can be used with keys being employee IDs and values being employee names. The tables below outline the structure of such nested dictionaries and how nested values can be accessed.

EXAMPLE 10.4

Defining nested dictionaries and accessing elements

Defining nested dictionaries

```python
company_org_chart = {
  "Marketing": {
    "ID234": "Jane Smith"
  },
  "Sales": {
    "ID123": "Bob Johnson",
    "ID122": "David Lee"
  },
  "Engineering": {
    "ID303": "Radhika Potlapally",
    "ID321": "Maryam Samimi"
  }
}
```

Table 10.8

Accessing nested dictionary items

```python
print(company_org_chart["Sales"]["ID122"])
print(company_org_chart["Engineering"]["ID321"])


David Lee
Maryam Samimi
```

Table 10.9

CONCEPTS IN PRACTICE

Nested dictionary structure

1. What is a nested dictionary in Python?
    a. A dictionary that contains only integers as keys and values.
    b. A dictionary that contains another dictionary as a value.
    c. A dictionary that contains only strings as keys and values.

d. A dictionary that contains only lists as keys and values.

2. How can a value be accessed in a nested dictionary in Python?
   a. by using the key of the outer dictionary
   b. by using the key of the inner dictionary
   c. By using both the keys of the outer and inner dictionaries

3. What is the syntax for creating a nested dictionary in Python?
   a. `{key: value}`
   b. `{key1: {key2: value}}`
   c. `{key: {value: key2}}`

Dictionary comprehension

Dictionary comprehension is a concise and efficient way to create a dictionary in Python. With dictionary comprehension, elements of an iterable object are transformed into key-value pairs. The syntax of dictionary comprehension is similar to list comprehension, but instead of using square brackets, curly braces are used to define a dictionary.

Here is a general syntax for dictionary comprehension:

SYNTAX FOR DICTIONARY COMPREHENSION

```
{key_expression: value_expression for element in iterable}
```

CHECKPOINT

Squares of numbers

Access multimedia content (https://openstax.org/books/introduction-python-programming/pages/10-5-nested-dictionaries-and-dictionary-comprehension)

CONCEPTS IN PRACTICE

Dictionary comprehension

4. What is the output of the following code?

```
numbers = [1, 2, 3, 4, 5]
my_dict = {x: x**2 for x in numbers if x % 2 == 0}
print(my_dict)
```

   a. `{1: 1, 3: 9, 5: 25}`
   b. `{2: 4, 4: 16}`

c. {1: 2, 2: 4, 3: 6, 4: 8, 5: 10}

5. What is the output of the following dictionary comprehension?

```
names = ["Alice ", "Bob ", "Charlie "]
name_lengths = {name: len(name) for name in names}
print(name_lengths)
```

a. { "Alice ": 5, "Bob ": 3, "Charlie ": 7}
b. {5: "Alice ", 3: "Bob ", 7: "Charlie "}
c. { "A ": 5, "B ": 3, "C ": 7}

6. What is the output of the following dictionary comprehension?

```
my_dict = {i: i**2 for i in range(4)}
print(my_dict)
```

a. {0: 0, 1: 1, 2: 4, 3: 9}
b. {0: 0, 1: 1, 2: 4}
c. {1: 1, 2: 4, 3: 9}

TRY IT

Product prices

Suppose you have a dictionary of product prices, where the keys are product names and the values are their respective prices in dollars. Write a Python program that uses dictionary comprehension to create a new dictionary that has the same keys as the original dictionary, but the values are the prices in euros. Assume that the exchange rate is 1 dollar = 0.85 euros.

Access multimedia content (https://openstax.org/books/introduction-python-programming/pages/10-5-nested-dictionaries-and-dictionary-comprehension)

TRY IT

Restructuring the company data

Suppose you have a dictionary that contains information about employees at a company. Each employee is identified by an ID number, and their information includes their name, department, and salary. You want to create a nested dictionary that groups employees by department so that you can easily see the names and salaries of all employees in each department. Write a Python program that when given a dictionary, employees, outputs a nested dictionary, dept_employees, which groups employees by department.

```
Input:
employees = {
    1001: {"name": "Alice", "department": "Engineering", "salary": 75000},
    1002: {"name": "Bob", "department": "Sales", "salary": 50000},
```

```
        1003: {"name": "Charlie", "department": "Engineering", "salary": 80000},
        1004: {"name": "Dave", "department": "Marketing", "salary": 60000},
        1005: {"name": "Eve", "department": "Sales", "salary": 55000}
}
```

Resulting dictionary:

```
{
"Engineering": {1001: {"name": "Alice", "salary": 75000}, 1003: {"name":
"Charlie", "salary": 80000}},
"Sales": {1002: {"name": "Bob", "salary": 50000}, 1005: {"name": "Eve",
"salary": 55000}},
"Marketing": {1004: {"name": "Dave", "salary": 60000}}
}
```

Access multimedia content (https://openstax.org/books/introduction-python-programming/pages/10-5-nested-dictionaries-and-dictionary-comprehension)

10.6 Chapter summary

Highlights from this chapter include:

- A dictionary in Python is a container object including key-value pairs.
- The `dict` type implements a dictionary in Python.
- A dictionary cannot have duplicate keys.
- A dictionary is a mutable object but keys in the dictionary must be immutable objects.
- A dictionary can be created using curly braces or the `dict()` method.
- Values in the dictionary can be obtained through square bracket notation or the `get()` method.
- Dictionary items, keys, and values can be obtained using `items()`, `keys()`, and `values()` methods, respectively.
- Existing items can be modified or new items can be added to a dictionary using square brackets notation or the `update()` method.
- Items can be removed from a dictionary using the `del` keyword or the `pop()` method.
- Conditional statements can be used with a dictionary to check if the dictionary contains specific keys, values, or key-value pairs.
- Looping on a dictionary can be done by iterating over keys, values, or items.
- Nested dictionaries are dictionaries that are stored as values within another dictionary.
- With dictionary comprehension, elements of an iterable object are transformed into key-value pairs.

At this point, you should be able to use dictionaries in your programs. The programming practice below ties together most topics presented in the chapter.

Concept	Description
Dictionary creation using curly braces	`my_dict = {key1:value1, key2:value2}`

Dictionary creation using the `dict()` method	`# Using a list`
	`my_list = [(key1, value1), (key2, value2)]`
	`my_dict = dict(my_list)`
	
	`# Using keyword arguments`
	`my_dict = dict(key1=value1, key2=value2)`
	
	`# From another dictionary`
	`old_dict = {key1: value1, key2: value2}`
	`new_dict = dict(old_dict)`

Accessing dictionary items	`my_dict = {key1: value1, key2: value2}`
	
	`# Accessing item using square bracket notation`
	`my_dict[key1]`
	
	`# Accessing item through get() method`
	`my_dict.get(key1)`

Accessing all dictionary items	`my_dict.items()`
Accessing all dictionary keys	`my_dict.keys()`
Accessing all dictionary values	`my_dict.values()`

Table 10.10 Chapter 10 reference.

Concept	Description
| Adding a new key-value pair or updating an existing key-value pair | ```
my_dict = {key1: value1, key2: value2}

# Updating an item using square bracket notation
my_dict[key1] = new_value
# Adding a new key-value pair using square bracket notation
my_dict[key3] = value3

# Updating an item using update() method
my_dict.update({key1: new_value})
# Adding a new key-value pair using update() method
my_dict.update({key3: value3})
``` |
| Deleting a key-value pair from a dictionary | ```
my_dict = {key1: value1, key2: value2}

# Using del keyword
del my_dict[key1]

# Using pop() method
deleted_value = my_dict.pop(key1)
``` |
| Iterating over a dictionary | ```
for key in dictionary: # Loop expression
    # Statements to execute in the loop

#Statements to execute after the loop
``` |

Table 10.10 Chapter 10 reference.
```

Concept	Description

Nested dictionaries	`{`
	`key_1:{key11:value11, key12:value12},`
	`key_2:{key21:value21, key22:value22}`
	`}`

Dictionary comprehension	`{key_expression: value_expression for element in iterable}`

Table 10.10 Chapter 10 reference.

TRY IT

Even and odd values

Given a list, create a dictionary with two keys, `"even"` and `"odd"`. The values associated with each key must be the list of corresponding even and odd values in the given list.

```
Input:
input_list = [3, 5, 6, 1]


Prints {"even": [6], "odd":[3, 5, 1]}
```

Access multimedia content (https://openstax.org/books/introduction-python-programming/pages/10-6-chapter-summary)

11 Classes

Figure 11.1 credit: modification of work "Fresh, bright apples newly picked", by Colorado State University Extension/Flickr, Public Domain

Chapter Outline

- 11.1 Object-oriented programming basics
- 11.2 Classes and instances
- 11.3 Instance methods
- 11.4 Overloading operators
- 11.5 Using modules with classes
- 11.6 Chapter summary

Introduction

A programmer can model real-world entities as objects for better program design and organization. A class defines a type of object with attributes and methods. Many instances of a class type can be created to represent multiple objects in a program.

Classes promote reusability. Classes add benefits like data abstraction and encapsulation, which organize code for better usability and extensibility.

 ## 11.1 Object-oriented programming basics

Learning objectives

By the end of this section you should be able to

- Describe the paradigm of object-oriented programming (OOP).
- Describe the concepts of encapsulation and abstraction as they relate to OOP, and identify the value of each concept.

Grouping into objects

Object-oriented programming (OOP) is a style of programming that groups related fields, or data members, and procedures into objects. Real-world entities are modeled as individual objects that interact with each other. Ex: A social media account can follow other accounts, and accounts can send messages to each other. An account can be modeled as an object in a program.

CHECKPOINT

Using objects to model social media

Access multimedia content (https://openstax.org/books/introduction-python-programming/pages/11-1-object-oriented-programming-basics)

CONCEPTS IN PRACTICE

OOP

1. Consider the example above. Which is a field in Ellis's 12/18/23 post?
    a. Ellis's followers list
    b. Ellis's username

2. What does an object typically model in object-oriented programming?
    a. program code
    b. real-world entity

Encapsulation

Encapsulation is a key concept in OOP that involves wrapping data and procedures that operate on that data into a single unit. Access to the unit's data is restricted to prevent other units from directly modifying the data. Ex: A ticket website manages all transactions for a concert, keeping track of tickets sold and tickets still available to avoid accidental overbooking.

CHECKPOINT

Encapsulating concert ticket information

Access multimedia content (https://openstax.org/books/introduction-python-programming/pages/11-1-object-oriented-programming-basics)

CONCEPTS IN PRACTICE

Encapsulation

3. Consider the example above. Suppose the venue has to be changed due to inclement weather. How should a programmer change the website object to allow changes to the Venue field?
    a. Add a procedure to change the field.
    b. Allow users direct access to the field.
    c. No valid way to allow changes to the field.

4. Which is a benefit of encapsulation when developing complex programs?

a. All objects can easily access and modify each other's data.
b. Each object's data is restricted for intentional access.

Abstraction

Abstraction is a key concept in OOP in which a unit's inner workings are hidden from users and other units that don't need to know the inner workings. Ex: A driver doesn't usually need to know their car engine's exact, numerical temperature. So the car has a gauge to display whether the engine temperature is within an appropriate range.

CHECKPOINT

Abstracting data in a countdown calculator

Access multimedia content (https://openstax.org/books/introduction-python-programming/pages/11-1-object-oriented-programming-basics)

CONCEPTS IN PRACTICE

Abstraction

5. Consider the car example in the paragraph above. Suppose the designer decided to remove the engine temperature indicator. Would this be a good use of abstraction?
   a. yes
   b. no

6. Which is a benefit of abstraction?
   a. improved view of information
   b. high visibility of information

11.2 Classes and instances

Learning objectives

By the end of this section you should be able to

- Create a class with instance attributes, class attributes, and the `__init__()` method.
- Use a class definition to create class instances to represent objects.

Classes and instances

In the previous section, a real-world entity, like a person's social media profile, was modeled as a single object. How could a programmer develop a software system that manages millions of profiles? A blueprint that defines the fields and procedures of a profile would be crucial.

In a Python program, a **class** defines a type of object with attributes (fields) and methods (procedures). A class is a blueprint for creating objects. Individual objects created of the class type are called **instances**.

CHECKPOINT

Representing a coffee order with a class

Access multimedia content (https://openstax.org/books/introduction-python-programming/pages/11-2-classes-and-instances)

CONCEPTS IN PRACTICE

Classes and instances

Consider the example below:

```python
class Cat:
    def __init__(self):
        self.name = 'Kitty'
        self.breed = 'domestic short hair'
        self.age = 1
    def print_info(self):
        print(self.name, 'is a ', self.age, 'yr old', self.breed)

pet_1 = Cat()
pet_2 = Cat()
```

1. What is the name of the class?
   a. Cat
   b. class Cat
   c. self

2. Which of the following is an instance of the Cat class?
   a. __init__
   b. name
   c. pet_1

3. Which of the following is an attribute?
   a. breed
   b. pet_2
   c. print_info

4. Suppose the programmer wanted to change the class to represent a pet cat. Which is the appropriate name that follows PEP 8 recommendations?
   a. petcat
   b. pet_cat
   c. PetCat

Creating instances with __init__()

__init__() is a special method that is called every time a new instance of a class is created. **self** refers to the instance of a class and is used in class methods to access the specific instance that called the method. __init__() uses self to define and initialize the instance's attributes.

CHECKPOINT

Creating multiple coffee orders and changing attributes

Access multimedia content (https://openstax.org/books/introduction-python-programming/pages/11-2-classes-and-instances)

CONCEPTS IN PRACTICE

instances and __init__()

Consider the example below:

```
1   class Rectangle:
2       def __init__(self):
3           self.length = 1
4           self.width = 1
5       def area(self):
6           return self.length * self.width
7   
8   room_1 = Rectangle()
9   room_1.length = 10
10  room_1.width = 15
11  print("Room 1's area:", room_1.area())
12  room_3 = Rectangle()
13  room_3.length = 12
14  room_3.width = 14
15  print("Room 3's area:", room_3.area())
```

5. How many times is __init__() called?
   a. 1
   b. 2
   c. 3

6. When line 11 executes, execution flow moves to line 5. What does self represent on line 5?
   a. the area of room_1
   b. the instance room_1
   c. the Rectangle class

7. Which line initializes the instance attribute length?
   a. 3
   b. 6
   c. 9

8. Suppose line 2 is changed to def __init__():. What would room_1's attributes be initialized to?
   a. length = 0, width = 0
   b. length = 1, width = 1
   c. Error

Instance attributes vs. class attributes

The attributes shown so far have been instance attributes. An **instance attribute** is a variable that is unique to each instance of a class and is accessed using the format instance_name.attribute_name. Another type of attribute, a **class attribute**, belongs to the class and is shared by all class instances. Class attributes are accessed using the format class_name.attribute_name.

CHECKPOINT

Using class attributes for shared coffee order information

Access multimedia content (https://openstax.org/books/introduction-python-programming/pages/11-2-classes-and-instances)

CONCEPTS IN PRACTICE

Instances and class attributes

Consider the example above.

9. Which is an instance attribute?
   a. loc
   b. order_id
   c. order_3

10. Suppose the line order_1.cup_size = 8 is added before order_3.print_order(). What is the new output?
    a. Cafe Coffee Order 3 : 8 oz
    b. Cafe Coffee Order 3 : 16 oz
    c. Error

11. Suppose the line CoffeeOrder.loc = 'Caffeine Cafe' is added before order_3.print_order(). What is the new output?
    a. Caffeine Cafe Order 3 : 16 oz
    b. Cafe Coffee Order 3 : 16 oz
    c. Error

12. Suppose the line self.cls_id = 5 is added to the end of __init__()'s definition. What is the new output?
    a. Cafe Coffee Order 5 : 16 oz
    b. Cafe Coffee Order 3 : 16 oz
    c. Error

TRY IT

Creating a class for an airline's flight tickets

Write a class, FlightTicket, as described below. Default values follow the attributes. Then create a flight ticket and assign each instance attribute with values read from input.

Instance attributes:

- flight_num: 1
- airport: JFK
- gate: T1-1
- time: 8:00
- seat: 1A
- passenger: unknown

Class attributes:

- airline: Oceanic Airlines
- airline_code: OA

Method:

- __init__(): initializes the instance attributes
- print_info(): prints ticket information (provided in template)

Given input:

```
2121
KEF
D22B
11:45
12B
Jules Laurent
```

The output is:

```
Passenger Jules Laurent departs on flight # 2121 at 11:45 from KEF D22B in seat 12B
```

Access multimedia content (https://openstax.org/books/introduction-python-programming/pages/11-2-classes-and-instances)

TRY IT

Creating a class for fantasy books

Write a class, Book, as described below. Then create two instances and assign each instance attribute with values read from input.

Instance attributes:

- title: "
- author: "
- year: 0
- pages: 0

Class attribute:

- imprint: Fantasy Tomes

Method:

- `__init__()`: initializes the instance attributes
- `print_info()`: prints book information (provided in template)

Given input:

```
Lord of the Bracelets
Blake R. R. Brown
1999
423
A Match of Thrones
Terry R. R. Thomas
2020
761
```

The output is:

```
Lord of the Bracelets by Blake R. R. Brown published by Fantasy Tomes
in 1999 with 423 pages
A Match of Thrones by Terry R. R. Thomas published by Fantasy Tomes
in 2020 with 761 pages
```

Access multimedia content (https://openstax.org/books/introduction-python-programming/pages/11-2-classes-and-instances)

11.3 Instance methods

Learning objectives

By the end of this section you should be able to

- Create and implement `__init__()` with multiple parameters including default parameter values.
- Describe what information an instance method has access to and can modify.

More about __init__()

In Python, `__init__()` is the special method that creates instances. `__init__()` must have the calling instance, `self`, as the first parameter and can have any number of other parameters with or without default parameter values.

CHECKPOINT

Creating patient vital signs instances

Access multimedia content (https://openstax.org/books/introduction-python-programming/pages/11-3-instance-methods)

CONCEPTS IN PRACTICE

Defining and using __init__() with parameters

Consider the example above.

1. Suppose the programmer wanted to make blood pressure a required parameter in __init__(). Which is the correct __init__() method header?
   a. def __init__(p_id, bp, self, tmp=-1.0, hr=-1, rr=-1):
   b. def __init__(self, p_id, bp, tmp=-1.0, hr=-1, rr=-1):
   c. def __init__(self, p_id, bp=[-1,-1], tmp=-1.0, hr=-1, rr=-1):

2. Which is a correct call to __init__() to create an instance with p_id=5241?
   a. patient_10 = Vitals(self, 5241)
   b. patient_10 = Vitals(5241)
   c. both

3. Suppose another __init__() definition is added after the first with the header as follows:

   def __init__(self, p_id, bp, tmp, hr, rr)

   What is the impact on the program?
   a. no change.
   b. Second __init__() definition produces an error.
   c. First two __init__() calls produce an error.

Instance methods

An **instance method** is used to access and modify instance attributes as well as class attributes. All methods shown so far, and most methods defined in a class definition, are instance methods.

EXAMPLE 11.1

Instance methods are often used to get and set instance information

```
class ProductionCar:
   def __init__(self, make, model, year, max_mph = 0.0):
      self.make = make
      self.model = model
      self.year = year
```

```python
    self.max_mph = max_mph

  def max_kmh(self):
    return self.max_mph * 1.609344

  def update_max(self, speed):
    self.max_mph = speed

car_1 = ProductionCar('McLaren', 'Speedtail', 2020) # car_1.max_mph is 0.0
car_1.update_max(250.0) # car_1.max_mph is 250.0
print(car_1.make, car_1.model, 'reaches', car_1.max_mph, 'mph (',
  car_1.max_kmh(), 'km/h)') # Prints McLaren Speedtail reaches 250.0 mph (402.336 km/h)
```

CONCEPTS IN PRACTICE

CoffeeOrder instance methods

Consider the example below:

```python
class CoffeeOrder:
  loc = 'Cafe Coffee'
  cls_id = 1

  def __init__(self, size=16, milk=False, sugar=False):
    self.order_id = CoffeeOrder.cls_id
    self.cup_size = size
    self.with_milk = milk
    self.with_sugar = sugar
    CoffeeOrder.cls_id += 1

  def change(self, milk, sugar):
    self.with_milk = milk
    self.with_sugar = sugar

  def print_order(self):
    print(CoffeeOrder.loc,'Order', self.order_id, ':', self.cup_size, 'oz')
    if self.with_milk:
      print('\twith milk')
    if self.with_sugar:
      print('\twith sugar')

order_1 = CoffeeOrder(8)
order_2 = CoffeeOrder(8, True, False)
```

```
order_1.change(False, True)
```

4. What does order_1 represent at the end of the program?
   a. 8 oz coffee
   b. 8 oz coffee with milk
   c. 8 oz coffee with sugar

5. Why is change() an instance method?
   a. can change attributes
   b. has multiple parameters
   c. can change an instance

6. Can print_order() be unindented?
   a. yes
   b. no

TRY IT

Creating a class for vending machines

Write a class, VendingMachine, as described below. Default values follow the attributes. Ex: count's default value is 0. Create a vending machine using a value read from input and call instance methods.

Instance attributes:

- count: 0
- max: 0

Methods:

- __init__(num): initializes count and max with num parameter
- refill(): assigns count with max's value and prints "Refilled"
- sell(order): assigns count with the value of count minus order and prints "Sold: [order]"
- print_stock(): prints "Current stock: [count]"

Given input:

```
100
25
```

The output is:

```
Current stock: 100
Sold: 25
Current stock: 75
```

```
Refilled
Current stock: 100
```

Access multimedia content (https://openstax.org/books/introduction-python-programming/pages/11-3-instance-methods)

11.4 Overloading operators

Learning objectives

By the end of this section you should be able to

- Identify magic methods and describe their purpose.
- Develop overloaded arithmetic and comparison operators for user-defined classes.

Magic methods and customizing

Magic methods are special methods that perform actions for users, typically out of view of users. Magic methods are also called dunder methods, since the methods must start and end with double underscores (__). Ex: `__init__()` is a magic method used alongside `__new__()` to create a new instance and initialize attributes with a simple line like `eng = Engineer()`. A programmer can explicitly define a magic method in a user-defined class to customize the method's behavior.

CHECKPOINT

Customizing __str__() in a user-defined class, Engineer

Access multimedia content (https://openstax.org/books/introduction-python-programming/pages/11-4-overloading-operators)

CONCEPTS IN PRACTICE

Magic methods

1. Which of the following is a magic method?
   a. add()
   b. _add_()
   c. __add__()

2. Why are magic methods special?
   a. can't be called by the user
   b. perform internal actions
   c. have fixed definitions

3. Consider the example above, and identify the magic method(s) in the updated program.
   a. __init__()
   b. __str__()
   c. __init__(), __str__()

Overloading arithmetic operators

Operator overloading refers to customizing the function of a built-in operator. Arithmetic operators are commonly overloaded to allow for easy changes to instances of user-defined classes.

> **CHECKPOINT**
>
> Overloading __add__() for a user-defined class, Account
>
> Access multimedia content (https://openstax.org/books/introduction-python-programming/pages/11-4-overloading-operators)

Arithmetic operator (Operation)	Magic method
+ (Addition)	__add__(self, other)
- (Subtraction)	__sub__(self, other)
* (Multiplication)	__mul__(self, other)
/ (Division)	__truediv__(self, other)
% (Modulo)	__mod__(self, other)
** (Power)	__pow__(self, other)

Table 11.1 Arithmetic operators and magic methods.

> **CONCEPTS IN PRACTICE**
>
> Arithmetic operator overloading
>
> 4. A programmer explicitly defining the modulo operator for their user-defined class is _____ the operator.
>   a. overloading
>   b. rewriting
>   c. implementing
>
> 5. Given the code below, which argument maps to the parameter other in the call to Account.__add__()?
>
> ```
> acct_a = Account("Ashe", 6492)
> acct_b = Account("Bevins", 5210)
>
> acct_ab = acct_a + acct_b
> ```
>
>   a. acct_a
>   b. acct_b
>   c. acct_ab

6. Which __sub__() definition overloads the - operator for the code below to work?

```
class Pair:
  def __init__(self, x=0, y=0):
    self.x = x
    self.y = y
  # Define __sub__()

p1 = Pair(10, 2)
p2 = Pair(8, 4)
p3 = p1 - p2
print(p3.x, p3.y)
```

   a.   `def __sub__(self):`
           `return Pair(self.x - other.x, self.y - other.y)`
   b.   `def __sub__(self, other):`
           `return self.x - other.x, self.y - other.y`
   c.   `def __sub__(self, other):`
           `return Pair(self.x - other.x, self.y - other.y)`

Overloading comparison operators

Comparison operators can also be overloaded like arithmetic operators.

Comparison operator (Operation)	Magic method
< (Less than)	__lt__(self, other)
> (Greater than)	__gt__(self, other)
<= (Less than or equal to)	__le__(self, other)
>= (Greater than or equal to)	__ge__(self, other)
== (Equal)	__eq__(self, other)
!= (Not equal)	__ne__(self, other)

Table 11.2 Comparison operators and magic methods.

EXAMPLE 11.2

Overloading comparison operators for the Account class

Code	Output
| ```python
class Account:
    def __init__(self, name="", amount=0):
        self.name = name
        self.amount = amount

    def __str__(self):
        return f"{self.name}: ${self.amount}"

    def __lt__(self, other):
        return self.amount < other.amount

    def __gt__(self, other):
        return self.amount > other.amount

    def __eq__(self, other):
        return self.amount == other.amount

acct_a = Account("Ashe", 6492)
acct_b = Account("Bevins", 5210)

print(acct_a < acct_b)
print(acct_a > acct_b)
acct_a.amount = 5210
print(acct_a == acct_b)
``` | False<br>True<br>True |

Table 11.3

CONCEPTS IN PRACTICE

Comparison operator overloading

Consider the example above.

7. How many operators are overloaded?
   a. 3
   b. 4
   c. 5

8. Which code appropriately overloads the <= operator?
```

a. ```
    def __le__(other):
        return self.amount <= other.amount
    ```
b.  ```
    def __le__(self, other):
        return self.amount <= other.amount
    ```
c. ```
    def __le__(self, other):
        return other.amount <= self.amount
    ```

9. Which type of value does __gt__() return?
   a. account instance
   b. Boolean
   c. integer

---

TRY IT

Combining exercise logs

The ExerciseLog class has two instance attributes: e_type, the type of exercise, and duration, the time spent exercising.

Overload the + operator to combine two ExerciseLogs such that:

- If the exercise types are different, combine them with " and " in between. Else, use the same type and don't duplicate.
- Add durations together.

Given input:

```
walk
5
run
30
```

The output is:

```
walk and run: 35 minutes
```

Access multimedia content (https://openstax.org/books/introduction-python-programming/pages/11-4-overloading-operators)

TRY IT

Expanding the Account class

Using isinstance() allows the programmer to define different behaviors depending on an object's type. The first parameter is the object, and the second parameter is the type or class. Ex: isinstance(my_var,
```

`int)` returns `True` if `my_var` is an integer.

Expand the existing `Account` example so that the addition operator can also be used to add an integer value to an `Account`'s amount attribute.

Access multimedia content (https://openstax.org/books/introduction-python-programming/pages/11-4-overloading-operators)

11.5 Using modules with classes

Learning objectives

By the end of this section you should be able to

- Construct an import statement that selectively imports classes.
- Create an alias to import a module.

Importing classes from modules

Import statements, as discussed in the Modules chapter, allow code from other files, including classes, to be imported into a program. Accessing an imported class depends on whether the whole module is imported or only selected parts.

Multiple classes can be grouped in a module. For good organization, classes should be grouped in a module only if the grouping enables module reuse, as a key benefit of modules is reusability.

CHECKPOINT

Importing classes from files

Access multimedia content (https://openstax.org/books/introduction-python-programming/pages/11-5-using-modules-with-classes)

CONCEPTS IN PRACTICE

Importing classes

1. Consider the example above. How many classes are imported in the second *main.py*?
    a. 1
    b. 2
    c. 3

2. Which line imports only the `Level` class from character?
    a. `import Level from character`
    b. `from character import Level`
    c. `import Level`

3. How many classes can be in a module?
    a. none
    b. only 1
    c. any number

Using aliases

Aliasing allows the programmer to use an alternative name for imported items. Ex: `import triangle as tri` allows the program to refer to the triangle module as tri. Aliasing is useful to avoid name collisions but should be used carefully to avoid confusion.

EXAMPLE 11.3

Using aliasing to import character

character.py

```python
class Level:
    def __init__(self, level=1):
        self.level = level
    ...
    def level_up(self):
        ...
class XP:
    def __init__(self, XP=0):
        self.XP = XP
    ...
    def add_xp(self, num):
        ...
```

main.py

```python
import character as c

bard_level = c.Level(1)
bard_XP = c.XP(0)
bard_XP.add_xp(300)
bard_level.level_up()
...
```

CONCEPTS IN PRACTICE

Using an alias

Consider the example above. Suppose a program imports the character module using `import character as game_char`.

4. How would the program create a Level instance?
    a. `rogue_level = character.Level()`
    b. `rogue_level = game_char.Level()`

c. `rogue_level = character.game_char.Level()`

5. Which code creates a name collision?
   a. `character = 'Ranger'`
   b. `Game_char = 'Ranger'`
   c. `game_char = 'Ranger'`

TRY IT

Missing import statement

Add the missing import statement to the top of the file. Do not make any changes to the rest of the code. In the end, the program should run without errors.

Access multimedia content (https://openstax.org/books/introduction-python-programming/pages/11-5-using-modules-with-classes)

TRY IT

Missing class import statement

Add the missing class import statement to the top of the file. Import only a class, not a full module. Do not make any changes to the rest of the code. In the end, the program should run without errors.

Access multimedia content (https://openstax.org/books/introduction-python-programming/pages/11-5-using-modules-with-classes)

11.6 Chapter summary

Highlights from this chapter include:

- Object-oriented programming involves grouping related fields and procedures into objects using data abstraction and encapsulation.
- Classes define a type of object with attributes and methods.
- Instances of a class type represent objects and are created using `__init__()`.
- Attributes may belong to the instance (unique for each instance) or the class (shared by all instances).
- Instance methods have the first parameter `self` to access the specific instance.
- Python uses magic methods to perform "under-the-hood" actions for users. Magic methods always start and end with double underscores.
- Python allows overloading of existing operators for user-defined classes.
- Classes can be imported from modules by name or can be renamed using aliases.

At this point, you should be able to write classes that have instance attributes, class attributes, and methods, and import classes from modules. You should also be able to overload operators when defining a class.

Construct	Description
Class definition	`class ClassName:` `    """Docstring"""`

__init__()	`class ClassName:`
	`    def __init__(self):`
	`        # Initialize attributes`

Attributes	`class ClassName:`
	`    class_attr_1 = [value]`
	`    class_attr_2 = [value]`
	
	`    def __init__(self):`
	`        instance_attr_1 = [value]`
	`        instance_attr_2 = [value]`
	`        instance_attr_3 = [value]`

Methods (instance)	`class ClassName:`
	
	`    def __init__(self):`
	`        instance_attr_1 = [value]`
	`        instance_attr_2 = [value]`
	`        instance_attr_3 = [value]`
	
	`    def method_1(self, val1, val2):`
	`        # Access/change attributes`
	
	`    def method_2(self):`
	`        # Access/change attributes`

Instances	`instance_1 = ClassName()`
	`instance_1.instance_attr_1 = [new value]`
	`instance_2 = ClassName()`
	`instance_2.method_2()`

Table 11.4 Chapter 11 reference.

Construct	Description
| Overloaded multiplication operator | ```
class ClassName:
  # Other methods

  def __mul__(self, other):
     return ClassName(self.instance_attr_3 * other.instance_attr_3)
``` |
| Import class from module with alias | `from class_module import ClassName as ClassAlias` |

Table 11.4 Chapter 11 reference.
```

12 Recursion

Figure 12.1 credit: modification of work "Rings from the Ocean", by Sue Corbisez/Flickr, CC BY 2.0

Chapter Outline

12.1 Recursion basics
12.2 Simple math recursion
12.3 Recursion with strings and lists
12.4 More math recursion
12.5 Using recursion to solve problems
12.6 Chapter summary

Introduction

Recursion is a powerful programming technique to write solutions compactly. Recursion simplifies programs by calling smaller versions of a given problem that are used to generate the solution to the overall problem.

In advanced programming, some programs are difficult to write without the use of recursion. So recursion is also a style of programming that enables us to simplify programs.

Recursion enables a piece of code, a function, to call the same piece of code, the same function, with different parameters.

12.1 Recursion basics

Learning objectives

By the end of this section you should be able to

- Describe the concept of recursion.
- Demonstrate how recursion uses simple solutions to build a better solution.

Recursion

Recursion is a problem solving technique that uses the solution to a simpler version of the problem to solve the bigger problem. In turn, the same technique can be applied to the simpler version.

CHECKPOINT

Three Towers

Access multimedia content (https://openstax.org/books/introduction-python-programming/pages/12-1-recursion-basics)

CONCEPTS IN PRACTICE

Three Towers and recursion

1. How is the problem of moving two rings solved using recursion?
   a. Move the small ring to the middle tower, move the bigger ring to the target tower, and move the small ring to the target tower.
   b. Move two rings from the source tower to the target tower.
   c. Cannot be solved with recursion.

2. How is the problem of moving three rings solved using recursion?
   a. Move three rings from the source tower to the target tower.
   b. Move two rings to the middle tower, then move the biggest ring to the target tower, and finally, move two rings to the target tower.
   c. Cannot be solved with recursion.

3. How many times is the two-ring solution used with three rings?
   a. 1
   b. 2
   c. 0

Recursion to find a complete solution

The recursion process continues until the problem is small enough, at which point the solution is known or can easily be found. The larger solution can then be built systematically by successively building ever larger solutions until the complete problem is solved.

CHECKPOINT

Solving Three Towers

Access multimedia content (https://openstax.org/books/introduction-python-programming/pages/12-1-recursion-basics)

CONCEPTS IN PRACTICE

Solving Three Towers

4. How many total steps does it take to solve two rings?
   a. 1
   b. 2

c. 3

5. How many total steps does it take to solve three rings?
   a. 3
   b. 4
   c. 7

6. How many total steps does it take to solve four rings?
   a. 15
   b. 7
   c. 3

12.2 Simple math recursion

Learning objectives

By the end of this section you should be able to

- Identify a recursive case and a base case in a recursive algorithm.
- Demonstrate how to compute a recursive solution for the factorial function.

Calculating a factorial

The factorial of a positive integer is defined as the product of the integer and the positive integers less than the integer.

Ex: 5! = 5 * 4 * 3 * 2 * 1

Written as a general equation for a positive integer n: n! = n * (n - 1) * (n - 2) * . . . * 1

The above formula for the factorial of n results in a recursive formula: n! = n * (n - 1)!

Thus, the factorial of n depends upon the value of the factorial at n - 1. The factorial of n can be found by repeating the factorial of n - 1 until (n - 1)! = 1! (we know that 1! = 1). This result can be used to build the overall solution as seen in the animation below.

CHECKPOINT

Finding the factorial of 5

Access multimedia content (https://openstax.org/books/introduction-python-programming/pages/12-2-simple-math-recursion)

CONCEPTS IN PRACTICE

Recognizing recursion

Can the following algorithms be written recursively?

1. The summation of 1 + 2 + 3 + . . . + (n - 1) + n where n is a positive integer.

2. Listing the odd numbers greater than 0 and less than a given number n.

3. Listing the primary numbers (prime numbers) greater than 3.
4. Listing the Fibonacci sequence of numbers.

Defining a recursive function

Recursive algorithms are written in Python as functions. In a recursive function different actions are performed according to the input parameter value. A critical part of a recursive function is that the function must call itself.

A value for which the recursion applies is called the **recursive case**. In the recursive case, the function calls itself with a smaller portion of the input parameter. Ex: In the recursive function `factorial()`, the initial parameter is an integer n. In the function's recursive case, the argument passed to `factorial()` is n - 1, which is smaller than n.

A value of n for which the solution is known is called the **base case**. The base case stops the recursion. A recursive algorithm must include a base case; otherwise, the algorithm may result in an infinite computation.

To calculate a factorial, a recursive function, `factorial()` is defined with an integer input parameter, n. When n > 1, the recursive case applies. The `factorial()` calls itself with a smaller argument, n - 1. When n == 1, the solution is known because 1! is 1; therefore, n == 1 is a base case.

Note: 0! is defined to be 1; therefore, n == 0 is a second base case for `factorial()`. When n < 1, an error is returned.

CHECKPOINT

Factorial using recursion

Access multimedia content (https://openstax.org/books/introduction-python-programming/pages/12-2-simple-math-recursion)

CONCEPTS IN PRACTICE

Programming recursion

For the questions below, the function `rec_fact()` is another recursive function that calculates a factorial. What is the result of each definition of `rec_fact()` if n = 17 is the initial input parameter?

5. ```
def rec_fact(n):
    return n * rec_fact(n - 1)
```

   a. 355687428096000
   b. 0
   c. no result / infinite computation

6. ```
def rec_fact(n):
    if n < 0:
        print("error")
```

```
    elif n == 0:
        return n
    else:
        return n * rec_fact(n - 1)
```

  a. 355687428096000
  b. 0
  c. no result / infinite computation

7. ```
   def rec_fact(n):
       if n < 0:
           print("error")
       elif n == 0:
           return 1
       else:
           return n * rec_fact(n - 1)
   ```

   a. 355687428096000
   b. 0
   c. no result / infinite computation

8. ```
   def rec_fact(n):
       if n < 0:
           return -1
       else:
           return n * rec_fact(n - 1)
   ```

   a. 355687428096000
   b. 0
   c. no result / infinite computation

TRY IT

Recursive summation

Write a program that uses a recursive function to calculate the summation of numbers from 0 to a user specified positive integer n.

Access multimedia content (https://openstax.org/books/introduction-python-programming/pages/12-2-simple-math-recursion)

TRY IT

Digits

Write a program that computes the sum of the digits of a positive integer using recursion.

Ex: The sum of the digits of 6721 is 16.

Hint: There are 10 base cases, which can be checked easily with the right condition.

Access multimedia content (https://openstax.org/books/introduction-python-programming/pages/12-2-simple-math-recursion)

12.3 Recursion with strings and lists

Learning objectives

By the end of this section you should be able to

- Demonstrate the use of recursion to solve a string problem.
- Demonstrate the use of recursion to solve a list problem.
- Use the built-in count() list function.

Recursion with strings

A word that is spelled the same forward and backward is called a palindrome. Ex: racecar.

Recursion can be used to identify whether a given word is a palindrome.

CHECKPOINT

Identifying a palindrome

Access multimedia content (https://openstax.org/books/introduction-python-programming/pages/12-3-recursion-with-strings-and-lists)

CONCEPTS IN PRACTICE

Recursion with strings

Refer to the animation above.

1. Which of the following does palindrome() recognize as a palindrome?
   a. madamm
   b. madaM
   c. madame

2. What would happen if the condition on line 4 of palindrome() is changed to if len(word) == 1:
   a. Only palindromes with an odd number of letters would be recognized correctly.
   b. Nothing. The function would work the same.
   c. The function would not recognize any palindromes.

3. What would happen if the condition in line 8 palindrome() is changed to if

palindrome(word.strip(word[0])).
   a. Nothing. The function would work the same: the first and last letter would be removed.
   b. Some words, such as "madamm", would be incorrectly recognized as a palindrome.

Recursion with lists

The animation below shows a recursive way to check whether two lists contain the same items but in different order.

The count() function returns a count of the number of items in a list that match the given item, and returns 0 otherwise. Ex: For list_num = [1, 3, 3, 4], list_num.count(3) returns 2.

CHECKPOINT

Checking list permutations

Access multimedia content (https://openstax.org/books/introduction-python-programming/pages/12-3-recursion-with-strings-and-lists)

CONCEPTS IN PRACTICE

List permutations

Refer to the above animation. What would permu_check() return for each pair of lists below?

4. list_num = [1, 7, 99, 2]
   other_list = [99, 7, 1, 2]

   a. True
   b. False

5. list_num = [22, 9, 15, 17, 15]
   other_list = [17, 9, 22, 22, 15]

   a. True
   b. False

6. honors_list = ["Bo", "Joe", "Sandy"]
   first_names_of_team_1 = ["Sandy", "Bo", "Joe"]

   a. True
   b. False

7. this_list = [1, 2, [3], [4], 5]
   that_list = [[3], 1, 5, [4], 2]

a. True
b. False

8. `list_1 = [1, 2, 3]`
   `list_2 = [1, 2, 3]`

   a. True
   b. False

TRY IT

Remove duplicates

Write a recursive `rem_dup()` function that removes duplicates from a list.

Ex: List [5, 5, 2, 1, 3, 1, 6] should result in an output list [5, 2, 1, 3, 6].

Access multimedia content (https://openstax.org/books/introduction-python-programming/pages/12-3-recursion-with-strings-and-lists)

12.4 | More math recursion

Learning objectives

By the end of this section you should be able to

- Define a recursive function to generate Fibonacci numbers.

Fibonacci sequence using recursion

The Fibonacci sequence is a sequence in which each number in the sequence is the sum of the previous two numbers in the sequence. The first two numbers are 0 and 1. Thus, starting from 0 and 1, the third number is 0 + 1 = 1, and the next number is 1 + 1 = 2. The sequence of numbers is 0, 1, 1, 2, 3, 5, 8, 13, 21, 34, ...

Recursion can be used to calculate the nth Fibonacci number. The base cases are 0 and 1. Thereafter, the nth number is given by adding the (n - 1)th and (n - 2)th number. Thus, `fib(n) = fib(n - 1) + fib(n - 2)`, which is a recursive definition ending with base cases `f(0) = 0`, and `f(1) = 1`.

For a recursion that calls multiple functions in the recursive case, tracing how the recursion proceeds is useful. A structure used to trace the calls made by a recursive function is called a **recursion tree**. The animation below traces the recursion tree for a call to a recursive function to calculate the Fibonacci number for n = 5.

EXAMPLE 12.1

Finding the nth Fibonacci number

The Fibonacci function recursion is more complex with the value at n depending on two function calls with smaller values.

```
""" Recursive Fibonacci function """

def fib(n):
  # Base case
  if n == 0 or n == 1:
    return n
  # Recursive case
  elif n > 1:
    return fib(n - 1) + fib(n - 2)
  # Error case
  else:
    print("Fibonacci numbers begin at 0.")
    return

# Test code
print(fib(7))
```

The above code's output is:

13

CHECKPOINT

Recursive Fibonacci function

Access multimedia content (https://openstax.org/books/introduction-python-programming/pages/12-4-more-math-recursion)

CONCEPTS IN PRACTICE

Fibonacci numbers

1. `fib(9)` results in ____.
   a. 13
   b. 21
   c. 34

2. How many calls to the base cases are made as a result of calling `fib(5)`?
   a. 2
   b. 5
   c. 8

3. A structure tracing the function calls made as a result of a complex recursive function call is called a ____.

a. tree
b. recursion tree
c. iteration tree

Greatest common divisor (GCD)

The greatest common divisor (GCD) of two positive integers is an integer that is a divisor for both integers. Ex: The GCD of 6 and 9 is 3 because 3 x 2 = 6, and 3 x 3 = 9.

The GCD is found easily using Euclid's method. Euclid's method recursively subtracts the smaller integer from the larger integer until a base case with equal integers is reached. The greatest common divisor is the integer value when the base case is reached.

EXAMPLE 12.2

Finding the GCD

```
""" Find GCD using recursive implementation of Euclid's method """

def gcd(a, b):
  if a == b: # Base case
    return a
  elif a < b: # Recursive case
    return gcd(a, b - a)
  else:
    return gcd(a - b, a)

# Test code
print(gcd(24, 30))
```

The above code's output is:

6

CONCEPTS IN PRACTICE

GCD

4. What is the GCD of 15 and 35?
    a. 15
    b. 20
    c. 5

5. How many recursive calls are made with gcd(24, 30)?
   a. 4
   b. 1
   c. 24

6. What is the GCD of 13 and 23?
   a. 13
   b. 1
   c. 23

7. How many recursive calls are made with gcd(13, 23)?
   a. 1
   b. 8
   c. 13

TRY IT

Recursive power

Write a recursive power() function, such that given an integer x and a positive integer y, power(x, y) returns x raised to y.

Ex: power(3, 4) returns 81.

Access multimedia content (https://openstax.org/books/introduction-python-programming/pages/12-4-more-math-recursion)

TRY IT

Recursive power (with any integer power)

Write a recursive rec_pow() function such that given two integers, x and y, it returns x raised to y.

(Note: this is an extension of the above problem but now works for any integer value of y, positive or negative. How should the recursive function change to deal with a negative value of y?)

Ex: rec_pow(2, -4) returns 0.0625.

Access multimedia content (https://openstax.org/books/introduction-python-programming/pages/12-4-more-math-recursion)

12.5 Using recursion to solve problems

Learning objectives

By the end of this section you should be able to

- Use recursion to efficiently search a list.
- Demonstrate a solution to the Three Towers problem.

Binary search

Searching a sorted list usually involves looking at each item. If the item being searched is not found, then the search can take a long time.

A binary search is a recursive algorithm used to efficiently search sorted lists. In each recursive step, about half the items are discarded as not being potential matches, so the search proceeds much faster.

A binary search begins by checking the middle element of the list. If the search key is found, the algorithm returns the matching location (base case). Otherwise, the search is repeated on approximately half the list. If the key is greater than the middle element, then the key must be on the right half, and vice versa. The process continues by checking the middle element of the remaining half of the list.

EXAMPLE 12.3

Binary search

```python
""" Binary Search """

def binary_search(search_list, low, high, key):

   # Check base case
   if high > low:
      mid = (high + low) // 2

      # If element is present at the middle itself (base case)
      if search_list[mid] == key:
         return mid

      # Recursive case: check which subarray must be checked
      # Right subarray
      elif key > search_list[mid]:
         return binary_search(search_list, mid + 1, high, key)

      # Left subarray
      else:
         return binary_search(search_list, low, mid - 1, key)

   else:
      # Key not found (other base case)
      return "Not found"

# Test list
in_list = [1, 3, 13, 16, 19, 22, 27, 32, 48, 66, 78, 99, 111, 122]

# Call binary search function
print(binary_search(in_list, 0, len(in_list)-1, 48)) # Key exists at index 8

print(binary_search(in_list, 0, len(in_list)-1, 86)) # Key does not exist
```

The above code's output is:

```
8
Not found
```

> **CHECKPOINT**
>
> **Binary search**
>
> Access multimedia content (https://openstax.org/books/introduction-python-programming/pages/12-5-using-recursion-to-solve-problems)

> **CONCEPTS IN PRACTICE**
>
> **Binary search**
>
> 1. Which list can be searched with the binary search algorithm?
>   a. [5, 2, 7, 1, 8]
>   b. [9, 8, 7, 6, 5]
>   c. [4, 5, 6, 7, 8]
>
> 2. If the `binary_search()` function is called with `low = 4`, and `high = 7`, mid computes to _____.
>   a. 5
>   b. 6
>   c. 11
>
> 3. How many calls to the `binary_search()` function occur in the animation?
>   a. 3
>   b. 4
>   c. 8
>
> 4. How many calls to the `binary_search()` function occur in the code example when searching 86?
>   a. 4
>   b. 14

Solving Three Towers

As discussed in an earlier section, the Three Towers problem can be solved using recursion. The solution depends on calling the solution to the next smaller problem twice. As shown in the code example below, the recursive solution can solve the problem for any number of rings.

EXAMPLE 12.4

Solving N towers

The solution to Three Towers is simple with recursion. In the code below, rings are numbered from the top down. The smallest ring is 1, the next ring is 2, and when solving for three rings, the bottom ring is 3.

```python
""" Solving the towers problem recursively """

def three_towers(N, source_tower, dest_tower, temp_tower):
    # Base case: simply move the single(bottom) ring from source to destination tower
    if N==1:
        print("Move ring 1 from tower", source_tower, "to tower", dest_tower)
        return # Exit when the base case is reached

    # Recursive case
    # Call the smaller version of the problem:
    # to move the N-1 stack to the middle tower
    three_towers(N-1, source_tower, temp_tower, dest_tower)

    # Move the N ring to the destination tower
    print("Move ring", N, "from tower", source_tower, "to tower", dest_tower)

    # Call the smaller version of the problem:
    # to now move the N-1 stack from the middle tower
    # to the destination
    three_towers(N-1, temp_tower, dest_tower, source_tower)

# Test code
print("Solution for 3 rings:")
three_towers(3, 't1', 't3', 't2') # t1, t2, t3 are the towers
```

The above code's output is:

```
Solution for 3 rings:
Move ring 1 from tower t1 to tower t3
Move ring 2 from tower t1 to tower t2
Move ring 1 from tower t3 to tower t2
Move ring 3 from tower t1 to tower t3
Move ring 1 from tower t2 to tower t1
Move ring 2 from tower t2 to tower t3
Move ring 1 from tower t1 to tower t3
```

CONCEPTS IN PRACTICE

Solving Three Towers

5. For four rings, how many total lines will be printed by `three_towers()`?
   a. 7
   b. 15

6. Would an iterative solution to the Three Towers problem be more complex or less complex?
   a. more complex
   b. less complex

TRY IT

Coin combinations

Write a recursive function `print_H_T()` that produces all possible combinations of heads (`"H"`) and tails (`"T"`) for a given number of coin tosses.

Ex: For three coins, the program should print the output shown below.

```
HHH
HHT
HTH
HTT
THH
THT
TTH
TTT
```

Access multimedia content (https://openstax.org/books/introduction-python-programming/pages/12-5-using-recursion-to-solve-problems)

12.6 Chapter summary

Highlights from this chapter include:

- Describe the concept of recursion.
- Demonstrate how recursion uses simpler solutions to build a bigger solution.
- Identify a recursive case and a base case in a recursive algorithm.
- Demonstrate how to compute a recursive solution for the factorial function.
- Demonstrate the use of recursion to solve a string problem.
- Demonstrate the use of recursion to solve a list problem.
- Use the built-in `count()` list function.
- Define a recursive function to generate Fibonacci numbers.
- Use recursion to efficiently search a list.
- Demonstrate a solution to the Three Towers problem.

At this point, you should be able to solve problems using recursion.

Function	Description
count(element)	Returns the number of times the element exists on the list on which the count() function is called.

Table 12.1 Chapter 12 reference.

13 Inheritance

Figure 13.1 credit: modification of work "Don't stare...only sheep dogs stare...", by Bernard Spragg. NZ/Flickr, Public Domain

Chapter Outline

13.1 Inheritance basics
13.2 Attribute access
13.3 Methods
13.4 Hierarchical inheritance
13.5 Multiple inheritance and mixin classes
13.6 Chapter summary

 Introduction

Real-world entities are often described in relation to other entities. Ex: A finch is a type of bird. Similarly, classes, which represent types of real-world entities, can be related to each other.

Inheritance describes the relationship in which one class is a type of another class. Classes within inheritance relationships can inherit attributes and methods from other classes without needing to redefine everything. Thus, inheritance in object-oriented programming reduces redundancy and promotes modularity.

13.1 Inheritance basics

Learning objectives

By the end of this section you should be able to

- Identify is-a and has-a relationships between classes.
- Differentiate between a subclass and a superclass.
- Create a superclass, subclass, and instances of each.

is-a vs has-a relationships

Classes are related to each other. An is-a relationship exists between a subclass and a superclass. Ex: A daffodil is a plant. A `Daffodil` class inherits from a superclass, `Plant`.

Is-a relationships can be confused with has-a relationships. A has-a relationship exists between a class that contains another class. Ex: An employee has a company-issued laptop. Note: The laptop is not an employee.

CHECKPOINT

is-a relationship between Employee and Developer

Access multimedia content (https://openstax.org/books/introduction-python-programming/pages/13-1-inheritance-basics)

CONCEPTS IN PRACTICE

Relationships between classes

1. What is the relationship between a `Doughnut` class and a `Pastry` class?
   a. is-a
   b. has-a

2. What is the relationship between a `Kitchen` class and a `Freezer` class?
   a. is-a
   b. has-a

3. A goalkeeper is a player. Goalkeeper is a _____ class. Player is a _____ class.
   a. super; sub
   b. sub; super

Inheritance in Python

Inheritance uses an is-a relationship to inherit a class from a superclass. The subclass inherits all the superclass's attributes and methods, and extends the superclass's functionality.

In Python, a subclass is created by including the superclass name in parentheses at the top of the subclass's definition:

```python
class SuperClass:
    # SuperClass attributes and methods

class SubClass(SuperClass):
    # SubClass attributes and methods
```

CHECKPOINT

Using inheritance to create subclasses

Access multimedia content (https://openstax.org/books/introduction-python-programming/pages/13-1-inheritance-basics)

CONCEPTS IN PRACTICE

Creating subclasses

4. How is a Daisy class that inherits from the Plant class defined?
   a. class Plant(Daisy):
   b. class Daisy(Plant):
   c. class Daisy:
      class Plant:

5. Suppose a CarryOn class is inherited from a Luggage class. How is a CarryOn instance created?
   a. small_bag = CarryOn()
   b. small_bag = Luggage(CarryOn)
   c. small_bag = CarryOn(Luggage)

6. Given the following SuperClass and SubClass, which of the following can an instance of SubClass access?

   ```
   class SuperClass():
     def func_1(self):
       print('Superclass function')

   class SubClass(SuperClass):
     def func_2(self):
       print('Subclass function')
   ```

   a. func_1() only
   b. func_2() only
   c. func_1() and func_2()

7. Given the following SuperClass and SubClass, which of the following can an instance of SuperClass access?

   ```
   class SuperClass():
     def func_1(self):
       print('Superclass function')

   class SubClass(SuperClass):
     def func_2(self):
       print('Subclass function')
   ```

   a. func_1() only
   b. func_2() only
   c. func_1() and func_2()

ALTERNATIVE INHERITANCE TERMS

Python documentation for inheritance uses multiple terms to refer to the class that is inherited from and the class that inherits. This book uses superclass/subclass throughout for consistency.

Class inherited from	Class that inherits
superclass	subclass
base class	derived class
parent class	child class

Table 13.1

TRY IT

Employee and Developer classes

Given the `Employee` class, create a `Developer` class that inherits from `Employee`. The `Developer` class has one method, `update_codebase()`, which prints `"Employee has updated the codebase"`. Then, use the `Developer` instance, `python_dev`, to call `print_company()` and `update_codebase()`.

Access multimedia content (https://openstax.org/books/introduction-python-programming/pages/13-1-inheritance-basics)

TRY IT

Polygon classes

Define three classes: `Polygon`, `Rectangle`, and `Square`:

- `Polygon` has the method `p_disp()`, which prints `"object is a Polygon"`.
- `Rectangle` inherits from `Polygon` and has the method `r_disp()`, which prints `"object is a Rectangle"`.
- `Square` inherits from `Rectangle` and has the method `s_disp()`, which prints `"object is a Square"`.

Create an instance of each class. Then, for each instance, call all the methods the instance has access to.

Access multimedia content (https://openstax.org/books/introduction-python-programming/pages/13-1-inheritance-basics)

13.2 Attribute access

Learning objectives

By the end of this section you should be able to

- Implement a subclass that accesses inherited attributes from the superclass.
- Write a subclass's `__init__()` that inherits superclass instance attributes and creates new instance attributes.

Creating a simple subclass

Subclasses have access to the attributes inherited from the superclass. When the subclass's __init__() isn't explicitly defined, the superclass's __init__() method is called. Accessing both types of attributes uses the same syntax.

CHECKPOINT

Defining a simple subclass

Access multimedia content (https://openstax.org/books/introduction-python-programming/pages/13-2-attribute-access)

CONCEPTS IN PRACTICE

Using simple subclasses

1. Consider the Employee and Developer example above. What is the value of dev_1.e_id?
   a. 1
   b. 2
   c. Error

2. Consider the following example. Line 13 executes and SubClass() is called. Which line does control flow move to?

   ```
   1  class SuperClass:
   2      def __init__(self):
   3          self.feat_1 = 1
   4          self.feat_2 = ""
   5
   6      def bc_display(self):
   7          print(f"Superclass: {self.feat_2}")
   8
   9  class SubClass(SuperClass):
   10     def dc_display(self):
   11         print(f"Subclass: {self.feat_2}")
   12
   13 dc_1 = SubClass()
   ```

   a. 2
   b. 10
   c. Error

3. Consider the following example. Which instance attribute(s) does dc_1 have?

   ```
   class SuperClass:
       def __init__(self):
           self.feat_1 = 1
           self.feat_2 = ""
   ```

```
    def bc_display(self):
        print(f"Superclass: {self.feat_2}")

class SubClass(SuperClass):
    def dc_display(self):
        print(f"Subclass: {self.feat_2}")

dc_1 = SubClass()
```

a. feat_2
b. feat_1 and feat_2
c. None

Using __init__() to create and inherit instance attributes

A programmer often wants a subclass to have new instance attributes as well as those inherited from the superclass. Explicitly defining a subclass's __init__() involves defining instance attributes and assigning instance attributes inherited from the superclass.

CHECKPOINT

Defining __init__() in a subclass

Access multimedia content (https://openstax.org/books/introduction-python-programming/pages/13-2-attribute-access)

CONCEPTS IN PRACTICE

Accessing a subclass's attributes

Consider the Employee and Developer example code:

```
class Employee:
    count = 0
    def __init__(self):
        Employee.count += 1
        self.e_id = Employee.count
        self.hire_year = 2023

    def emp_display(self):
        print(f"Employee {self.e_id} hired in {self.hire_year}")

class Developer(Employee):
    def __init__(self):
        Employee.count += 1
        self.e_id = Employee.count
```

```
        self.hire_year = 2023
        self.lang_xp = ["Python", "C++", "Java"]

    def dev_display(self):
        print(f"Proficient in {self.lang_xp}")

emp_1 = Employee()
dev_1 = Developer()
```

4. What would be the output of `dev_1.dev_display()`?
   a. `Employee 2 hired in 2023`
   b. `Proficient in ['Python', 'C++', 'Java']`
   c. `Error`

5. What would be the output of `emp_1.dev_display()`?
   a. `Employee 1 hired in 2023`
   b. `Proficient in ['Python', 'C++', 'Java']`
   c. `Error`

6. Suppose `dev_display()` should be modified to display the developer's ID along with their proficiencies. Ex: `dev_1.dev_display()` would output `Employee 2 proficient in ['Python', 'C++', 'Java']`. Which is the appropriate new `print()` call in `dev_display()`?
   a. `print(f"Employee {self.e_id} proficient in {self.lang_xp}")`
   b. `print(f"Employee {self.Employee.e_id} proficient in {self.lang_xp}")`
   c. `print(f"Employee 2 proficient in {self.lang_xp}")`

TRY IT

Creating a subclass with an instance attribute

Given a class `Dessert`, create a class, Cupcake, inherited from `Dessert`. Cupcake class methods:

- `__init__(self)`: initializes inherited instance attribute ingredients with ["butter", "sugar", "eggs", "flour"], and initializes instance attribute frosting with "buttercream"
- `display(self)`: prints a cupcake's ingredients and frosting

Then call the `display()` method on a new Cupcake object. The output should match:

```
Made with ["butter", "sugar", "eggs", "flour"] and topped with buttercream frosting
```

Access multimedia content (https://openstax.org/books/introduction-python-programming/pages/13-2-attribute-access)

13.3 Methods

Learning objectives

By the end of this section you should be able to

- Write overridden methods to change behavior of inherited methods.
- Use `super()` to access superclass methods.
- Identify applications of polymorphism in method and function use.

Overriding methods

Sometimes a programmer wants to change the functions a subclass inherits. `Mint` is a subclass that has the same functionality as `Plant`, except for one function. A subclass can **override** a superclass method by defining a method with the same name as the superclass method.

CHECKPOINT

Overriding a superclass method

Access multimedia content (https://openstax.org/books/introduction-python-programming/pages/13-3-methods)

CONCEPTS IN PRACTICE

Overriding methods

1. Suppose a programmer inherits the `ContractTax` class from class `Tax` and wants to override `Tax`'s `calc_tax()`. What should the programmer do?
   a. Define another `calc_tax()` method in `Tax`.
   b. Define a `calc_tax()` method in `ContractTax`.
   c. Define a function that takes a `ContractTax` instance.

2. Which is the error in the program that attempts to override `calc_tax()` for `ContractTaxDE`?

   ```
   class Tax:
       def calc_tax(self):
           print('Calculating tax')

   class ContractTax(Tax):
       def calc_tax(self):
           print('Calculating contract tax')

   class ContractTaxDE(ContractTax):
       def calc_tax():
           print('Calculating German contract tax')

   my_tax = ContractTaxDE()
   my_tax.calc_tax()
   ```

   a. `ContractTaxDE` must inherit from `Tax`, not `ContractTax`.

b. `ContractTaxDE`'s definition of `calc_tax()` is missing a parameter.
c. `ContractTaxDE` can't override `calc_tax()` since `ContractTax` already has.

3. The following program doesn't override `calc_tax()`. Why?

   ```
   class Tax:
     def calc_tax(self):
       print('Calculating tax')
       total = 0 # To replace with calculation
       return total

   class ContractTax:
     def calc_tax(self):
       print('Calculating contract tax')
       total = 0 # To replace with calculation
       return total

   my_tax = ContractTax()
   my_tax.calc_tax()
   ```

   a. An overridden method cannot return a value.
   b. Tax doesn't specify `calc_tax()` can be overridden.
   c. `ContractTax` isn't inherited from Tax.

super()

`super()` is a special method that provides a temporary superclass object instance for a subclass to use. `super()` is commonly used to call superclass methods from a subclass. `super()` is commonly used in a subclass's `__init__()` to assign inherited instance attributes. Ex: `super().__init__()`.

CHECKPOINT

Using super() to call the superclass __init__() method

Access multimedia content (https://openstax.org/books/introduction-python-programming/pages/13-3-methods)

CONCEPTS IN PRACTICE

Using super()

Consider the following program.

```
1  class Polygon:
2      def __init__(self, num_sides=3):
3          self.num_sides = num_sides
4
5      class Rectangle(Polygon):
```

```
 6          def __init__(self, ln=1, wd=1):
 7              super().__init__(4)
 8              self.length = ln
 9              self.width = wd
10
11      class Square(Rectangle):
12          def __init__(self, side=1):
13              super().__init__(side, side)
14              self.side = side
15
16      sq_1 = Square(5)
17      print(sq_1.num_sides)
```

4. Line 16 executes and Square's __init__() is called on line 12. Line 13 executes and the superclass's __init__() is called. Which line does control flow move to next?
   a. 2
   b. 6
   c. 14

5. The next line executes. Which line does control flow move to next?
   a. 2
   b. 6
   c. 14

6. The method call returns. Lines 8 and 9 execute to initialize length and width, and Rectangle's __init__() returns. Which line does control flow move to next?
   a. 12
   b. 14
   c. 17

7. Square's __init__() returns and control flow moves to line 17. What is the output?
   a. 3
   b. 4
   c. 5

Polymorphism

Polymorphism is the concept of having many forms. In programming, a single name can be used for multiple functionalities. Within inheritance, polymorphism is the basis of method overriding, as multiple methods have the same name.

EXAMPLE 13.1

Polymorphism and inheritance

The name `display()` maps to multiple methods. The class type of the calling object determines which `display()` method is executed.

```
class Plant:
  def display(self):
    print("I'm a plant")

class Mint(Plant):
  def display(self):
    print("I'm a mint")

class Lavender(Mint):
  def display(self):
    print("I'm a lavender")

mint_1 = Mint()
mint_1.display()

lavender_1 = Lavender()
lavender_1.display()
```

The code's output is:

```
I'm a mint
I'm a lavender
```

Polymorphism can also be used with methods of unrelated classes. The class type of the calling object determines the method executed.

EXAMPLE 13.2

Polymorphism and methods

Tax and ContractTax are unrelated classes that each define calc_tax(). calc_tax() isn't overridden as ContractTax isn't inherited from Tax.

```
class Tax:
  def __init__(self, value):
    self.value = value

  def calc_tax(self):
    print("Calculating tax")
    total = 0.10 * self.value   # To replace with calculation
    return total
```

```python
class ContractTax:
    def __init__(self, value):
        self.value = value

    def calc_tax(self):
        print("Calculating contracts tax")
        total = 0.15 * self.value    # To replace with calculation
        return total

my_tax = ContractTax(value=1000)    # Replace 1000 with any value
result = my_tax.calc_tax()
print(f"Total tax: ${result}")
```

The code's output is:

```
Calculating contracts tax
Total tax: $150.00
```

Polymorphism allows methods to be called with different parameter types. Many built-in operators and functions have this utility.

EXAMPLE 13.3

Polymorphism and functions

`len()` can be called with multiple types, including lists and strings.

```python
tree_list = ["ash", "hazel", "oak", "yew"]
tree_1 = tree_list[0]
print(len(tree_list))
print(len(tree_1))
```

The code's output is:

```
4
3
```

CONCEPTS IN PRACTICE

Polymorphism in practice

8. Consider the example. What is the output?

   ```
   class Polygon:
      def print_type(self):
         print("Polygon type")

   class Rectangle(Polygon):
      def print_type(self):
         print("Rectangle type")

   class Square(Rectangle):
      def print_type(self):
         print("Square type")

   sq_1 = Square()
   sq_1.print_type()
   ```

   a. `Polygon type`
   b. `Rectangle type`
   c. `Square type`

9. Which is an example of polymorphism for the multiplication operator?
   a. `x = 3 * 4`
      `y = 3 * "la"`
   b. `x = 3 * 4`
      `y = str(x)`
   c. `x = 3 * 4`
      `y = x * x`

TRY IT

Overriding methods

Given the Pet class, create a Bird class inherited from Pet and a Finch class inherited from Bird. Override the `display()` method in Bird and Finch such that the program output is:

```
Pet type: Bird
Bird type: Finch
```

Access multimedia content (https://openstax.org/books/introduction-python-programming/pages/13-3-methods)

TRY IT

Using super()

Given the Employee class, create a Developer class inherited from Employee with methods `__init__()` and `print_info()` such that:

`__init__()`

- Uses `super()` to call Employee's `__init__()` to initialize `e_id` and `hire_year`.
- Assigns `lang_xp` with list parameter `lang_xp`.

`print_info()`

- Uses `super()` to print `e_id` and `hire_year`.
- Prints `"Language(s):"` followed by `lang_xp`.

Access multimedia content (https://openstax.org/books/introduction-python-programming/pages/13-3-methods)

13.4 Hierarchical inheritance

Learning objectives

By the end of this section you should be able to

- Label relationships between classes as types of inheritance.
- Construct classes that form hierarchical inheritance.

Hierarchical inheritance basics

Hierarchical inheritance is a type of inheritance in which multiple classes inherit from a single superclass. **Multilevel inheritance** is a type of inheritance in which a subclass becomes the superclass for another class. Combining hierarchical and multilevel inheritance creates a tree-like organization of classes.

CHECKPOINT

Hierarchical organization and types of inheritance

Access multimedia content (https://openstax.org/books/introduction-python-programming/pages/13-4-hierarchical-inheritance)

CONCEPTS IN PRACTICE

Hierarchical organization

1. Which is an example of hierarchical inheritance?
    a. Class B inherits from Class A
       Class C inherits from Class A
    b. Class B inherits from Class A
       Class C inherits from Class B
    c. Class B inherits from Class A

Class C inherits from Class D

2. Which group of classes is hierarchical inheritance appropriate for?
   a. `Cat, Dog, Bird`
   b. `Employee, Developer, SalesRep`
   c. `Dessert, BakedGood, ApplePie`

Implementing hierarchical inheritance

Multiple classes can inherit from a single class by simply including the superclass name in each subclass definition.

EXAMPLE 13.4

Choir members

```python
class ChoirMember:
  def display(self):
    print("Current choir member")

class Soprano(ChoirMember):
  def display(self):
    super().display()
    print("Part: Soprano")

class Soprano1(Soprano):
  def display(self):
    super().display()
    print("Division: Soprano 1")

class Alto(ChoirMember):
  def display(self):
    super().display()
    print("Part: Alto")

class Tenor(ChoirMember):
  def display(self):
    super().display()
    print("Part: Tenor")

class Bass(ChoirMember):
  def display(self):
    super().display()
    print("Part: Bass")

mem_10 = Alto()
```

```
        mem_13 = Tenor()
        mem_15 = Soprano1()

        mem_10.display()
        print()
        mem_13.display()
        print()
        mem_15.display()
```

The code's output is:

```
Current choir member
Part: Alto

Current choir member
Part: Tenor

Current choir member
Part: Soprano
Division: Soprano 1
```

CONCEPTS IN PRACTICE

Implementing hierarchical inheritance

Consider the program:

```
class A:
    def __init__(self, a_attr=0):
        self.a_attr = a_attr

class B(A):
    def __init__(self, a_attr=0, b_attr=0):
        super().__init__(a_attr)
        self.b_attr = b_attr

class C(A):
    def __init__(self, a_attr=0, c_attr=0):
        super().__init__(a_attr)
        self.c_attr = c_attr

class D(B):
    def __init__(self, a_attr=0, b_attr=0, d_attr=0):
```

```
        super().__init__(a_attr, b_attr)
        self.d_attr = d_attr

b_inst = B(2)
c_inst = C(c_attr=4)
d_inst = D(6, 7)
```

3. What is the value of b_inst.b_attr?
    a. 0
    b. 2
    c. Error

4. Which attributes does c_inst have access to?
    a. a_attr
    b. a_attr, c_attr
    c. c_attr

5. Which attributes does d_inst have access to?
    a. b_attr, d_attr
    b. a_attr, b_attr, d_attr
    c. d_attr

TRY IT

Overriding methods

Define three classes: Instrument, Woodwind, and String.

- Instrument has instance attribute owner, with default value of "unknown".
- Woodwind inherits from Instrument and has instance attribute material with default value of "wood".
- String inherits from Instrument and has instance attribute num_strings, with default value of 4.

The output should match:

```
This flute belongs to unknown and is made of silver
This cello belongs to Bea and has 4 strings
```

Access multimedia content (https://openstax.org/books/introduction-python-programming/pages/13-4-hierarchical-inheritance)

13.5 Multiple inheritance and mixin classes

Learning objectives

By the end of this section you should be able to

- Construct a class that inherits from multiple superclasses.
- Identify the diamond problem within multiple inheritance.
- Construct a mixin class to add functionality to a subclass.

Multiple inheritance basics

Multiple inheritance is a type of inheritance in which one class inherits from multiple classes. A class inherited from multiple classes has all superclasses listed in the class definition inheritance list. Ex: `class SubClass(SuperClass_1, SuperClass_2)`.

CHECKPOINT

Multiple inheritance organization

Access multimedia content (https://openstax.org/books/introduction-python-programming/pages/13-5-multiple-inheritance-and-mixin-classes)

CONCEPTS IN PRACTICE

Implementing multiple inheritance

Consider the program:

```
class A:
   def __init__(self, a_attr=2):
      self.a_attr = a_attr

class B:
   def __init__(self, b_attr=4):
      self.b_attr = b_attr

class C(A, B):
   def __init__(self, a_attr=5, b_attr=10, c_attr=20):
      A.__init__(self, a_attr)
      B.__init__(self, b_attr)
      self.c_attr = c_attr

b_inst = B(2)
c_inst = C(1, 2)
```

1. What is the value of `c_inst.a_attr`?
   a. 1
   b. 5

c. Error

2. What is the value of c_inst.c_attr?
   a. 2
   b. 20
   c. Error

3. What is the value of b_inst.a_attr?
   a. 2
   b. 4
   c. Error

The diamond problem and mixin classes

Multiple inheritance should be implemented with care. The **diamond problem** occurs when a class inherits from multiple classes that share a common superclass. Ex: Dessert and BakedGood both inherit from Food, and ApplePie inherits from Dessert and BakedGood.

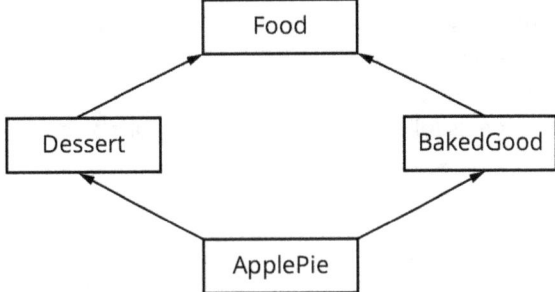

Figure 13.2 The diamond problem. If both Dessert and BakedGood override a Food method, the overridden Food method that ApplePie inherits is ambiguous. Thus, diamond shaped inheritance should be avoided.

Mixin classes promote modularity and can remove the diamond problem. A mixin class:

- Has no superclass
- Has attributes and methods to be added to a subclass
- Isn't instantiated (Ex: Given MyMixin class, my_inst = MyMixin() should never be used.)

Mixin classes are used in multiple inheritance to add functionality to a subclass without adding inheritance concerns.

CONCEPTS IN PRACTICE

Creating a mixin class

The following code isn't correct, as not all plants are carnivorous. Follow the programmer through the programmer's edits to improve the program. Note: Rose, Pitcher, and VenusFlyTrap represent plants that all photosynthesize. Pitcher and VenusFlyTrap represent plants that are also carnivorous and can eat.

A pass statement is used in Python to indicate that code is to be written later and prevents certain errors that would result if no code was written or a comment was used instead.

```
class Plant:
  def photosynth(self):
    print("Photosynthesizing")

  def eat(self):
    print("Eating")

class Rose(Plant):
  pass

class Pitcher(Plant):
  pass

class VenusFlyTrap(Plant):
  pass
```

4. Which edit is appropriate?
   a. Move eat() to a different class.
   b. Remove Plant as a superclass.

5. The programmer edits the code as follows. How can the program be improved?

```
class Plant:
  def photosynth(self):
    print("Photosynthesizing")

class Rose(Plant):
  pass

class Pitcher(Plant):
  def eat(self):
    print("Eating")

class VenusFlyTrap(Plant)
  def eat(self):
    print("Eating")
```

   a. Move photosynth() into Rose.
   b. Remove redundancy of eat().

6. The programmer edits the code to create a mixin class containing eat(). Which class name, replacing X, is most appropriate for the mixin?

```
class Plant:
  def photosynth(self):
    print("Photosynthesizing")
```

```
class X:
  def eat(self):
    print("Eating")

class Rose(Plant):
  pass

class Pitcher(Plant, X):
  pass

class VenusFlyTrap(Plant, X)
  pass
```

a. CarnivClass
b. CarnivMixin

TRY IT

Fixing the diamond problem with a mixin class

The program below represents multiple inheritance and has the diamond problem. Edit the program to use a mixin class, OnlineMixin. OnlineMixin:

- Replaces OnlineShop.
- Is a superclass of FoodFast.
- Has one method, process_online(), which prints "Connecting to server" and is called by FoodFast's process_order().

The output should match:

```
Processing meal order
Connecting to server
Enjoy your FoodFast order
```

Access multimedia content (https://openstax.org/books/introduction-python-programming/pages/13-5-multiple-inheritance-and-mixin-classes)

13.6 Chapter summary

Highlights from this chapter include:

- Inheritance describes an is-a relationship between classes. One class, the subclass, inherits from another class, the superclass.
- Subclasses can access inherited attributes and methods directly.
- Subclasses can override superclass methods to change or add functionality.
- super() allows a subclass to access the methods of the superclass.

- Polymorphism describes a single representation for multiple forms and is applied in Python to define multiple methods with the same name and allow the same method to take different arguments.
- Hierarchical inheritance is a type of inheritance in which multiple classes inherit from a single superclass.
- Multiple inheritance is a type of inheritance in which one class inherits from multiple classes.
- Mixin classes are used in multiple inheritance to add functionality to a subclass without adding inheritance concerns.

At this point, you should be able to write subclasses that inherit instance attributes and methods, and subclasses that have unique attributes and overridden methods. You should also be able to create hierarchical inheritance relationships and multiple inheritance relationships between classes.

Task	Example
Define a subclass	```class SuperClass: passclass SubClass(SuperClass): pass```
Define a subclass's __init__() using super()	```class SubClass(SuperClass): def __init__(self): super().__init__() # Calls superclass __init__() # Initialize subclass instance attributes```
Override a superclass method	```class SuperClass: def display(self): print('Superclass method')class SubClass(SuperClass): def display(self): # Same name as superclass method print('Subclass method')```

Table 13.2 Chapter 13 reference.

Task	Example
| Implement hierarchical inheritance | ```python
class SuperClass:
  def display(self):
    print('Superclass method')

class SubClass1(SuperClass):
  def display(self):
    print('Subclass 1 method ')
class SubClass2(SuperClass):
  def display(self):
   print('Subclass 2 method')

class SubClass3(SuperClass):
  def display(self):
    print('Subclass 3 method')
``` |
| Implement multiple inheritance | ```python
class SuperClass1:
    pass

class SuperClass2:
    pass

class SubClass(SuperClass1, SuperClass2):
    pass
``` |

Table 13.2 Chapter 13 reference.

14 Files

Figure 14.1 credit: Larissa Chu, CC BY 4.0

Chapter Outline

14.1 Reading from files
14.2 Writing to files
14.3 Files in different locations and working with CSV files
14.4 Handling exceptions
14.5 Raising exceptions
14.6 Chapter summary

 Introduction

Programming often involves reading information from files and writing information into files. This chapter begins by introducing how to read from and write into files in Python.

Reading and writing files can lead to exceptions when the file specified cannot be found. There are many other situations in which exceptions can occur. The second half of the chapter introduces exceptions and how to handle exceptions in Python.

14.1 Reading from files

Learning objectives

By the end of this section you should be able to

- Understand how to open a file using the open() function.
- Demonstrate how to read information from a file using read(), readline(), and readlines().

Opening a file

Reading information from and writing information to files is a common task in programming.

Python supports the opening of a file using the **open()** function.

CHECKPOINT

Opening a file

Access multimedia content (https://openstax.org/books/introduction-python-programming/pages/14-1-reading-from-files)

CONCEPTS IN PRACTICE

Opening files

1. What is the correct way to open a file named *firstfile.txt* so that the file's contents can be read into a Python program?
   a. `open("firstfile")`
   b. `open("firstfile.txt")`
   c. `fileobj = open("firstfile.txt")`

2. Suppose that there is no file named *input.txt*. What is the result of trying to execute `open("input.txt")`?
   a. `Error`
   b. `nothing`
   c. `"input.txt" file is created.`

3. What is the result of the following code?

   ```
   fileobj = open("newfile.txt")
   print(fileobj)
   ```

   a. `Error`
   b. Information about the object `fileobj` is printed.
   c. The contents of *newfile.txt* are printed.

Using read() and reading lines

Python provides functions that can be called on a file object for reading the contents of a file:

- The **read()** function reads the contents of a file and returns a string.
- The **readline()** function reads the next line in a file and returns a string.
- The **readlines()** function reads the individual lines of a file and returns a string list containing all the lines of the file in order.

EXAMPLE 14.1

Using read() and readlines()

A file called *input.txt* has the following contents:

```
    55
    5
    91



    """Demonstrating read() and readlines()"""

    # Using read()
    # Open the file and associate with a file object
    infile = open("input.txt")

    # Read the contents of the file into a string
    str1 = infile.read()

    # Print str1
    print("Result of using read():")
    print(str1)

    # Always close the file once done using the file
    infile.close()

    # Using read()
    # Open the file and associate with a file object
    infile2 = open("input.txt")

    # Read the contents of the file into a string list
    str_list = infile2.readlines()

    # Printing the third item in the string list.
    print("Result of using readlines() and printing the third item in the string
list:")
    print(str_list[2])

    # Always close the file once done using the file
    infile2.close()
```

The code's output is:

```
    Result of using read():
    12
    55
    5
    91
    Result of using readlines() printing the third item in the string list:
    5
```

CHECKPOINT

read() and readline()

Access multimedia content (https://openstax.org/books/introduction-python-programming/pages/14-1-reading-from-files)

CONCEPTS IN PRACTICE

Reading files

Suppose `fileobj = open("input.txt")` has already been executed for each question below.

input.txt:

```
Hello world!
How are you?
```

4. What is the correct way to use the `read()` function to read the contents of *input.txt* into a string `file_str`?
   a. `file_str = read(fileobj)`
   b. `file_str = read("input.txt")`
   c. `file_str = fileobj.read()`

5. What is the correct way to use the `readlines()` function?
   a. `file_lines = readlines(fileobj)`
   b. `file_lines = fileobj.readlines()`

6. What is printed as a result of executing `print(fileobj.readline())`?
   a. The first line of *input.txt* is printed.
   b. The contents of the file *input.txt* are printed.
   c. `Error`

TRY IT

Reading from a file

Open the file *test.txt* and print the file's contents.

Access multimedia content (https://openstax.org/books/introduction-python-programming/pages/14-1-reading-from-files)

> **TRY IT**
>
> Reading from a file line by line
>
> The file *input.txt* is shown. The file represents a set of integers. Line 1 of the file specifies how many integers follow. Write a program that reads from this file and determines the average of the numbers following the first line.
>
> *input.txt*
>
> ```
> n: 5
> 25
> 13
> 4
> 6
> 19
> ```
>
> Access multimedia content (https://openstax.org/books/introduction-python-programming/pages/14-1-reading-from-files)

14.2 Writing to files

Learning objectives

By the end of this section you should be able to

- Understand how to open a file for writing.
- Explain different modes for opening a file in Python.
- Demonstrate the use of the `write()` function to write to a file.
- Understand the importance of closing a file.

Opening a file for writing

A file may be opened for reading, allowing no changes, or for writing, allowing changes to occur in the file. The **mode** defines whether a file is opened for reading only or for writing. The default mode of the `open()` function is reading only. A second mode parameter defines the mode.

Ex: `open("output.txt", 'w')` opens the *output.txt* file in writing mode. The following table lists common modes.

Parameter	Mode name and description	Example

`'r'`	Read mode:
	Open the specified file for reading.
	If the file does not exist, an error occurs.
	When no mode parameter is used, the default is to open a file in read mode.
		`fileobj = open("input.txt")`
		same as:
		`fileobj = open("input.txt", 'r')`

`'w'`	Write mode: Open the specified file for writing. If the file does not exist, then the file is created. If the file already exists, the contents of the file are overwritten.	`fileobj = open("output.txt", 'w')`
`'a'`	Append mode: Open the specified file for appending, which means adding information to the end of the existing file. If the file does not exist, then the file is created.	`fileobj = open("log.txt", 'a')`

Table 14.1 Modes for the `open()` function.

CONCEPTS IN PRACTICE

File modes

Assume that a file named *logfile.txt* exists.

1. To read *logfile.txt*, which of the following lines of code works best?
   a. `logfile = open("logfile.txt")`
   b. `logfile = open("logfile.txt", 'w')`
   c. `logfile = open("logfile.txt", 'a')`

2. Additions are to be made to *logfile.txt*. Which of the following lines of code works best?
   a. `infile = open("logfile.txt")`
   b. `infile = open("logfile.txt", 'w')`
   c. `infile = open("logfile.txt", 'a')`

3. A new file called *newlog.txt* must be created. Which of the following lines of code works best?
   a. `logfile = open("newlog.txt")`
   b. `logfile = open("newlog.txt", 'w')`
   c. `logfile = open("newlog.txt", 'a')`

Using `write()` and `close()`

The `write()` function is used to write to an already opened file. The `write()` function will only accept a string parameter. Other variable types must be cast to string before writing using `write()`.

The `write()` function does not automatically add a newline character as the `print()` function does. A newline must be added explicitly by adding a newline (`'\n'`) character.

The write() function writes automatically to a temporary store called the file buffer. To ensure that the information is written to a file, the close() function must be used. The close() function finalizes changes and closes the file.

EXAMPLE 14.2

Writing and appending to a file

```python
"""Operations for writing and appending to files."""

# Create a new file
opfile = open("output.txt", 'w')

# Writing to the file
opfile.write("Writing to a new file.")

# To add another line the newline character must be used
opfile.write("\nSecond line.")

# Ensure changes are saved by closing the file
opfile.close()

# Read and display the contents of the file
infile = open("output.txt")
print("\nRead the original file:\n")
print(infile.read())
infile.close()

# Reopen the file in append mode to add to the file
opfile = open("output.txt", 'a')

# Note the use of newline characters
opfile.write("\nAdding to the file.")
opfile.write("\nAdding another line.")

# Ensure changes are saved by closing the file
opfile.close()

# Read and display the contents of the modified file
infile = open("output.txt")
print("\nRead the modified file:\n")
print(infile.read())
infile.close()
```

The code's output is:

```
Read the original file:

Writing to a new file.
Second line.

Read the modified file:

Writing to a new file.
Second line.
Adding to the file.
Adding another line.
```

CHECKPOINT

write() and close()

Access multimedia content (https://openstax.org/books/introduction-python-programming/pages/14-2-writing-to-files)

CONCEPTS IN PRACTICE

Writing to files

resources.txt already exists. What would happen for each of the following snippets of code?

4. ```
   outfile = open("resources.txt", 'w')
   outfile.write("new content")
   ```

   a. nothing
   b. The contents of the *resources.txt file* is overwritten with the line `"new content"`.
   c. The *resources.txt* file is overwritten, but the contents of *resources.txt* are uncertain.

5. ```
   outfile = open("resources.txt", 'w')
   outfile.write("new content")
   outfile.close()
   ```

   a. The content of the *resources.txt* file is overwritten with the line `"new content"`.
   b. The line `"new content"` is added to the end of *resources.txt*.

6. ```
   outfile = open("resources.txt", 'a')
   outfile.write("new content")
   outfile.close()
   ```

   a. The content of the *resources.txt* file is overwritten with the line `"new content"`.
   ```

b. The line `"new content"` is added to the end of *resources.txt*.

TRY IT

Writing to a new file

Write a line of text to a file called *out.txt*. Don't forget to use `close()`. *out.txt* should only have the line of text that you have written.

Access multimedia content (https://openstax.org/books/introduction-python-programming/pages/14-2-writing-to-files)

TRY IT

Writing to an existing file

Add two lines of text to the file called *out.log*, such that *out.log* has three lines after the code executes.

Hint: Don't forget that you need a newline character.

Access multimedia content (https://openstax.org/books/introduction-python-programming/pages/14-2-writing-to-files)

14.3 Files in different locations and working with CSV files

Learning objectives

By the end of this section you should be able to

- Demonstrate how to access files within a file system.
- Demonstrate how to process a CSV file.

Opening a file at any location

When only the filename is used as the argument to the `open()` function, the file must be in the same folder as the Python file that is executing. Ex: For `fileobj = open("file1.txt")` in *files.py* to execute successfully, the *file1.txt* file should be in the same folder as *files.py*.

Often a programmer needs to open files from folders other than the one in which the Python file exists. A **path** uniquely identifies a folder location on a computer. The path can be used along with the filename to open a file in any folder location. Ex: To open a file named *logfile.log* located in `/users/turtle/desktop` the following can be used:

`fileobj = open("/users/turtle/desktop/logfile.log")`

Operating System	File location	`open()` function example
Mac	`/users/student/`	`fileobj = open("/users/student/output.txt")`
Linux	`/usr/code/`	`fileobj = open("/usr/code/output.txt")`
Windows	`c:\projects\code\`	`fileobj = open("c:/projects/code/output.txt")` or `fileobj = open("c:\\projects\\code\\output.txt")`

Table 14.2 Opening files on different paths. In each of the following cases, a file called output.txt is located in a different folder than the Python folder. Windows uses backslash \ characters instead of forward slash / characters for the path. If the backslash is included directly in `open()`, then an additional backslash is needed for Python to understand the location correctly.

CONCEPTS IN PRACTICE

Opening files at different locations

For each question, assume that the Python file executing the `open()` function is not in the same folder as the *out.txt* file.

Each question indicates the location of *out.txt*, the type of computer, and the desired mode for opening the file. Choose which option is best for opening *out.txt*.

1. `/users/turtle/files` on a Mac for reading
   a. `fileobj = open("out.txt")`
   b. `fileobj = open("/users/turtle/files/out.txt")`
   c. `fileobj = open("/users/turtle/files/out.txt", 'w')`

2. `c:\documents\` on a Windows computer for reading
   a. `fileobj = open("out.txt")`
   b. `fileobj = open("c:/documents/out.txt", 'a')`
   c. `fileobj = open("c:/documents/out.txt")`

3. `/users/turtle/logs` on a Linux computer for writing
   a. `fileobj = open("out.txt")`
   b. `fileobj = open("/users/turtle/logs/out.txt")`
   c. `fileobj = open("/users/turtle/logs/out.txt", 'w')`

4. `c:\proj\assets` on a Windows computer in append mode
   a. `fileobj = open("c:\\proj\\assets\\out.txt", 'a')`
   b. `fileobj = open("c:\proj\assets\out.txt", 'a')`

Working with CSV files

In Python, files are read from and written to as Unicode by default. Many common file formats use Unicode such as text files (*.txt*), Python code files (*.py*), and other code files (*.c*,*.java*).

Comma separated value (CSV, *.csv*) files are often used for storing tabular data. These files store cells of information as Unicode separated by commas. CSV files can be read using methods learned thus far, as seen in the example below.

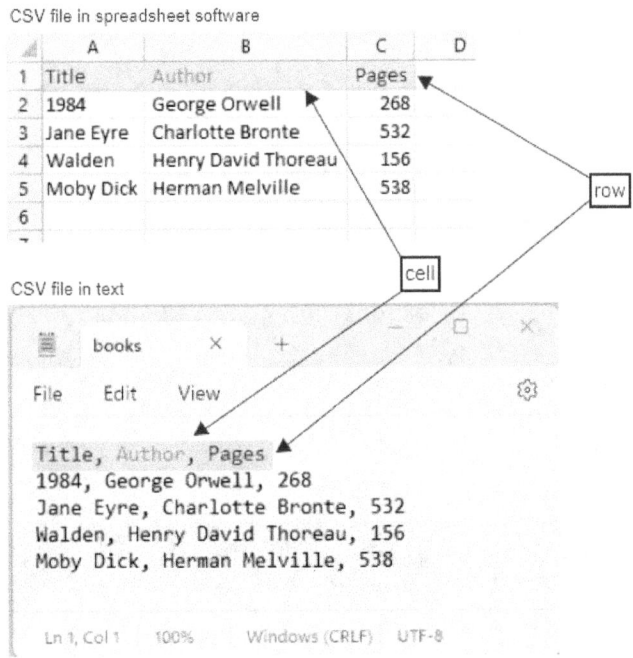

Figure 14.2 CSV files. A CSV file is simply a text file with rows separated by newline \n characters and cells separated by commas.

Raw text of the file:

Title, Author, Pages\n1984, George Orwell, 268\nJane Eyre, Charlotte Bronte, 532\nWalden, Henry David Thoreau, 156\nMoby Dick, Herman Melville, 538

EXAMPLE 14.3

Processing a CSV file

```
"""Processing a CSV file."""
# Open the CSV file for reading
file_obj = open("books.csv")

# Rows are separated by newline \n characters, so readlines() can be used to read in all rows into a string list
csv_rows = file_obj.readlines()

list_csv = []

# Remove \n characters from each row and split by comma and save into a 2D structure
for row in csv_rows:
```

```python
        # Remove \n character
        row = row.strip("\n")
        # Split using commas
        cells = row.split(",")
        list_csv.append(cells)

        # Print result
    print(list_csv)
```

The code's output is:

```
[['Title', ' Author', ' Pages'], ['1984', ' George Orwell', ' 268'], ['Jane
Eyre', ' Charlotte Bronte', ' 532'], ['Walden', ' Henry David Thoreau', ' 156'],
['Moby Dick', ' Herman Melville', ' 538']]
```

CONCEPTS IN PRACTICE

File types and CSV files

5. Why does `readlines()` work for reading the rows in a CSV file?
   a. `readlines()` reads line by line using the newline \n character.
   b. `readlines()` is not appropriate for reading a CSV file.
   c. `readlines()` automatically recognizes a CSV file and works accordingly.

6. For the code in the example, what would be the output for the statement `print(list_csv[1][2])`?
   a. 532
   b. 268
   c. Jane Eyre

7. What is the output of the following code for the *books.csv* seen above?

   ```
   file_obj = open("books.csv")

   csv_read = file_obj.readline()

   print(csv_read)
   ```

   a. `['Title, Author, Pages\n', '1984, George Orwell, 268\n', 'Jane Eyre, Charlotte Bronte, 532\n', 'Walden, Henry David Thoreau, 156\n', 'Moby Dick, Herman Melville, 538']`
   b. `[['Title', ' Author', ' Pages'], ['1984', ' George Orwell', ' 268'], ['Jane Eyre', ' Charlotte Bronte', ' 532'], ['Walden', ' Henry David Thoreau', ' 156'], ['Moby Dick', ' Herman Melville', ' 538']]`
   c. `Title, Author, Pages`

> **EXPLORING FURTHER**
>
> Files such as Word documents (.*docx*) and PDF documents (.*pdf*), image formats such as Portable Network Graphics (PNG, .*png*) and Joint Photographic Experts Group (JPEG, .*jpeg* or .*jpg*) as well as many other file types are encoded differently.
>
> Some types of non-Unicode files can be read using specialized libraries that support the reading and writing of different file types.
>
> PyPDF (https://openstax.org/r/100readthedocs) is a popular library that can be used to extract information from PDF files.
>
> BeautifulSoup (https://openstax.org/r/100software) can be used to extract information from XML and HTML files. XML and HTML files usually contain unicode with structure provided through the use of angled <> bracket tags.
>
> python-docx (https://openstax.org/r/100readwrtedocx) can be used to read and write DOCX files.
>
> Additionally, csv (https://openstax.org/r/100csvlibrary) is a built-in library that can be used to extract information from CSV files.

> **TRY IT**
>
> Processing a CSV file
>
> The file *fe.csv* contains scores for a group of students on a final exam. Write a program to display the average score.
>
> Access multimedia content (https://openstax.org/books/introduction-python-programming/pages/14-3-files-in-different-locations-and-working-with-csv-files)

14.4 Handling exceptions

Learning objectives

By the end of this section you should be able to

- Describe two exceptions that may occur when reading files.
- Write `try`/`except` statements that handle built-in exceptions.

Runtime errors

Various errors may occur when reading a file:

- `FileNotFoundError`: The filename or path is invalid.
- `IndexError`/`ValueError`: The file's format is invalid.
- Other errors caused by invalid contents of a file.

When an error occurs, the program terminates with an error message.

> ### EXAMPLE 14.4
>
> Typo in a file
>
> A file named food_order.txt has the following contents:
>
> ```
> 5 sandwiches
> 4 chips
> 1 pickle
> soft drinks
> ```
>
> The following program expects each line of the file to begin with an integer:
>
> ```python
> for line in open("food_order.txt"):
>     space = line.index(" ")
>     qty = int(line[:space])
>     item = line[space+1:-1]
>     print(qty, item)
> ```
>
> Unfortunately, the line `"soft drinks"` does not begin with an integer. As a result, the program terminates and displays an error message:
>
> ```
> Traceback (most recent call last):
>   File "food_order.py", line 3
>     qty = int(line[:space])
> ValueError: invalid literal for int() with base 10: 'soft'
> ```

> ### CONCEPTS IN PRACTICE
>
> Common exceptions
>
> What error might occur in each situation?
>
> 1. The line `"soft drinks"` is changed to `"3-4 soft drinks"`.
>   a. FileNotFoundError
>   b. IndexError
>   c. ValueError
>
> 2. `for line in open("food_order.text"):`
>   a. FileNotFoundError
>   b. IndexError
>   c. ValueError

3. ```
   parts = line.split()
   qty = parts[0]
   item = parts[1]
   ```

   a. `FileNotFoundError`
   b. `IndexError`
   c. `ValueError`

> **EXPLORING FURTHER**
>
> The Built-in Exceptions (https://openstax.org/r/100exceptions) page of the Python Standard Library explains the meaning of each exception.

Try and except

Programs can be designed to handle exceptions, rather than terminate. A **try** statement runs code that might raise an exception. An `except` clause runs code in response to the exception.

EXAMPLE 14.5

Try to open a file

The following program, named *try_open.py*, asks the user for a filename and counts the number of lines in the file.

```
name = input("Enter a filename: ")
try:
    file = open(name)
    lines = file.readlines()
    count = len(lines)
    print(name, "has", count, "lines")
except FileNotFoundError:
    print("File not found:", name)
print("Have a nice day!")
```

When running this program with the input *try_open.py*, the name of the program file, the output is:

```
Enter a filename: try_open.py
try_open.py has 9 lines
Have a nice day!
```

If the filename does not exist, a `FileNotFoundError` is raised on line 3. The program then jumps to the except clause on line 7 and continues to run. The resulting output is:
```

```
Enter a filename: try_open.txt
File not found: try_open.txt
Have a nice day!
```

CONCEPTS IN PRACTICE

Predicting output with exceptions

For each code snippet, what is the output?

4.
```
word = "one"
try:
    number = int(word)
    print(word, "equals", number)
except ValueError:
    print(word, "is not a number")
```

a. one equals 1
b. one is not a number
c. ValueError: invalid literal for int() with base 10: 'one'

5.
```
word = "one"
try:
    number = int(word)
    print(word, "equals", number)
except IndexError:
    print(word, "is not a number")
```

a. one equals 1
b. one is not a number
c. ValueError: invalid literal for int() with base 10: 'one'

6.
```
word = "one"
try:
    char = word[3]
    print("The char is", char)
except:
    print("That didn't work")
```

a. The char is e
b. That didn't work
c. IndexError: string index out of range

TRY IT

Type analyzer

Analysis programs often need to find numbers in large bodies of text. How can a program tell if a string like "123.45" represents a number? One approach is to use exceptions:

1. Try converting the string to an integer. If no ValueError is raised, then the string represents an integer.
2. Otherwise, try converting the string to a float. If no ValueError is raised, then the string represents a float.
3. Otherwise, the string does not represent a number.

Implement the get_type() function using this approach. The provided main block calls get_type() for each word in a file. get_type() should return either "int", "float", or "str", based on the word. The output for the provided data.txt is:

```
str: Hello
int: 100
str: times!
float: 3.14159
str: is
str: pi.
```

Access multimedia content (https://openstax.org/books/introduction-python-programming/pages/14-4-handling-exceptions)

TRY IT

United countries

Write a program that prompts the user to input a word and a filename. The program should print each line of the file that contains the word. Here is an example run of the program (user input in bold):

United
```
    Enter a filename: countries.csv
    United Arab Emirates,9890402,83600,118
    United Kingdom,67886011,241930,281
    United States of America,331002651,9147420,36

    Enter a word: United
    Enter a filename: countries.csv
    United Arab Emirates,9890402,83600,118
    United Kingdom,67886011,241930,281
    United States of America,331002651,9147420,36
```

This example uses a file named countries.csv based on the alphabetical list of countries (https://openstax.org/r/100countries) from Worldometer. Each line of the file includes a country's name, population, land area, and population density, separated by commas.

The user might incorrectly type the filename (Ex: *countries.txt* instead of *countries.csv*). Your program should output an error message if the file is not found, and keep prompting the user to input a filename until the file is found:

```
countries
    File not found: countries
    Enter a filename: countries.txt
    File not found: countries.txt
    Enter a filename: countries.csv
    ...


    ...
    Enter a filename: countries
    File not found: countries
    Enter a filename: countries.txt
    File not found: countries.txt
    Enter a filename: countries.csv
    ...
```

Hint: Try to open the file specified by the user. A `FileNotFoundError` is raised if the filename is invalid.

Access multimedia content (https://openstax.org/books/introduction-python-programming/pages/14-4-handling-exceptions)

14.5 Raising exceptions

Learning objectives

By the end of this section you should be able to

- Use a `raise` statement to indicate that user input is invalid.
- Explain the flow of execution when an exception is raised.

The raise statement

A program can raise an exception when an error is detected. Raising an exception forces a program to deal with the error. If the exception is not handled using `try` and `except`, the program displays an error message and terminates.

EXAMPLE 14.6

Invalid pizza size

The following class represents a pizza for sale. The `SIZES` dictionary maps an abbreviation to a size's name and price. Line 11 checks if the size received by the constructor is in the dictionary. Line 12 raises a `ValueError` with specific error message.

```
1  class Pizza:
```

```
 2
 3          SIZES = {
 4              "S": ("Small", 5.99),
 5              "M": ("Medium", 7.99),
 6              "L": ("Large", 9.99),
 7              "XL": ("X-Large", 11.99),
 8          }
 9
10      def __init__(self, size):
11          if size not in Pizza.SIZES:
12              raise ValueError(f"Unknown size '{size}'")
13          self.size = size
14
15      def __str__(self):
16          name, price = Pizza.SIZES[self.size]
17          return f"{name} pizza for ${price}"
18
19  if __name__ == "__main__":
20      p1 = Pizza("L")
21      print(p1)
22      p2 = Pizza("Z")
23      print(p2)
```

```
Large pizza for $9.99
Traceback (most recent call last):
  File "pizza.py", line 23, in <module>
    p2 = Pizza("Z")
  File "pizza.py", line 12, in __init__
    raise ValueError(f"Unknown size '{size}'")
ValueError: Unknown size 'Z'
```

Raising an exception in a constructor prevents an invalid object from being constructed. In the example, p1 is constructed but p2 is not constructed.

CONCEPTS IN PRACTICE

Predicting output with raise

For each code snippet, what is the output?

1. ```
   p3 = Pizza("M")
   print(p3)
   ```

   a. Medium pizza for $7.99
   b. ValueError: Unknown size 'M'
   ```

c. `TypeError: missing argument`

2. `raise PizzaError("Invalid size")`
   a. `Invalid size`
   b. `PizzaError: Invalid size`
   c. `NameError: name 'PizzaError' is not defined`

3. `raise ValueError`
   a. `ValueError`
   b. `NameError: name 'ValueError' is not defined`
   c. `SyntaxError: Missing parenthesis in call to 'ValueError'`

TRY IT

Language objects

The file top27.csv is based on Wikipedia's list of languages by number of native speakers (https://openstax.org/r/100languages). A linguist would like to work with this data in an object-oriented way and has already defined a Language class. However, the code is not working correctly because of errors in the CSV file. (The CSV program cannot be changed because the program's purpose is to detect these kinds of errors.)

Your task is to modify the constructor to raise a `ValueError` in the following situations:

- If the line does not have exactly four values (separated by commas).
- If the number of speakers is not a positive floating point number.

Note: The provided top27.csv includes mistakes for English, Korean, and French. Your program should raise a `ValueError` only for these languages. No other errors (including `IndexError`) should be raised.

Access multimedia content (https://openstax.org/books/introduction-python-programming/pages/14-5-raising-exceptions)

TRY IT

Looking up keys

When looking up a value in a dictionary, a key has to match exactly. Ex: Given `fruit = {"apple": 1, "banana": 2}`, the expression `fruit["Apple"]` raises a `KeyError` because `"Apple"` is not the same as `"apple"`. Likewise, `fruit["NANA"]` raises a `KeyError` because `"nana"` does not exactly match `"banana"`.

Implement the `lookup()` function. This function tries to find a key in the dictionary that matches the search term. A key matches if the search term is a substring of the key, ignoring case. Ex: The key `"banana"` matches the search term `"NANA"`.

If no matching keys are found, `lookup()` should raise a `KeyError` with the message `"search term not found"`. If multiple matches are found, `lookup()` should raise a `KeyError` with the message `"multiple keys found"`. Otherwise, `lookup()` should return both the key and the value for the matching item in the dictionary.

Given the books.csv file, the output should be:

```
Found: ('Pride and Prejudice', 9780141439518)
Found: ('The Hobbit', 9780547928227)
Error: search term not found
Error: multiple keys found
```

Access multimedia content (https://openstax.org/books/introduction-python-programming/pages/14-5-raising-exceptions)

14.6 Chapter summary

Highlights from this chapter include:

- Python can read and write data in files using the built-in `open()` function.
- Due to buffering, changes to a file may not be visible until the file is closed.
- Newline characters need to be removed/added when reading/writing files.
- Comma-separate-value (CSV) files are commonly used to represent data.
- Exceptions that cause a program to terminate can be handled using `try` and `except`.
- Raising an exception is an alternative way to return from a function when an error occurs.

Statement	Description
`file = open("myfile.txt")`	Open a file for reading.
`file = open("myfile.txt", 'w')`	Open a file for writing.
`file = open("myfile.txt", 'a')`	Open a file for appending.
`file.close()`	Close a file after making changes.
`data = file.read()`	Read the entire contents of a file. The variable `data` is a string.
`data = file.readline()`	Read the next line of a file. The variable `data` is a string.

Table 14.3 Chapter 14 reference.

Statement	Description
`data = file.readlines()`	Read all lines of a file. The variable `data` is a list of strings.
`file.write("Have a nice day!\n")`	Writes a line to a file. In contrast to `print()`, the `write()` function does not automatically append a newline.
`file.write(["Line 1\n", "Line 2\n"])`	Writes multiple lines to a file. As with `write()`, a newline is not automatically added at the end of each line.

`try:`
`    # Statements`
`except:`
`    # Statements`
	Try to run statements that might raise an error. If any error is raised, run other statements.

`try:`
`    # Statements`
`except ValueError:`
`    # Statements`
	Try to run statements that might raise a `ValueError`. If a `ValueError` is raised, run other statements.

`try:`
`    # Statements`
`except ValueError as err:`
`    # Statements`
	Try to run statements that might raise a `ValueError`. If a `ValueError` is raised, run other statements. The variable `err` contains more details about the `ValueError`.

`raise ValueError`	Raises a `ValueError` with no specific error message.
`raise ValueError("number is prime")`	Raises a `ValueError` with the message `"number is prime"`.

Table 14.3 Chapter 14 reference.

15 Data Science

Figure 15.1 credit: modification of work by Sebastian Sikora/Flickr, CC BY 2.0

Chapter Outline

15.1 Introduction to data science
15.2 NumPy
15.3 Pandas
15.4 Exploratory data analysis
15.5 Data visualization
15.6 Summary

Introduction

Data Science provides the ability to derive insights and make informed decisions from data. Data science helps people make decisions in disciplines as diverse as healthcare, business, education, politics, environmental science, and social sciences.

This chapter aims to provide an introduction to the field of data science and the data science life cycle. The resources provided in this chapter are meant to guide readers using Python to further explore data science.

15.1 Introduction to data science

Learning objectives

By the end of this section you should be able to

- Describe data science.
- Identify different stages of the data science life cycle.
- Name data science tools and software.
- Use Google Colaboratory to run code.

Data science life cycle

Data science is a multidisciplinary field that combines collecting, processing, and analyzing large volumes of data to extract insights and drive informed decision-making. The **data science life cycle** is the framework followed by data scientists to complete a data science project. The data science life cycle is an iterative process that starts with data acquisition, followed by data exploration. The data acquisition stage may involve obtaining data from a source or collecting data through surveys and other means of data collection that are domain-specific. During the data exploration stage, data scientists will ensure that the data are in the right format for the data analysis stage through data cleanup and they may also visualize the data for further inspection. Once the data are cleaned, data scientists can perform data analysis, which is shared with stakeholders using reports and presentations. The **data analysis** stage involves using data to generate insights or make a predictive model. Data science is increasingly being adopted in many different fields, such as healthcare, economics, education, and social sciences, to name a few. The animation below demonstrates different stages of the data science life cycle.

CHECKPOINT

Data science life cycle

Access multimedia content (https://openstax.org/books/introduction-python-programming/pages/15-1-introduction-to-data-science)

CONCEPTS IN PRACTICE

What is data science?

1. What is the first stage of any data science life cycle?
    a. data visualization
    b. data cleanup
    c. data acquisition

2. How many stages does the data science life cycle have?
    a. 3
    b. 4
    c. 5

3. What does a data scientist do in the data exploration stage?
    a. document insights and visualization
    b. analyze data
    c. data cleaning and visualization

Data science tools

Several tools and software are commonly used in data science. Here are some examples.

- Python programming language: Python is widely used in data science. It has a large system of libraries designed for data analysis, machine learning, and visualization. Some popular Python libraries for data science include NumPy, Pandas, Matplotlib, Seaborn, and scikit-learn. In this chapter, you will explore some of these libraries.
- R programming language: R is commonly used in statistical computing and data analysis, and it offers a wide range of packages and libraries tailored for data manipulation, statistical modeling, and visualization.
- Jupyter Notebook/JupyterLab: **Jupyter Notebook** and **JupyterLab** are web-based interactive computing environments that support multiple programming languages, including Python and R. They allow a

programmer to create documents that contain code, visualizations, and text, making them suitable for data exploration, analysis, and reporting.
- Google Colaboratory: **Google Colaboratory** is a cloud-based Jupyter Notebook environment that allows a programmer to write, run, and share Python code online. In this chapter, you will use Google Colaboratory to practice data science concepts.
- Kaggle Kernels: **Kaggle Kernels** is an online data science platform that provides a collaborative environment for building and running code. Kaggle Kernels support Python and R and offers access to datasets, pre-installed libraries, and computational resources. Kaggle also hosts data science competitions and provides a platform for sharing and discovering data science projects.
- Excel/Sheets: **Microsoft Excel** and **Google Sheets** are widely used spreadsheet applications that offer basic data analysis and visualization capabilities. They can help beginners get started with data manipulation, basic statistical calculations, and simple visualizations.

CHECKPOINT

Google Colaboratory ecosystem

Access multimedia content (https://openstax.org/books/introduction-python-programming/pages/15-1-introduction-to-data-science)

CONCEPTS IN PRACTICE

Data science tools and software

4. Between Python, R, and Java, which is the most popular language in data science?
    a. Python
    b. R
    c. Java

5. Which of the following is a data science-related library in Python?
    a. list
    b. NumPy
    c. array

6. Google Colaboratory can be used for reporting and sharing insights.
    a. true
    b. false

Programming practice with Google

Open the Google Colaboratory document below. To open the Colaboratory document, you need to login to a Google account, if you have one, or create a Google account. Run all cells. You may also attempt creating new cells or modifying existing cells. To save a copy of your edits, go to "File > Save a Copy in Drive", and the edited file will be stored in your own Google Drive.

Google Colaboratory document (https://openstax.org/r/100colabdoc)

15.2 NumPy

Learning objectives

By the end of this section you should be able to

- Describe the NumPy library.
- Create a NumPy array object.
- Choose appropriate NumPy functions to process arrays of numerical data.

NumPy library

NumPy (Numerical Python) is a Python library that provides support for efficient numerical operations on large, multi-dimensional arrays and serves as a fundamental building block for data analysis in Python. The conventional alias for importing NumPy is np. In other words, NumPy is imported as `import numpy as np`. NumPy implements the **ndarray** object, which allows the creation of a multi-dimensional array of homogeneous data types (columns with the same data type) and efficient data processing. An ndarray object can have any number of dimensions and can store elements of various numeric data types. To create a NumPy ndarray object, one of the following options can be used:

- Creating an ndarray by converting a Python list or tuple using the `np.array()` function.
- Using built-in functions like `np.zeros()` and `np.ones()` for creating an array of all 0's or all 1's, respectively.
- Generating an array with random numbers using `np.random.rand(n, m)`, where n and m are the number of rows and columns, respectively.
- Loading data from a file. Ex: `np.genfromtxt('data.csv', delimiter=',')`.

CHECKPOINT

Creating an ndarray object

Access multimedia content (https://openstax.org/books/introduction-python-programming/pages/15-2-numpy)

CONCEPTS IN PRACTICE

NumPy library

1. Which of the following creates an ndarray object with one row and two columns?
   a. `np.array([2, 3])`
   b. `np.zeros(1, 2)`
   c. `np.zeros((1, 2))`

2. Which of the following is a NumPy data type?
   a. `ndarray`
   b. `list`
   c. `array`

3. What is the benefit of using an `ndarray` object compared to a list?
   a. computational efficiency

b. array-oriented computing
c. memory efficiency
d. all the above

NumPy operations

In addition to the ndarray data type, NumPy's operations provide optimized performance for large-scale computation. The key features of NumPy include:

- Mathematical operations: NumPy provides a range of mathematical functions and operations that can be applied to entire arrays or specific elements. These operations include arithmetic, trigonometric, exponential, and logarithmic functions.
- Array manipulation: NumPy provides various functions to manipulate the shape, size, and structure of arrays. These include reshaping, transposing, concatenating, splitting, and adding or removing elements from arrays.
- Linear algebra operations: NumPy offers a set of linear algebra functions for matrix operations, like matrix multiplication, matrix inversion, eigenvalues, and eigenvectors.

CHECKPOINT

NumPy array operations

Access multimedia content (https://openstax.org/books/introduction-python-programming/pages/15-2-numpy)

CONCEPTS IN PRACTICE

NumPy operations

4. What is the output of the following code?

   ```
   import numpy as np

   arr = np.array([[1, 2], [3, 4]])
   out = 2 * arr
   print(out)
   ```

   a. [[2 4]
       [8 16]]
   b. [[2 4]
       [6 8]]
   c. [[1 2]
       [3 4]]

5. Which of the following results in a 2 by 3 ndarray?
   a. ```
      import numpy as np
      arr = np.array(2, 3)
      ```
   b. ```
      import numpy as np
      ```

```
       arr = np.array([[1, 2], [1, 2], [1, 2]])
    c. import numpy as np
       arr = np.array([[1, 2], [1, 2], [1, 2]]).T
```

6. The function np.multiply(arr1, arr2) receives two ndarray objects arr1 and arr2 with the same dimensions, and performs element-wise multiplication. What is the output of the following code?

```
import numpy as np

arr1 = np.array([[1, 2], [3, 4]])
arr2 = np.array([[1, 0], [0, 1]])
out = np.multiply(arr1, arr2)
print(out)
```

   a. [[1 0]
       [0 4]]
   b. [[1 2]
       [3 4]]
   c. [[2 2]
       [3 5]]

> **EXPLORING FURTHER**
>
> Please refer to the NumPy user guide for more information about the NumPy library.
>
> - NumPy User Guide (https://openstax.org/r/100numpyguide)

Programming practice with Google

Use the Google Colaboratory document below to practice NumPy functionalities to extract statistical insights from a dataset.

Google Colaboratory document (https://openstax.org/r/100numpycolab)

15.3 Pandas

Learning objectives

By the end of this section you should be able to

- Describe the Pandas library.
- Create a DataFrame and a Series object.
- Choose appropriate Pandas functions to gain insight from heterogeneous data.

Pandas library

Pandas is an open-source Python library used for data cleaning, processing, and analysis. Pandas provides data structures and data analysis tools to analyze structured data efficiently. The name "Pandas" is derived from the term "panel data," which refers to multidimensional structured datasets. Key features of Pandas include:

- Data structure: Pandas implements two main data structures:
    - Series: A **Series** is a one-dimensional labeled array.
    - DataFrame: A **DataFrame** is a two-dimensional labeled data structure that consists of columns and rows. A DataFrame can be thought of as a spreadsheet-like data structure where each column represents a Series. DataFrame is a heterogeneous data structure where each column can have a different data type.
- Data processing functionality: Pandas provides various functionalities for data processing, such as data selection, filtering, slicing, sorting, merging, joining, and reshaping.
- Integration with other libraries: Pandas integrates well with other Python libraries, such as NumPy. The integration capability allows for data exchange between different data analysis and visualization tools.

The conventional alias for importing Pandas is pd. In other words, Pandas is imported as `import pandas as pd`. Examples of DataFrame and Series objects are shown below.

DataFrame example				Series example	
	Name	Age	City	0	Emma
0	Emma	15	Dubai	1	Gireeja
1	Gireeja	28	London	2	Sophia
2	Sophia	22	San Jose	dtype:	object

Table 15.1

Data input and output

A DataFrame can be created from a dictionary, list, NumPy array, or a CSV file. Column names and column data types can be specified at the time of DataFrame instantiation.

Description	Example	Output			Explanation

DataFrame from a dictionary	`import pandas as pd`
	
	`# Create a dictionary of columns`
	`data = {`
	`  "Name": ["Emma", "Gireeja", "Sophia"],`
	`  "Age": [15, 28, 22],`
	`  "City": ["Dubai", "London", "San Jose"]`
	`}`
	
	`# Create a DataFrame from the dictionary`
	`df = pd.DataFrame(data)`
	
	`# Display the DataFrame`
	`df`
			Name	Age	City	The `pd.DataFrame()` function takes in a dictionary and converts it into a DataFrame. Dictionary keys will be column labels and values are stored in respective columns.

		0	Emma	15	Dubai	
		1	Gireeja	28	London	
		2	Sophia	22	San Jose	

DataFrame from a list	`import pandas as pd`
	
	`# Create a list of rows`
	`data = [`
	`  ["Emma", 15, "Dubai"],`
	`  ["Gireeja", 28, "London"],`
	`  ["Sophia", 22, "San Jose"]`
	`]`
	
	`# Define column labels`
	`columns = ["Name", "Age", "City"]`
	
	`# Create a DataFrame from list using column labels`
	`df = pd.DataFrame(data, columns=columns)`
	
	`# Display the DataFrame`
	`df`
			Name	Age	City	The `pd.DataFrame()` function takes in a list containing the records in different rows of a DataFrame, along with a list of column labels, and creates a DataFrame with the given rows and column labels.

		0	Emma	15	Dubai	
		1	Gireeja	28	London	
		2	Sophia	22	San Jose	

Table 15.2 DataFrame creation.

Description	Example	Output	Explanation
| DataFrame from a NumPy array | ```python
import numpy as np
import pandas as pd

# Create a NumPy array
data = np.array([
  [1, 0, 0],
  [0, 1, 0],
  [2, 3, 4]
])

# Define column labels
columns = ["A", "B", "C"]

# Create a DataFrame from the NumPy array
df = pd.DataFrame(data, columns=columns)

# Display the DataFrame
df
``` | |   | A | B | C |
|---|---|---|---|
0	1	0	0
1	0	1	0
2	2	3	4		A NumPy array, along with column labels, are passed to the pd.DataFrame() function to create a DataFrame object.

Table 15.2 DataFrame creation.
```

Description	Example	Output	Explanation

DataFrame from a CSV file	`import pandas as pd`
	
	`# Read the CSV file into a DataFrame`
	`df = pd.read_csv("data.csv")`
	
	`# Display the DataFrame`
	`df`
		The content of the CSV file will be printed in a tabular format.	The pd.read_csv() function reads a CSV file into a DataFrame and organizes the content in a tabular format.

DataFrame from a Excel file	`import pandas as pd`
	
	`# Read the Excel file into a DataFrame`
	`df = pd.read_excel("data.xlsx")`
	
	`# Display the DataFrame`
	`df`
		The content of the Excel file will be printed in a tabular format.	The pd.read_excel() function reads an Excel file into a DataFrame and organizes the content in a tabular format.

Table 15.2 DataFrame creation.

CONCEPTS IN PRACTICE

Pandas basics

1. Which of the following is a Pandas data structure?
    a. Series
    b. dictionary
    c. list

2. A DataFrame object can be considered as a collection of Series objects.
    a. true
    b. false

3. What are the benefits of Pandas over NumPy?
    a. Pandas provides integration with other libraries.
    b. Pandas supports heterogeneous data whereas NumPy supports homogenous numerical data.
    c. Pandas supports both one-dimensional and two-dimensional data structures.

Pandas for data manipulation and analysis

The Pandas library provides functions and techniques to explore, manipulate, and gain insights from the data. Key DataFrame functions that analyze this code are described in the following table.

```
import pandas as pd
import numpy as np

# Create a sample DataFrame
days = {
    'Season': ['Summer', 'Summer', 'Fall', 'Winter', 'Fall', 'Winter'],
    'Month': ['July', 'June', 'September', 'January', 'October', 'February'],
    'Month-day': [1, 12, 3, 7, 20, 28],
    'Year': [2000, 1990, 2020, 1998, 2001, 2022]
}
df = pd.DataFrame(days)
```

	Season	Month	Month-day	Year
0	Summer	July	1	2000
1	Summer	June	12	1990
2	Fall	September	3	2020
3	Winter	January	7	1998
4	Fall	October	20	2001
5	Winter	February	28	2022

Table 15.3

Function name	Explanation	Example	Output
`head(n)`	Returns the first n rows. If a value is not passed, the first 5 rows will be shown.	`df.head(4)`	<table><tr><th></th><th>Season</th><th>Month</th><th>Month-day</th><th>Year</th></tr><tr><td>0</td><td>Summer</td><td>July</td><td>1</td><td>2000</td></tr><tr><td>1</td><td>Summer</td><td>June</td><td>12</td><td>1990</td></tr><tr><td>2</td><td>Fall</td><td>September</td><td>3</td><td>2020</td></tr><tr><td>3</td><td>Winter</td><td>January</td><td>7</td><td>1998</td></tr></table>
`tail(n)`	Returns the last n rows. If a value is not passed, the last 5 rows will be shown.	`df.tail(3)`	<table><tr><th></th><th>Season</th><th>Month</th><th>Month-day</th><th>Year</th></tr><tr><td>3</td><td>Winter</td><td>January</td><td>7</td><td>1998</td></tr><tr><td>4</td><td>Fall</td><td>October</td><td>20</td><td>2001</td></tr><tr><td>5</td><td>Winter</td><td>February</td><td>28</td><td>2022</td></tr></table>
`info()`	Provides a summary of the DataFrame, including the column names, data types, and the number of non-null values. The function also returns the DataFrame's memory usage.	`df.info()`	``` <class 'pandas.core.frame.DataFrame'> RangeIndex: 6 entries, 0 to 5 Data columns (total 4 columns): # Column Non-Null Count Dtype --- ------ -------------- ----- 0 Season 6 non-null object 1 Month 6 non-null object 2 Month-day 6 non-null int64 3 Year 6 non-null int64 dtypes: int64(2), object(2) memory usage: 320.0+ bytes ```

Table 15.4 DataFrame functions.

Function name	Explanation	Example	Output		
describe()	Generates the column count, mean, standard deviation, minimum, maximum, and quartiles.	df.describe()		Month-day	Year
			count	6.000000	6.000000
			mean	11.833333	2005.166667
			std	10.457852	12.875040
			min	1.000000	1990.000000
			25%	4.000000	1998.500000
			50%	9.500000	2000.500000
			75%	18.000000	2015.250000
			max	28.000000	2022.000000
value_counts()	Counts the occurrences of unique values in a column when a column is passed as an argument and presents them in descending order.	df.value_counts \('Season')	Season Fall 2 Summer 2 Winter 2 dtype: int64		
unique()	Returns an array of unique values in a column when called on a column.	df['Season'] \.unique()	['Summer' 'Fall' 'Winter']		

Table 15.4 DataFrame functions.

> **CONCEPTS IN PRACTICE**
>
> DataFrame operations
>
> 4. Which of the following returns the top five rows of a DataFrame?
>   a. `df.head()`
>   b. `df.head(5)`
>   c. both
>
> 5. What does the `unique()` function do in a DataFrame when applied to a column?
>   a. returns the number of unique columns
>   b. returns the number of unique values in the given column
>   c. returns the unique values in the given column
>
> 6. Which function generates statistical information of columns with numerical data types?
>   a. `describe()`
>   b. `info()`
>   c. `unique()`

> **EXPLORING FURTHER**
>
> Please refer to the Pandas user guide for more information about the Pandas library.
>
> - Pandas User Guide (https://openstax.org/r/100pandaguide)

Programming practice with Google

Use the Google Colaboratory document below to practice Pandas functionalities to extract insights from a dataset.

Google Colaboratory document (https://openstax.org/r/100googlecolab)

15.4 Exploratory data analysis

Learning objectives

By the end of this section you should be able to

- Describe exploratory data analysis.
- Inspect DataFrame entries through appropriate indexing.
- Use filtering and slicing to obtain a subset of a DataFrame.
- Identify `Null` values in a DataFrame.
- Remove or replace `Null` values in a DataFrame.

Exploratory data analysis

Exploratory Data Analysis (EDA) is the task of analyzing data to gain insights, identify patterns, and understand the underlying structure of the data. During EDA, data scientists visually and statistically examine data to uncover relationships, anomalies, and trends, and to generate hypotheses for further analysis. The main goal of EDA is to become familiar with the data and assess the quality of the data. Once data are understood and cleaned, data scientists may perform feature creation and hypothesis formation. A **feature** is an individual variable or attribute that is calculated from the raw data in the dataset.

Data indexing can be used to select and access specific rows and columns. Data indexing is essential in examining a dataset. In Pandas, two types of indexing methods exist:

- Label-based indexing using `loc[]`: **loc[]** allows you to access data in a DataFrame using row/column labels. Ex: `df.loc[row_label, column_label]` returns specific data at the intersection of `row_label` and `column_label`.
- Integer-based indexing using `iloc[]`: **iloc[]** allows you to access data in a DataFrame using integer-based indexes. Integer indexes can be passed to retrieve specific data. Ex: `df.iloc[row_index, column_index]` returns specific data at the index `row_index` and `column_index`.

CHECKPOINT

Indexing a DataFrame

Access multimedia content (https://openstax.org/books/introduction-python-programming/pages/15-4-exploratory-data-analysis)

CONCEPTS IN PRACTICE

DataFrame indexing

Given the following code, respond to the questions below.

```
import pandas as pd

# Create sample data
data = {
    "A": ["a", "b", "c", "d"],
    "B": [12, 20, 5, -10],
    "C": ["C", "C", "C", "C"]
}

df = pd.DataFrame(data)
```

1. What is the output of `print(df.iloc[0, 0])`?
   a. a
   b. b
   c. IndexError

2. What is the output of `print(df.iloc[1, 1])`?
   a. a
   b. b
   c. 20

3. What is the output of `print(df.loc[2, 'A'])`?
   a. c
   b. C

c. b

Data slicing and filtering

Data slicing and filtering involve selecting specific subsets of data based on certain conditions or index/label ranges. **Data slicing** refers to selecting a subset of rows and/or columns from a DataFrame. Slicing can be performed using ranges, lists, or Boolean conditions.

- Slicing using ranges: Ex: df.loc[start_row:end_row, start_column:end_column] selects rows and columns within the specified ranges.
- Slicing using a list: Ex: df.loc[[label1, label2, ...], :] selects rows that are in the list [label1, label2, ...] and includes all columns since all columns are selected by the colon operator.
- Slicing based on a condition: df[condition] selects only the rows that meet the given condition.

Data filtering involves selecting rows or columns based on certain conditions. Ex: In the expression df[df['column_name'] > threshold], the DataFrame df is filtered using the selection operator ([]) and the condition(df['column_name'] > threshold) that is passed. All entries in the DataFrame df where the corresponding value in the DataFrame is True will be returned.

CHECKPOINT

Indexing on a flight dataset

Access multimedia content (https://openstax.org/books/introduction-python-programming/pages/15-4-exploratory-data-analysis)

CONCEPTS IN PRACTICE

DataFrame slicing and filtering

Given the following code, respond to the questions.

```
import pandas as pd

# Create sample data
data = {
  "A": [1, 2, 3, 4],
  "B": [5, 6, 7, 8],
  "C": [9, 10, 11, 12]
}

df = pd.DataFrame(data)
```

4. Which of the following returns the first three rows of column A?
   a. df.loc[1:3, "A"]
   b. df.loc[0:2, "A"]
   c. df.loc[0:3, "A"]

5. Which of the following returns the second row?
   a. df.iloc[2]
   b. df[2]
   c. df.loc[1]

6. Which of the following returns the first column?
   a. df.loc[0, :]
   b. df.iloc[:, 0]
   c. df.loc["A"]

7. Which of the following results in selecting the second and fourth rows of the DataFrame?
   a. df[df.loc[:, "A"] % 2 == 0]
   b. df[df[:, "A"] % 2 == 0]
   c. df[df.loc["A"] % 2 == 0]

Handling missing data

Missing values in a dataset can occur when data are not available or are not recorded properly. Identifying and removing missing values is an important step in data cleaning and preprocessing. A data scientist should consider ethical considerations throughout the EDA process, especially when handling missing data. They might consider answering questions such as "Why are the data missing?", "Whose data are missing?", and "Considering the missing data, is the dataset still a representative sample of the population under study?". The functions below are useful in understanding and analyzing missing data.

- isnull(): The isnull() function can be used to identify Null entries in a DataFrame. The return value of the function is a Boolean DataFrame, with the same dimensions as the original DataFrame with True values where missing values exist.
- dropna(): The dropna() function can be used to drop rows with Null values.
- fillna(): The fillna() function can be used to replace Null values with a provided substitute value. Ex: df.fillna(df.mean()) replaces all Null values with the average value of the specific column.

To define a Null value in a DataFrame, you can use the np.nan value from the NumPy library. Functions that aid in identifying and removing null entries are described in the table below the following code.

```python
import pandas as pd
import numpy as np

# Create sample data
data = {
  "Column 1": ["A", "B", "C", "D", "E"],
  "Column 2": [np.NAN, 200, 500, 0, -10],
  "Column 3": [True, True, False, np.NaN, np.NaN]
}

df = pd.DataFrame(data)
```

	Column 1	Column 2	Column 3
0	A	NaN	True
1	B	200.0	True
2	C	500.0	False
3	D	0.0	NaN
4	E	-10.0	NaN

Table 15.5

Function	Example	Output				Explanation
isnull()	df.isnull()		Column 1	Column 2	Column 3	The df.isnull() function returns a Boolean array with Boolean values representing whether each entry is Null.
		0	False	True	False	
		1	False	False	False	
		2	False	False	False	
		3	False	False	True	
		4	False	False	True	
fillna()	df["Column 2"] =\ df["Column 2"].fillna(df["Column 2"] .mean())		Column 1	Column 2	Column 3	Null values in Column 2 are replaced with the mean of non-Null values in the column.
		0	A	172.5	True	
		1	B	200.0	True	
		2	C	500.0	False	
		3	D	0.0	NaN	
		4	E	-10.0	NaN	
dropna()	# Applied after the run # of the previous row df = df.dropna()		Column 1	Column 2	Column 3	All rows containing a Null value are removed from the DataFrame.
		0	A	172.5	True	
		1	B	200.0	True	
		2	C	500.0	False	

Table 15.6 Null identification and removal examples.

> **CONCEPTS IN PRACTICE**
>
> Missing value treatment
>
> 8. Which of the following is used to check the DataFrame for Null values?
>   a. isnan()
>   b. isnull()
>   c. isnone()
>
> 9. Assuming that a DataFrame df is given, which of the following replaces Null values with zeros?
>   a. df.fillna(0)
>   b. df.replacena(0)
>   c. df.fill(0)
>
> 10. Assuming that a DataFrame df is given, what does the expression df.isnull().sum() do?
>   a. Calculates sum of the non-Null values in each column
>   b. Calculates the number of Null values in the DataFrame
>   c. Calculates the number of Null values in each column

Programming practice with Google

Use the Google Colaboratory document below to practice EDA on a given dataset.

Google Colaboratory document (https://openstax.org/r/100edapractice)

15.5 Data visualization

Learning objectives

By the end of this section you should be able to

- Explain why visualization has an important role in data science.
- Choose appropriate visualization for a given task.
- Use Python visualization libraries to create data visualization.

Why visualization?

Data visualization has a crucial role in data science for understanding the data. Data visualization can be used in all steps of the data science life cycle to facilitate data exploration, identify anomalies, understand relationships and trends, and produce reports. Several visualization types are commonly used:

Visualization type	Description	Benefits/common usage
Bar plot	Rectangular bars	Compare values across different categories.
Line plot	A series of data points connected by line segments	Visualize trends and changes.

Table 15.7 Common visualization types.

Visualization type	Description	Benefits/common usage
Scatter plot	Individual data points representing the relationship between two variables	Identify correlations, clusters, and outliers.
Histogram plot	Rectangular bars representing the distribution of a continuous variable by dividing the variable's range into bins and representing the frequency or count of data within each bin	Summarizing the distribution of the data.
Box plot	Rectangular box with whiskers that summarize the distribution of a continuous variable, including the median, quartiles, and outliers	Summarizing the distribution of the data and comparing different variables.

Table 15.7 Common visualization types.

CHECKPOINT

Visualization types

Access multimedia content (https://openstax.org/books/introduction-python-programming/pages/15-5-data-visualization)

CONCEPTS IN PRACTICE

Comparing visualization methods

1. Which of the following plot types is best suited for comparing the distribution of a continuous variable?
    a. scatter plot
    b. histogram plot
    c. line plot

2. Which of the following plot types is best suited for visualizing outliers and quartiles of a continuous variable?
    a. histogram plot
    b. bar plot
    c. box plot

3. Which of the following plot types is effective for displaying trends and changes over time?
    a. line plot
    b. bar plot
    c. histogram plot

Data visualization tools

Many Python data visualization libraries exist that offer a range of capabilities and features to create different plot types. Some of the most commonly used frameworks are Matplotlib, Plotly, and Seaborn. Here, some useful functionalities of `Matplotlib` are summarized.

Plot type	Method
Bar plot	The `plt.bar(x, height)` function takes in two inputs, x and height, and plots bars for each x value with the height given in the height variable.
Example	**Output**
| ```
import matplotlib.pyplot as plt

# Data
categories = ["Course A", "Course B", "Course C"]
values = [25, 40, 30]

# Create the bar chart
fig = plt.bar(categories, values)

# Customize the chart
plt.title("Number of students in each course')
plt.xlabel("Courses")
plt.ylabel("Number of students")

# Display the chart
plt.show()
``` | A bar chart titled "Number of Students in Each Course" with Course A at 25, Course B at 40, and Course C at 30. |

Table 15.8 Matplotlib functionalities. Bar plot.
```

Plot type	Method
Line plot	The `plt.plot(x, y)` function takes in two inputs, x and y, and plots lines connecting pairs of (x, y) values.
Example	**Output**

| ```python
import matplotlib.pyplot as plt

# Data
month = ["Jan", "Feb", "Mar", "Apr", "May"]
inflation = [6.41, 6.04, 4.99, 4.93, 4.05]

# Create the line chart
plt.plot(month, inflation,
marker="o",
linestyle="-",
color="blue")

# Customize the chart
plt.title("Inflation trend in 2023")
plt.xlabel("Month")
plt.ylabel("Inflation")

# Display the chart
plt.show()
``` | Inflation Trend in 2023 line chart showing inflation decreasing from 6.41 in Jan to 4.05 in May. |

Table 15.9 Matplotlib functionalities. Line plot.
```

Plot type	Method
Scatter plot	The `plt.scatter(x, y)` function takes in two inputs, x and y, and plots points representing `(x, y)` pairs.
Example	**Output**
| ```
import matplotlib.pyplot as plt

# Data
x = [1, 2, 3, 4, 5, 6, 7, 8, 9, 10]
y = [10, 8, 6, 4, 2, 5, 7, 9, 3, 1]

# Create the scatter plot
plt.scatter(x, y, marker="o", color="blue")

# Customize the chart
plt.title("Scatter Plot Example")
plt.xlabel("X")
plt.ylabel("Y")

# Display the chart
plt.show()
``` | (Scatter Plot Example chart) |

Table 15.10 Matplotlib functionalities. Scatter plot.
```

Plot type	Method
Histogram plot	The `plt.hist(x)` function takes in one input, x, and plots a histogram of values in x to show distribution or trend.
Example	**Output**

| ```python
import matplotlib.pyplot as plt
import numpy as np

# Data: random 1000 samples
data = np.random.randn(1000)

# Create the histogram
plt.hist(data, bins=30, edgecolor="black")

# Customize the chart
plt.title("Histogram of random values")
plt.xlabel("Values")
plt.ylabel("Frequency")

# Display the chart
plt.show()
``` | *Histogram of Random Values — bell-shaped distribution centered near 0, ranging from -4 to 3, frequency up to ~100.* |

Table 15.11 Matplotlib functionalities. Histogram plot.
```

Plot type	Method
Box plot	The `plt.boxplot(x)` function takes in one input, x, and represents minimum, maximum, first, second, and third quartiles, as well as outliers in x.
Example	**Output**
``‍`python
import matplotlib.pyplot as plt
import numpy as np

# Data: random 100 samples
data = [np.random.normal(0, 5, 100)]

# Create the box plot
plt.boxplot(data)

# Customize the chart
plt.title("Box Plot of random values")
plt.xlabel("Data Distribution")
plt.ylabel("Values")

# Display the chart
plt.show()
``‍` | Box Plot of Random Values |

Table 15.12 Matplotlib functionalities. Box plot.

CONCEPTS IN PRACTICE

Matplotlib methods

4. Given the following code, which of the function calls is appropriate in showing association between x and y?

```
import matplotlib.pyplot as plt

# Data
```

```
x = [1, 2, 3, 4, 5]
y = [10, 15, 12, 18, 20]
```

a. `plt.boxplot(x)`
b. `plt.hist(y)`
c. `plt.scatter(x, y)`

5. What is being plotted using the code below?

```
import matplotlib.pyplot as plt

# Data
categories = ['A', 'B', 'C', 'D']
values = [10, 15, 12, 18]
plt.bar(categories, values)
```

a. a histogram plot
b. a bar plot
c. a line plot

6. Which library in Python is more commonly used for creating interactive visualizations?
a. Matplotlib
b. Plotly
c. Pandas

EXPLORING FURTHER

Please refer to the following user guide for more information about the Matplotlib, Plotly, and Seaborn libraries.

- Matplotlib User Guide (https://openstax.org/r/100matplotguide)
- Plotly User Guide (https://openstax.org/r/100plotlyguide)
- Seaborn User Guide (https://openstax.org/r/100seabornguide)

Programming practice with Google

Use the Google Colaboratory document below to practice a visualization task on a given dataset.

Google Colaboratory document (https://openstax.org/r/100visualization)

15.6 Summary

Highlights from this chapter include:

- Data science is a multidisciplinary field that combines collection, processing, and analysis of large volumes of data to extract insights and drive informed decision-making.
- The data science life cycle is the framework followed by data scientists to complete a data science project.
- The data science life cycle includes 1) data acquisition, 2) data exploration, 3) data analysis, and 4) reporting.

- Google Colaboratory is a cloud-based Jupyter Notebook environment that allows programmers to write, run, and share Python code online.
- NumPy (Numerical Python) is a Python library that provides support for efficient numerical operations on large, multi-dimensional arrays and serves as a fundamental building block for data analysis in Python.
- NumPy implements an ndarray object that allows the creation of multi-dimensional arrays of homogeneous data types and efficient data processing.
- NumPy provides functionalities for mathematical operations, array manipulation, and linear algebra operations.
- Pandas is an open-source Python library used for data cleaning, processing, and analysis.
- Pandas provides Series and DataFrame data structures, data processing functionality, and integration with other libraries.
- Exploratory Data Analysis (EDA) is the task of analyzing data to gain insights, identify patterns, and understand the underlying structure of the data.
- A feature is an individual variable or attribute that is calculated from raw data in a dataset.
- Data indexing can be used to select and access specific rows and columns.
- Data slicing refers to selecting a subset of rows and/or columns from a DataFrame.
- Data filtering involves selecting rows or columns based on certain conditions.
- Missing values in a dataset can occur when data are not available or were not recorded properly.
- Data visualization has a crucial role in data science for understanding the data.
- Different types of visualizations include bar plot, line plot, scatter plot, histogram plot, and box plot.
- Several Python data visualization libraries exist that offer a range of capabilities and features to create different plot types. These libraries include Matplotlib, Seaborn, and Plotly.
- The conventional aliases for importing NumPy, Pandas, and Matplotlib.pyplot are np, pd, and plt, respectively.

At this point, you should be able to write programs to create data structures to store different datasets and explore and visualize datasets.

Function	Description
np.array()	Creates an ndarray from a list or tuple.
np.zeros()	Creates an array of zeros.
np.ones()	Creates an array of ones.
np.random.rand(n, m)	Creates an array of random numbers with n rows and m columns
np.genfromtxt('data.csv', delimiter=',')	Creates an array from a CSV file.
pd.DataFrame()	Creates a DataFrame from a list, dictionary, or an array.
pd.read_csv()	Creates a DataFrame from a CSV file.

Table 15.13 Chapter 15 reference.

Function	Description
df.head()	Returns the first few rows of a DataFrame.
df.tail()	Returns the last few rows of a DataFrame.
df.info()	Provides a summary of the DataFrame, including the column names, data types, and the number of non-Null values.
df.describe()	Generates the column count, mean, standard deviation, minimum, maximum, and quartiles.
df.value_counts()	Counts the occurrences of unique values in a column and presents them in descending order.
df.unique()	Returns an array of unique values in a column.
loc[]	Allows for accessing data in a DataFrame using row/column labels.
iloc[]	Allows for accessing data in a DataFrame using row/column integer-based indexes.
df[condition]	Selects only the rows that meet the given condition.
df.loc[start_row:end_row, start_column:end_column]	Slices using label ranges.
df.loc[[label1, label2, ...], :]	Slices rows that are in the list [label1, label2, ...].
df.isnull()	Returns a Boolean array with Boolean values representing whether each entry has been Null.
fillna()	Replaces Null values.
dropna()	Removes all rows containing a Null value.
plt.bar(x, height)	Takes in two inputs, x and height, and plots bars for each x value with the height given in the height variable.
plt.plot(x, y)	Takes in two inputs, x and y, and plots lines connecting pairs of (x, y) values.

Table 15.13 Chapter 15 reference.

Function	Description
`plt.scatter(x, y)`	Takes in two inputs, x and y, and plots points representing (x, y) pairs.
`plt.hist(x)`	Takes in one input, x, and plots a histogram of values in x to show distribution or trend.
`plt.boxplot(x)`	Takes in one input, x, and represents minimum, maximum, first, second, and third quartiles, as well as outliers in x.

Table 15.13 Chapter 15 reference.

Answer Key
Chapter 1
1.1 Background

1. b. Each image in the animation represents a different type of computer program.
2. a. This type of analysis requires basic knowledge of programming.
3. c. Like mobile apps, wi-fi speakers run small programs that connect to servers.
4. b. This book assumes readers understand the basics of algebra, but nothing too difficult.
5. c. Python's syntax is more concise than Java's.
6. a. Python does not require a semicolon at the end of each line. Braces are also not required.

1.2 Input/output

1. c. The hello world program is just one line of code.
2. c. The end="" option removes the newline character after hello, producing Hello world! on the same line.
3. c. The default space character that separates multiple items has been replaced with the dash character.
4. c. The user input is stored in memory and can be referenced using today_is.
5. b. The print() function outputs "You entered:" followed by a space character, followed by the input data, Sophia, which is referenced by the variable name.
6. a. The input is stored exactly as the user enters the input. So, the retrieved value is displayed exactly as entered by the user.

1.3 Variables

1. c. This would produce the output string, "The city where you live is Chicago".
2. b. These two lines of code would produce the output string, "Total = 6".
3. c. The single = character is the assignment operator.
4. a. An assignment statement has the variable name on the left side and the value on the right side of the assignment statement.
5. a. median is a descriptive name for a variable that stores a median value.
6. b. A variable name can contain, but not start with, a digit.
7. c. The name clearly indicates the value being stored is a zip code.
8. a. Snake case separates each word with an underscore and uses only lowercase letters.

1.4 String basics

1. c. A string that is enclosed by matching double quotes is a valid string. Note that '7 days' is also a string.
2. c. The string, fred78@gmail.com, is enclosed in matching double quotes, and is assigned to the variable email. A string can contain characters such as "@" or "." in addition to letters and numbers.
3. c. The string has matching double quotes. Since a single quote is a part of this string, double quotes must be used.
4. c. Note that the enclosing single quotes (') are not part of the string but the double quotes (") are.
5. c. The len() function returns the number of characters in the string. 6 characters exist in "Hi Ali" which are "H", "i", " ", "A", "l", and "i".
6. b. The length of an empty string equals 0.
7. b. The number_of_digits variable's value is 2, and as such, the output is "Number 12 has 2 digits.".
8. c. The 1 and 0 are enclosed in quotes indicating valid strings, and the + is not, indicating a concatenation operation. Thus, the string "10" is produced. Note that concatenation operator does not include any default separator characters like the space character.

9. c. `"A"` and `"wake"` are valid strings, and the + is not enclosed in quotes, indicating a concatenation operation. Thus the string `"Awake"` is produced. Note that the concatenation operator does not include any default separator characters like the space character.
10. c. Note that space characters must be explicitly included when using the concatenation operator.
11. c. A concatenation of the two strings is assigned to the variable `holiday`. Note that `"one-sided"` would assign the same string to `holiday`.

1.5 Number basics

1. c. `x = 1` is an integer, and when printing the type of an integer variable, the output is `<class 'int'>`.
2. b. `y = 2.0` is floating-point number.
3. a. Any value defined within quotation marks is a string value regardless of the content.
4. c. Line 2 of the code evaluates as follows: `c = x - z = 7 - 2 = 5`. Line 3 increments variable c by 1, making the total equal to 6.
5. b. The output of `3.5-1.5` equals `2.0`, which is a floating-point number.
6. c. The result of the division operation is a floating-point number that isn't rounded down. `7/2 = 3.5`.
7. c. The output of the `20/2` equals `10.0` because the division operation results in a float.
8. c. The output of an arithmetic operator on any floating-point operand results in a floating-point value. `2 * 1.5 = 3.0`.
9. a. 3 raised to the power 2 is 9, times 4 is 36, plus 1 is 37.
10. b. Although addition has lower precedence than exponentiation, the parentheses cause `1 + 3` to be evaluated first.
11. a. In Python, exponentiation, or raising to a power, has higher precedence than making a value negative. Python's `-16` result can be confusing because, in math, `"-4 squared"` is `16`.
12. c. The statement uses the assignment operator (=), the negative operator (-), and the exponentiation operator (**).

1.6 Error messages

1. b. The filename can be found after the last slash (/). Other names, like Desktop, refer to folders.
2. b. Line 2 is mentioned immediately after the filename.
3. b. The type of error is always the first word on the last line of the error message.
4. a. The middle three lines are indented. In Python, lines may not begin with spaces or tabs unexpectedly.
5. c. The quote marks are missing at the end of the input prompt.
6. b. The name for `"input"` is misspelled.

1.7 Comments

1. b. Comments help explain the purpose of code so that other programmers understand what the code intends.
2. a. The hash character indicates the beginning of a comment.
3. b. Having one space after the # is the community standard.
4. c. This comment explains the intent of the code. If the code had a mistake, the programmer reading the comment might notice the mistake more easily.
5. a. A blank line separates the input from the output.
   Then again, inserting a blank line in a three-line program is generally unnecessary.
6. c. The # symbol "comments out" the line without removing the line permanently.
7. a. The docstring is primarily written for others who will use the program.
8. c. Docstrings must be a valid string, not a multi-line comment. Docstrings are stored in the program's memory, but comments are ignored.
9. b. The amount of information in this docstring is just right. In most cases, the docstring should not be longer than the code.

1.8 Why Python?

1. a. The language was named after Monty Python. Just for fun, the official documentation makes subtle references to Monty Python comedy sketches.
2. b. Python's first release was in 1991, after being developed in the late 1980's.
3. c. Making Python open source early on allowed for many programmers to provide feedback.
4. b. For 20 years, Java and C traded places as the top language until Python took over in 2021!
5. a. The line for Python crosses the line for JavaScript in the middle of 2018.
6. b. TIOBE started tracking language popularity in 2001, several years after web search engines became popular.

Chapter 2
2.1 The Python shell

1. a. Most programming languages are high-level and meant to be understood by humans.
2. c. The most basic line of Python code is a single expression, such as the integer `1`.
3. b. After the input is stored in memory, the shell displays a prompt for the next line.
4. c. The up arrow displays the previous line, and the left arrow moves within that line.
5. a. Pressing the up arrow twice moves to the line before the previous line.

2.2 Type conversion

1. a. `book_rating` was assigned with `3.5` on line 5 and converted from an integer to a float by the interpreter. `book_rating` isn't modified after line 5.
2. a. Combining a float and an integer in a calculation produces a float. `book_rating` would be assigned with `4.0`.
3. a. A calculation with a float and an integer produces a float. x is a float, `42.0`, after the code executes.
4. a. `float()` converts the input number of slices from a string to a float for the pizza order calculation.
5. b. `int()` removes any fractional part. Many calculations will produce a fractional part. Ex: 46 people with 3.0 slices per person will need 138 slices or 17.25 pizzas. `int(17.25)` is `17`, so adding `1` produces `18` pizzas, a better estimate to ensure enough pizza is ordered.
6. a. `y = int(4.5) = 4`. The fractional part, 0.5, is removed.
7. b. `str(4.5)` produces `"4.5"`.
8. a. `float(y) = float(4) = 4.0`.The fractional part, 0.5, was removed during the integer conversion, `int(x)`.

2.3 Mixed data types

1. b. Multiplying an integer and a float produces a float.
2. a. Multiplying two integers produces an integer.
3. b. Dividing two integers produces a float, even when the result is a whole number.
4. b. Dividing two integers produces a float and does not round.
5. b. Dividing a float by an integer produces a float, even when the result is a whole number.
6. a. Subtraction of a float from an integer produces a float.
7. b. Subtraction of a float from an integer produces a float and does not round.
8. b. `34 + 56` produces `90`, an integer.
9. a. `'12' + ' red roses'` performs string concatenation.
10. c. Multiplying a string by an integer is a useful shortcut.
11. c. Adding `'5.2'`, a string, and `7`, an integer, is not an accepted operation and leads to an error.
12. b. Adding a float and an integer produces a float.
13. b. `'3.14'` and `'159'` are concatenated.
14. c. String repetition only works with strings and integers.

2.4 Floating-point errors

1. b. An overflow error occurs because the value is larger than the upper limit of the floating-point range.
2. a. The digits starting from the eighteenth place after the decimal are inaccurate due to approximation, so a round-off error occurs.
3. c. `round(6.6)` = `7` as 7 is the closest whole number to 6.6.
4. c. `round(3.5, 2)` = `3.50` as the input is rounded to two decimal places.
5. b. When `round()` is applied to an integer value without specifying the number of decimal places, there will be no change to the value.
6. a. The `round(0.1, 1)` rounds the value `0.1` to one decimal place, which is `0.1`.

2.5 Dividing integers

1. b. 13 divided by 5 is 2 and 3/5. The / operator computes the result as a float.
2. c. 5 goes into 13 two times, remainder 3. The % operator computes the remainder.
3. a. 4 goes into 1 zero times, remainder 1. The // operator computes the quotient.
4. c. Dividing by zero is undefined in math. Python raises an error when dividing by zero.
5. b. The modulus is the amount to divide by. To convert hours to minutes, a program divides by 60.
6. a. Programs that use floor division often use modulo on the next line.

2.6 The math module

1. c. The import statement defines the math variable needed to access the module.
2. b. The `round()` function, for rounding floating-point numbers, is built-in.
3. a. `abs()` is a built-in function. The math module does not have an `abs()` function.
4. b. Tau is equal to 2π, so tau divided by 2 is π.
5. a. The `math.sqrt()` function returns a float, even when given an integer.
6. b. This expression is a concise way to write πr^2.
7. a. When given integers, the ** operator returns an integer result.

2.7 Formatting code

1. a. The code has one space before and after the assignment operator (=).
2. c. Each operator (=, +) has one space both before and after.
3. b. The comma is followed by a space.
4. a. The expressions b**2 and 4*a*c are evaluated first. Adding space around the - operator makes the order of operations more readable.
5. b. The two consecutive strings are automatically combined into one string before printing.
6. a. The original strings do not have a space between the words `"is"` and `"a"`.
7. c. The literal `"Hello,"` and the variable name cannot be concatenated without using a + operator. Alternatively, the two values could be separated by a comma in the print function.
8. b. The backslash, when used at the end of a line, indicates a multi-line statement.
9. a. Using one print statement with parentheses joins the lines implicitly and does not increase the number of statements.
10. c. The first line assigns `"Happy "` to the variable saying. The second line has no effect on the program.

2.8 Python careers

1. d. Python is one of the most-used programming languages in the world, especially in fields outside of CS and IT.
2. a. Matplotlib is a popular library for creating charts, plots, and other visualizations.
3. b. As of 2023, Instagram is the largest deployment of the Python Django web framework.

Chapter 3
3.1 Strings revisited
1. a. Since index values start at 0, the index 1 refers to the second character of the string.
2. b. The character at index 1 is y, and the character at index -1 is !.
3. c. The result of s[0] is "P", which is a string of length 1.
4. b. Code points 65 to 90 are used for uppercase letters.
5. b. The code point for the character "0" is 48.
6. b. Tilde (~) is the character for code point 126. The chr() function returns a string of length one.
7. c. An escape sequence is two characters long and begins with a backslash (\).
8. c. The first backslash indicates an escape sequence, and the second backslash indicates the character.
9. c. The escape sequence \n produces a new line. print("Enter\nhere") produces the same result.

3.2 Formatted strings
1. b. The same variable, says, is used in three replacement fields.
2. a. The string is not an f-string, so the brace characters (around temp and food) are printed literally.
3. c. Using an f-string allows the entire output to be specified without commas and extra quote marks.
4. a. The format specifier 02d appends a 0 to the front of the integer when the integer is only one digit.
5. c. The format specifier ".2f" (with a period) means fixed-point, rounded to two decimal places.
6. b. This format specifier is useful for displaying large amounts of money.

3.3 Variables revisited
1. b. Each line of the program in the animation is an assignment statement.
2. c. The program assigns the int object 10 and the float object 9.7, as shown in the memory diagram.
3. a. An arrow shows which object a variable currently refers to.
4. a. An object's identity is an integer representing the memory location.
5. c. The type function returns an object's class name like int, float, or str.
6. b. A variable refers to an object, so the variable's value is the object's value.

3.4 List basics
1. b. A list of numbers can be set up using an assignment operator.
2. a. Individual elements in a list must be separated by a comma. Python does not understand what is meant by 2 3.
3. c. Since indexes start at 0, the required number is one less than the position being accessed.
4. a. The index -1 always refers to the last element of a list. The expression len(name_list)-1, which evaluates to 3 and refers to the last element in a list of 4 elements, can also be used in place of -1 here.

3.5 Tuple basics
1. a. The first element, 2, is at index 0.
2. c. Tuples can have elements of the same type as well as elements of different types.
3. a. A tuple must be created using commas. Parentheses are optional but recommended. The three elements are "a", "b", and "c".
4. b. my_tuple is initially assigned with the tuple (0.693, 0.414, 3.142). Then my_tuple is assigned with the new tuple, (0.693, 1.414, 3.142), to correct a mistake with the second element.
5. a. Tuples are immutable. No changes, including appending, can be made after the tuple is created.
6. b. Tuples are immutable, so attempted changes produce errors. Using a tuple would protect the constants from accidental changes.

Chapter 4

4.1 Boolean values

1. c. `"True"` uses quotation marks, so the value is a string.
2. b. `is_vegetable` is an integer and can be used in arithmetic operations.
3. a. A variable assigned with either `True` or `False` is a Boolean variable.
4. a. A Boolean variable represents the value `True` or `False`.
5. b. `True` and `False` are the only two values for a Boolean variable.
6. b. Assigning a bool with an `int` results in implicit type conversion. The type conversion can cause issues later in the code if the programmer assumes `is_dessert` is still a Boolean.
7. b. Any numeric type representing 0 converts to `False`. Non-zero numbers convert to `True`.
8. a. A negative number is non-zero and converts to `True`.
9. b. The empty string is the only string that converts to `False`.
10. a. `"0"` is a non-empty string and is converted to `True`.
11. a. The input is read in as a string, so `bool("False")` is `True`.
12. b. `True` converted to a float is `1.0`. `False` converted to a float is `0.0`.
13. b. `True` converted to a string is `"True"`. `False` converted to a string is `"False"`.
14. b. When a Boolean is converted to a numeric type, `True` is converted to `1`, and `False` is converted to `0`.
15. b. 14 is greater than 13, so 14 is not less than or equal to 13.
16. a. 0 is less than 0.4, so 0 is not equal to 0.4.
17. b. 4 is equal to 4.0, so 4 is not less than 4.0.
18. c. Numeric types cannot be compared to strings using the comparison operators: >, <, >=, <=. Using == or != will produce a Boolean.
19. b. Strings are compared by comparing each character's Unicode values. Letters have ascending Unicode values in alphabetical order (and are case sensitive). `"c"` and `"c"` are equal, so `"i"` is compared to `"o"`. `"i"` is not equal to `"o"` so `False` is produced, though cilantro and coriander come from the same plant.
20. b. Letters have ascending Unicode values in alphabetical order (and are case sensitive). `"d"` is greater than, not less than, `"c"`, so `False` is produced.

4.2 If-else statements

1. b. `age < 12` is between `"if"` and `":"` and is an expression that evaluates to `True` or `False`.
2. c. The program executes the body when the condition is true.
3. b. The body, line 3, isn't executed because the condition is false.
4. c. `-10 < 0` is true, so num is assigned with `25`. Then `25 < 100`, so num is assigned with `25 + 50`, which is `75`.
5. b. Line 4 is not indented, so `positive_num` is always assigned with `0`. The positive input value is lost.
6. c. The `if` branch is taken when x `>= 15`, so the `else` branch is taken when x is not greater than or equal to `15`.
7. a. `40 > 30`, so the body of the `if` statement is executed. y = 40 - 10 = 30.
8. b. One of the branches is always taken in an `if-else` statement. Depending on x's value, y will either have a final value of `30` or `105`.

4.3 Boolean operations

1. a. `2500 < 3000` is `True`, and `2.5 > 1.0` is `True`, so Jaden can enter.
2. b. `3000 > 3000` is `False`. False and True is `False`. False and False is `False`. So no value of `hrs_to_close` will allow Darcy to enter.
3. b. False and True is `False`.

4. b. `(8 < 10) and (21 > 20)` evaluates to `True and True`, which is `True`. So the body of the `if` is executed, and z is assigned with `5`.
5. a. `(21 < 30) or False` evaluates to `True or False`, which is `True`.
6. c. The discount does not apply for ages between 12 and 65 inclusive.
7. a. `(9%2==0 and 10%2 ==1)` evaluates to `(False and False)`, which is `False`. `(9%2 == 1 and 10%2 == 0)` evaluates to `(True and True)`, which is `True`. `False or True` is `True`. The `if` statement checks whether the numbers form an even-odd or odd-even pair.
8. a. `not(13 < 10)` evaluates to `not(False)`, which is `True`.
9. b. `not(18 > 15 and 18 < 20)` evaluates to `not(True and True)`, then `not(True)`, and finally, `False`.
10. a. `65 > 60` is `True`, so is_turn is assigned with `not(False)`, which is `True`.

4.4 Operator precedence

1. b. Exponentiation has the highest precedence, then division, then addition.
2. a. Multiplication has the highest precedence, then greater than, then not.
3. b. Division has the highest precedence, then equality and less than, then and.
4. b. Multiplication and division have the highest precedence, are left associative, and have higher precedence than addition.
5. b. Exponentiation is right associative and has higher precedence than multiplication.
6. c. The expression is valid and is separated into comparisons connected with and.
7. a. The equality operator, ==, has higher precedence than the logical and.
8. a. The expression is evaluated as `x + (3*y) - 5`. `8 + (3*9) - 5 = 30`.
9. b. The expressions in parentheses are evaluated first. `(8+3) * (9-5) = 11 * 4 = 44`.

4.5 Chained decisions

1. b. `elif` will evaluate condition_2 if condition_1 is `False` and execute Body 2 if condition_2 is `True`.
2. b. `x > 44`, `42 > 44`, is `False`, so `x < 50` is evaluated. `42 < 50` is `True`, so `y = 0 + 5`. Only one of the `if` and `elif` branches is taken.
3. a. If `x < 0`, Body 1 executes. Else if `x == 0`, Body 2 executes.
4. a. The `elif` must be chained to a preceding statement and at the same indentation level.
5. c. The `if` and `if-elif` statements are not chained. The first `if` evaluates to `True` and executes. Then the `if-elif` is evaluated and the `elif` branch executes.
6. b. The third branch executes if `hour < 8` and `hour < 12` is `False` and `hour < 13` is `True`.
7. c. An `elif` can be chained to another `elif` to form a longer chained decision.
8. a. Only one branch is executed in a chained decision statement. `-1 < 0` and `-2 < 0` is `True`, so `y = 10`.
9. c. The first branch executes if `price < 9.99`. The second branch executes if `price < 19.99` and the first condition fails: that is, `price >= 9.99`. The third branch executes if the first and second conditions fail: that is, `price >= 19.99`. Chaining can simplify decision statements.

4.6 Nested decisions

1. c. `leaf_count == 3` is `False`, so the outer `else`'s body is executed.
2. c. num_dancers is positive, so the `else` branch is taken. num_dancers is odd, so the error is printed before the program continues after the nested `if` and prints num_dancers.
3. b. `256 == 513` is `False`, and `256 < 513` is `True`, so the `elif` branch is taken and Body 2 executes. `513 >= 512` is `True`, so Body 3 executes.
4. c. The first `else` isn't indented and is treated as the `else` to the original `if`. Thus the second `else` is not connected to an `if` statement and produces an error.

4.7 Conditional expressions

1. c. The conditional expression will assign `response` with `"even"` if x is even. `response` is assigned with `"odd"` if x is odd.
2. a. `100 < 100` is `False` so `result` is assigned with `x - offset` = 100 - 10 = 90.
3. c. `min_num` cannot be assigned with `min_num = y`. The correct expression is `min_num = x if x < y else y"`
4. b. Conditional expressions that evaluate to a Boolean are redundant. The Boolean expression should be used instead.
5. b. The expression is evaluated as `(fee + 10) if hours > 12 else 2`. So if hours > 12, the result will be fee + 10; otherwise, the result will be 2.

Chapter 5
5.1 While loop

1. b. The loop runs six times for values of g = 1 , 2 , 3 , 5 , 8 , and 13 .
2. c. 21 is the first Fibonacci number larger than 20, and for g = 21, the condition will evaluate to `False` for the first time.
3. a. The code first prints the variable f's initial value. Then, at each iteration, g's value is printed, and g's value throughout the code's execution will be 1 , 2 , 3 , 5 , 8 , and 13 . Thus, all printed values are 1 , 1 , 2 , 3 , 5 , 8 , and 13 .
4. b. The loop runs for n = 4, 3 , 2 , 1 .
5. b. The loop's termination condition is n = 0; therefore, the value of n after the loop equals 0 . The last printed line will be: `value of n after the loop is 0`.
6. c. Since the initialization value for n equals 4 and the value of n is only increasing, the loop condition will always remain true. The loop will never terminate.

5.2 For loop

1. b. Eight characters exist in the `str_var`. Iterating over all characters and incrementing the value of `count` variable at each iteration results in the `count`'s value of 8 .
2. a. Since the initial `count`'s value is 0 , multiplying `count` by any number results in the output of 0 .
3. c. The added line prints each character that is looped on (character c), and prints an additional * after the character.
4. a. The output will be an increasing sequence between 10 and 22 (inclusive of both): 10 , 13 , 16 , 19 , and 22 .
5. c. The expression starts a sequence from 5 , decreases by 1 at every step, and ends at 1 .
6. a. The `range()` function generates a descending sequence, beginning from -1 until -2. Hence, the output is -1.
7. c. When the step size is negative, the generated sequence will be in descending order. Hence, `start` must be larger than end; otherwise, no sequence will be generated.
8. c. When two arguments are provided to the `range()` function, arguments are considered as `start` and end of the sequence, and the step size will be 1 . When step size is positive, the generated sequence will be in ascending order, and hence, `start` must be less than end. Otherwise, no sequence will be generated.

5.3 Nested loops

1. b. The combination of i and j values, (i, j), that meet the inner and outer loop conditions are as follows:
   (1, 1), (1, 2), (1, 3), (1, 4),
   (2, 1), (2, 2), (2, 3),

(3, 1), (3, 2),
(4, 1)

2. b. Each inner loop's full execution prints three "*" characters, and the outer loop executes twice.
3. b. Each line i of the output (i = 1, 2, 3, and 4) contains i times values 1 through 4. Hence, the outer loop executes while i <= 4, and the inner loop iterates over j while j's value is less than or equal to 4.
4. a. The outer loop's execution range is 0, 1, and 2; hence, the outer loop executes three times.
5. b. The inner loop is evaluated four times (j = 0, 1, 2, and 3) for every i's value set by the outer loop. In the given example i = 0, 1, and 2; hence, the total number of times the inner loop executes is 3 * 4 = 12.
6. c. The printed output displays three rows with each row i displaying i * values in the range of 0 to 3. Hence, the code must iterate over row ID in the outer loop, and in each row, iterate over elements' ID in the range of 0 to 3.

5.4 Break and continue

1. c. The code prints all characters before the first occurrence of a space character in separate lines. Hence the output is:

   H
   e
   l
   l
   o

2. b. As soon as the print statement is executed, the break statement causes the loop's termination. Also, for i = 15, the condition (i%3 == 0 and i%5 == 0) is met, and hence the print statement will be executed exactly once.
3. b. The loop finds the first five numbers that are divisible by 2 or 3. These numbers are 2, 3, 4, 6, and 8, and thus 8 is the final i's value.
4. b. The print statement is executed for numbers within the range of 0 and 10 (inclusive) that are divisible by 3. The printed output is:

   9
   6
   3
   0

5. b. The loop checks whether the character being evaluated is a space character or not. If so, the remainder of the loop will be skipped and the space character will not be printed.

5.5 Loop else

1. b. The variable i is initialized to 16, and the while loop executes with i = 16, 8, 4, and 2. In each loop's iteration, the variable exp's value is incremented by 1. Hence, at the end of the loop, exp = 4. Since the loop terminates without interruption, the else statement after the loop is executed and prints 16 is 2 to the 4.
2. a. The initial i's value is 7. Hence, in the first loop's iteration, the else statement within the loop executes, and the break statement terminates the loop. Since the loop's execution is interrupted, the else after the loop will not execute and there will be no output.
3. b. The loop iterates over all integer values in the list. If a value is less than 5, the value will be printed, and if the value is greater than 5, the code prints "Not all numbers are less than 5." and the code's

execution terminates.

Chapter 6
6.1 Defining functions

1. c. The `print()` function is called to output the variable, `offset_num`.
2. b. Lines 1, 4, and 5 each call `print()` once. Lines 2 and 3 call a different function, `input()`.
3. b. Line 1 is a comment that is not executed. Lines 2 and 3 each call `float()` and `input()`. Line 3 calls `print()` for a total of five function calls.
4. b. The corrected line is `def water_plant():` .
5. c. The main program outputs `"User info:"` and then calls `print_phone_num()`, which outputs the phone number.
6. b. A function call includes the function name and parentheses.
7. a. `calc_tax` is concise, in snake case, and indicates the function's task.
8. c. Each calculation uses four statements to read in the x,y values of a pair of points. The original program performs three calculations by repeating code for a total of 12 input statements. The revised program performs three calculations by executing the four input statements multiple times with function calls.
9. c. The benefits of a function's reusability is highlighted by many function calls that drastically reduce the amount of cluttered, redundant code. Calling `calc_distance()` 10 times is equivalent to 60 statements in the original program.

6.2 Control flow

1. c. Line 5 is the start of the main program, which is not indented. `park_greet()` is called on line 6 and executed.
2. b. Control flow moves to where `park_greet()` is defined, at line 4.
3. c. Control flow returns to the line that called the function. Line 12 contains the function call to `extra_lot()`, so control flow returns to line 12.
4. c. The program has an indentation mistake. `print("Open ...")` is unindented, so the statement is not a part of `park_greet()` and is executed first. Then, `park_greet()` is called, and `print("Welcome ...")` is executed.
5. c. The `for` loop has three iterations. Each iteration calls `print_book_club()`, which calls `print_conf()`. So the program calls `print_book_club()` three times and `print_conf()` three times.
6. b. Control flow returns to line 11, which called `print_conf()`. Then `print_book_club()` finishes, and control flow returns to line 16, which called `print_book_club()`.

6.3 Variable scope

1. c. Both `num` and `num_sq` are created outside of functions and are global variables.
2. a. `num` is created outside of a function and is global. `num_sq` is created in `print_square()` and is not global.
3. c. `num` is global and can be accessed anywhere in the program, including both `print_double()` and `print_square()`.
4. b. `out_str` is the only variable declared in `print_time()` and is a local variable.
5. c. `out_str` is accessed in `print_greeting()` but created in statements outside of `print_greeting()`.
6. b. `print_time()` creates `out_str` as a local variable. `out_str` is only in scope in `print_time()` and cannot be accessed elsewhere.
7. a. The global variable `hour` is not edited in `update_hour()`. `tmp` is the local variable edited. `tmp` is discarded after `update_hour()` finishes.
8. c. `new_hour` is a local variable that the print statement tries to access after `update_hour()` finishes. `new_hour` is out of scope, so an error is produced.

9. b. The `global` keyword can be used to create a global variable from within a function. `new_hour` has global scope and can be accessed outside `update_hour()`.

6.4 Parameters

1. b. `username` is the argument passed to `print_welcome()`. `name` is `print_welcome()`'s parameter that is assigned with `username`'s value.
2. a. `name` is the only parameter defined with `print_welcome()`. `username` is the argument passed on line 5's function call.
3. a. `name` is a parameter that exists only within a call to `print_welcome()`.
4. a. The program would run correctly. Arguments and parameters can have the same name, and a local variable called `name` would still be created in `print_welcome()`. Scope can be confusing with variables of the same name.
5. a. `p1_x` is the first argument used in line 9's function call. `x1` is defined as the first parameter of `calc_distance()`.
6. b. `y1` is defined as `calc_distance()`'s second parameter. `p1_y` is the second argument on line 9's function call.
7. c. `3` is a literal passed as the third argument, which corresponds to `x2`, the third parameter.
8. a. A list is mutable, so the object referred to by `wknd_temps` and `temps` is modified without needing a local copy.
9. b. A string is immutable, so `convert_temps()` makes a new object for `unit` to refer to.
10. a. An immutable object's value cannot be changed.
11. b. `unit` no longer exists after `convert_temps()` finishes and returns to line 14.

6.5 Return values

1. a. `calc_mpg()` specifies `mpg` to be returned with the `return` statement.
2. b. `return` is a valid statement to end the function and return to the calling code without a specified value. `calc_sqft()` should return `sqft` with the line `return sqft`.
3. c. If the return value or `return` statement is not specified, the function returns `None`.
4. b. `num == 3` is `True`, so the `return "dk"` statement executes.
5. a. For `inc_volume(9,10)`, `return level` returns `9`, and `level += 1` is never reached.
6. b. `bill += tax(bill) + auto_tip(bill)` evaluates to `bill += 6.0 + 20.0` to `bill = 100.0 + 6.0 + 20.0` to `126.0`.
7. a. `val2 = sq(offset(5))` evaluates to `val2 = sq(3)` to `9`.

6.6 Keyword arguments

1. d. The function call uses all keyword arguments to assign values to the named parameters.
2. b. `"Hiya"` is the value of `msg` and `"Ash"` is the value of `name` in the function.
3. a. `"Welcome"` is unnamed and assigned correctly to `count`. Positional arguments must come before keyword arguments.
4. b. The positional arguments, `"Hi"` and `"Bea"`, follow the keyword argument `count=1`, which produces an error.
5. b. `name`'s default value is `"Friend"`, and `count`'s default value is `1`. `msg` does not have default value.
6. c. `msg` is a required argument assigned with `"Greetings"`. `name` and `count` use the default values. `"Greetings Friend"` is printed.
7. b. `msg="Hello"`, `name="Friend"`, and `count=0`, so the call is valid. The function executes but doesn't enter the `for` loop because `count=0`.

Chapter 7

7.1 Module basics

1. b. The code has ten `def` statements, each of which defines a function.
2. a. Many modules consist of function definitions only. The functions are intended to be called in other modules.
3. c. `area.cube(5)` is `6 * 5**2`, which is `6 * 25`, which is `150`.
4. a. When importing a module from another file, the suffix *.py* is removed.
5. b. The circle function must be called using the area variable that refers to the module.
6. b. Adding the function to the area module makes the function easier to reuse in other programs.

7.2 Importing names

1. a. This statement imports the sqrt function defined in the math module.
2. b. A variable is defined for each function imported: sin, cos, and tan.
3. b. A name error occurs when a variable name is not found, which might be due to a missing import statement.
4. b. This statement replaces the previously imported circle function, even though `circle()` and `area.circle()` have different parameters.
5. a. Assigning the area variable replaces the previously imported module with the integer `51`. The variable can no longer be used to call functions in the area module.
6. b. The most recent definition of `hello()` requires one argument, so this line would result in an error.

7.3 Top-level code

1. b. Whenever this module is imported, Python will output `"Defining sphere function"` as a side effect.
2. a. Even though nothing is printed, calling the sphere function ten million times causes a delay in the main program.
3. a. All code is at the top level, and no functions are defined. Importing this module would run all code as a side effect.
4. c. The variable __name__ is the module's name, unless the module was run as the main program. In that case, __name__ is `"__main__"`.
5. a. Since *test.py* was imported, the value of __name__ is `"test"`.
6. c. This line is found in many Python modules to check if the module was run as the main program.

7.4 The help function

1. b. The digits have 0 red and 0 green, so the color must be a shade of blue. Navy is a darker version of standard blue, *#0000FF*.
2. c. FF in hexadecimal is 255, the maximum amount of red, green, or blue in a color.
3. a. The red, green, and blue values for orange are higher than the red, green, and blue values for green.
4. b. The hexadecimal for YELLOW is *#FFFF00*, meaning 255 red + 255 green + 0 blue.
5. c. Both the `darken` function and the BLUE variable must be accessed via the `colors` variable.
6. a. Function names that begin with an underscore are intended to be used only within the current module.
7. b. Only docstrings are included in the documentation. All comments are ignored by the help function.
8. a. The functions are sorted alphabetically by name to make looking up a function easier.
9. a. Functions that begin with an underscore are intended to be used only within a module, not in other modules.

7.5 Finding modules

1. a. This reference describes the standard library, including built-in functions, types, and modules.
2. b. As explained in the documentation of the `calendar` module, MONDAY is `0` and SUNDAY is `6`.
3. a. The `tkinter` module stands for Tk interface. Tk is a standard toolkit for creating windows, text boxes,

buttons, and other graphical widgets.
4. c. `MoviePy` is a module for video editing, and `Pillow` is a module for image processing.
5. a. According to the "Features" section of the documentation, `Arrow`'s is a "fully-implemented, drop-in replacement for `datetime`."
6. a. This function converts a color code to a color name. Ex: `hex_to_name("#daa520")` returns `"goldenrod"` .

Chapter 8
8.1 String operations
1. a. Since a's ASCII value is less than b's ASCII value, the output for `"aaa" < "aab"` is True.
2. b. Since `"a"` is shorter than `"aa"` , and the prefix `"aa"` with length 1 equals the second operand (`"a"`), the shorter string is considered smaller. As such, `"aa" < "a"` evaluates to False.
3. c. While all characters in `"aples"` exist in `"apples"` , the characters are not sequential, so the string `"aples"` is not a substring of `"apples"` . Therefore, `"aples" in "apples"` returns False.
4. a. `"aBbA".lower()` converts all characters to lowercase, and the output is `"abba"` .
5. b. `"aBbA".upper()` converts all characters to uppercase, and the output is `"ABBA"` .
6. a. The `upper()` converts `"a"` to uppercase (`"A"`). When checking `"a".upper() == "A"`, the output is True.

8.2 String slicing
1. b. Since indexing starts from 0, the character at index 1 is the second character in the string, which is `"e"` .
2. b. Since negative indexing starts from -1 from the right of the string to the left, `"u"` is at index -2.
3. a. Character `"e"` in the string `"chance"` has index of -1 (negative indexing) and 5 (positive indexing).
4. b. `a_string[2:4]` is a slice including the third and fourth characters, which is `"ll"` .
5. b. The slice `[-3:-1]` includes characters at index -3 and -2, which are `"oo"` .
6. b. The string slice of `greeting[3:]` is the substring starting from index 3 up to the end of the string, which is `"Leila"` .
7. b. To modify string content, a new variable must be created with desired modifications.
8. a. Attempting to assign a value to an index or range of indexes in a string results in `TypeError: 'str' object does not support item assignment`.
9. c. The character at index 1, `"o"` , is replacing the content of variable `str` . As such, the print statement prints `"o"` .

8.3 Searching/testing strings
1. c. Since `"a"` is a substring of `"an umbrella"` , the output of `"a" in "an umbrella"` is True .
2. b. `"ab"` is not a substring of `"arbitrary"` ; hence, the output is False .
3. a. Since `""` is a substring of length 0 for `"string"` , the output is True .
4. a. The `for` loop iterates through the characters in `"string"` and prints all character without any separator character.
5. c. The given code iterates over characters in string `"abca"` , and each time character `"a"` is observed, a counter variable is increased by 1. Since `"a"` appears twice in `"abca"` , the output will be 2 .
6. c. The code iterates over the characters in `"cab"` and prints each character's uppercase equivalent. Therefore, the output is `"CAB"` .
7. c. `"aaa".count("a")` returns 3 , which is the number of occurrences of `"a"` in string `"aaa"` .
8. a. Zero occurrence of `"b"` exists in `"weather"` ; hence, the output of `"weather".count("b")` is 0 .
9. b. Two substrings `"aa"` exist in `"aaa"` , one starting from index 0 and one starting from index 1.
10. a. The `find()` method returns the index for the first occurrence of the substring in the given string. The

index for the first occurrence of `"a"` is 1.
11. b. Since `"c"` is not a substring in `"banana"`, the `find()` method returns `-1`.
12. a. Since `"banana"` is not a substring of `"b"`, `-1` is returned.
13. a. The `index()` method returns the index of the start of the first occurrence of a substring in the given string. The index of the first occurrence of `"o"` in `"school"` is 3.
14. c. Substring `"ooo"` does not exist in the string `"ooo"` and hence the `index()` method returns a `ValueError`.
15. a. `sentence.index(" ")` returns the index of the first space character. The print statement prints the prefix of the sentence ending just before the first space character, so the output is `"This"`.

8.4 String formatting

1. c. `"Ana"` is substituted for the replacement field `{}` in the template and hence the output is `"Hello Ana!"`.
2. b. The two arguments are passed to the template `"{}:{}"` that outputs `"One:1"`.
3. a. The arguments for the `format()` function are passed in order and will be substituted for the replacement fields. Additional arguments may be ignored by the template and remain unused.
4. c. `"Bengio"` is substituted in the named replacement field associated with the tag name; hence, the output is `"Hey Bengio!"`.
5. b. Since the string template uses a named argument, inputs are only accepted through the corresponding keys. Hence, the code generates `KeyError: 'name'`.
6. b. The greeting variable with value `"Hi"` is substituted for the greeting replacement field. The same is also done for the name replacement field and the name variable. The output is `"Hi Jess"`.
7. b. The template specifies the minimum length for the name field to be 12, so `len(formatted_name)` is 12.
8. c. The alignment and the field length specifications format the greeting field to be six characters in length and right-aligned. Therefore, the variable `formatted_greeting` will take value `" Hello"`, and character 0 of the string is a space character.
9. c. The field length specification enforces the minimum length of the string. Inputs that are longer than the specified minimum length will not be modified.
10. c. The `.3` format specification shows that the output precision must be three decimal places.
11. a. The `{:1>3d}` specification outputs a 3-digit number in the output, and if the given argument does not have three digits, the number will be padded with 1's from the left side.
12. b. `{:+d}` formats the decimal number by adding the positive sign.

8.5 Splitting/joining strings

1. b. When `"1*2*3*"` is broken into substrings using the `'*'` delimiter, the output is `["1", "2", "3"]`.
2. c. When `"a year includes 12 months"` is broken into substrings using blank space characters, the list `["a", "year", "includes", "12", "months"]` is created.
3. b. When splitting the multi-line string, the output is `['This', 'is', 'a', 'test']`.
4. c. Elements of the list `elements` are concatenated together using a comma, so the output is `'A,beautiful,day,for,learning'`.
5. b. The output of `"sss".join(["1","2"])` is `"1sss2"`, which has a length of 5.
6. b. Since the separator is an empty string, elements of the list will be concatenated without a separator and the output will be `"12"`.

Chapter 9
9.1 Modifying and iterating lists

1. b. The `append()` operation adds an element to the end of a list.

2. c. The element to be removed is passed as a parameter to the remove operation. The remove is performed on the specified list.
3. c. Both `pop()` and `remove()` can be used to remove the last element of a list. `pop()` automatically removes the last element, whereas `remove()` requires the last element be specified.
4. a. The length of the list is 5, so the iterative `for` loop executes five times.
5. b. `len(my_list)` is 5. A counting `for` loop ends at 1 less than the second value in the range function, so the final value of `i` is 4 .
6. a. The `for` loop steps by two each time, so index 0, 2, and 4 are printed. Due to the `"end="` in the print statement, all elements are printed on one line.

9.2 Sorting and reversing lists

1. b. Sorting in descending order means to arrange the elements from largest to smallest. -3 is the smallest element of the list and would be the last element when the list is sorted in descending order.
2. a. For strings, ascending order refers to dictionary order.
3. c. In alphabetical order, "h" comes before "k". The first four characters are the same, so `"flash"` comes before `"flask"` .
4. b. The `sort()` function must be applied on the list. The default for the `sort()` function is to arrange elements in ascending order.
5. a. The correct syntax for the `reverse()` function requires the function to be applied to the list.
6. a. `"go"` is the first element of `board_games`, so `"go"` would be the last element once `board_games` is reversed.

9.3 Common list operations

1. a. The `min()` function takes a list as a parameter and returns the minimum for the list.
2. b. `"Austin City Limits"` is the first string in dictionary order.
3. c. The summation of the given floats is 12.4 .
4. c. `list2` refers to the same list as `my_list`, so any changes made to `list2` also reflect on `my_list`. 18 is the summation of the values in the list.
5. a. 3 is the maximum value in the list `my_list`. Line 3 changes the value of the first element in `list2`.
6. b. `sum()` function is not defined for string values.

9.4 Nested lists

1. a. Each row of the matrix is represented as a list in the larger list-of-lists, `matA`. `matA` represents the complete matrix.
2. c. 6 is in the 2nd row and 3rd column. Using zero-indexing results in index 1 for the row and 2 for the column.
3. c. The first element of the list `matA` is a list `[7, 4, 5]` representing the first row of the matrix.
4. a. The outer `for` loop iterates row by row. The inner `for` loop iterates through each element in a row. So all the numbers are printed, starting from 7 and ending in -5.
5. c. The outer `for` loop runs for three iterations because there are three elements in the list-of-lists. The inner `for` loop iterates through each element of each row using the length of each row.

9.5 List comprehensions

1. a. The expression tells Python what element to put in the new list.
2. c. `i+2` results in adding 2 to each element of `a_list` to generate `b_list`.
3. b. The `for` loop starts at 1 and steps by three, so it begins at 1 and ends at 13. Dividing using the `//` operator results in dropping the part after the decimal.
4. c. The list comprehension filters for negative numbers in `my_list`.
5. b. The list comprehension selects vowels from the given string.

6. a. The `for` loop ranges from 0 through 20, stepping by two, but each iterated element is even, so nothing is added to new_list.

Chapter 10
10.1 Dictionary basics

1. a. The first item in each key-value pair is the key. Hence `"Sunday"`, `"Monday"`, `"Tuesday"` are key items.
2. b. The second item in each key-value pair is the value. Hence `1`, `2`, `3` are value items.
3. b. Based on the days dictionary object, the value assigned to `"Sunday"` is `1`.
4. b. The type of a dictionary object is `dict`.
5. b. A dictionary cannot have duplicate keys, and `"a"` and `"A"` are two different keys because `"a"` and `"A"` are different characters.
6. a. A dictionary can have duplicate values, but not duplicate keys.

10.2 Dictionary creation

1. b. Curly braces can be used to create an empty dictionary.
2. c. `{"one": 1}` creates a dictionary object with one item `"one": 1`.
3. b. Two pairs of items exist in the my_dict dictionary. The two pairs are `"a": 1` and `"b": 2`.
4. b. `dict()` function, along with keyword arguments, can be used to create a dictionary object.
5. a. my_dict is a dictionary with one key-value pair, `"a": 1`.
6. b. The `dict()` function can create a dictionary object from a list of tuples. The first element of each tuple acts as the key, and the second element is the value.

10.3 Dictionary operations

1. c. The value associated with the key `"Jaya"` is `"Student"`.
2. b. When a key does not exist in a dictionary, `None` is returned by default.
3. b. The second argument to the `get()` function will be returned if the key is not found in the dictionary.
4. a. The return type of `keys()` function is `dict_keys`.
5. c. The values in the numbers dictionary are `1`, `2`, and `3`. When printing `numbers.values()`, `dict_values([1, 2, 3])` is printed.
6. b. Keys in the dictionary are `"one"`, `"two"`, `"three"`. Using the `list()` constructor, a list object containing all keys is returned.
7. c. When accessing a dictionary key and assigning a new value, the associated value for the key will be updated.
8. b. Using the `del` keyword, items can be deleted from a dictionary using the key.
9. a. The `update()` function modifies the value associated with the key `"Kabob"` and adds a new item, `"Sushi": "$16"`.

10.4 Conditionals and looping in dictionaries

1. a. `"apple"` is a key in the dictionary and exists in the returned keys from `fruit_count.keys()`.
2. b. The key `"orange"`, with associated value `5`, exists in the dictionary and the return value is `True`.
3. b. Conditional statements can be written to examine keys and values.
4. b. The `values()` method iterates over values in a dictionary.
5. a. The loop iterates over the keys `"apple"`, `"orange"`, and `"banana"`, and prints the keys space-separated.
6. c. The loop multiplies all values by 2 and prints the output. So, `4`, `10`, and `2` are printed.

10.5 Nested dictionaries and dictionary comprehension

1. b. A nested dictionary contains another dictionary.
2. c. Both outer and inner keys must be used to index into both outer and inner dictionaries, respectively, to obtain an inner value.
3. b. A nested dictionary is a value of another dictionary, representing the data in a two-layer structure.
4. b. Keys in the dictionary are even values in the list numbers, and associated values are the powers of two.
5. a. Dictionary keys are string values in the names list, and associated values are the length of each string.
6. a. The dictionary is created from key values from 0 up to and including 3. The associated values are powers of two of the keys.

Chapter 11
11.1 Object-oriented programming basics

1. b. Ellis's username represents the post creator.
2. b. An object models a real-world entity with fields and procedures.
3. a. A procedure, such as Change venue, can make changes to the field and protect the field from inappropriate access.
4. b. Limiting data access prevents accidental changes and makes relationships between objects clearer.
5. b. Correct abstraction makes only necessary information visible. An overheated engine can cause irreparable damage, so an indicator is necessary for the driver.
6. a. Showing only the necessary information reduces clutter and improves the overall experience.

11.2 Classes and instances

1. a. Cat follows the class keyword at the top of the class definition and is the name of the class.
2. c. pet_1 is an instance of the Cat class created by calling Cat(). The other instance is pet_2.
3. a. breed is an instance attribute defined in __init__(). The other instance attributes are name and age.
4. c. CapWords style, with all words capitalized and no spaces between words, is recommended for class names. "Pet" and "cat" are separate words, so each is capitalized and one directly follows the other.
5. b. Two instances, room_1 and room_3, are created by calling Rectangle(), which calls the constructor __init__().
6. b. room_1 is the instance that called the method area(), so self represents the specific instance.
7. a. Line 3 is in __init__(), which initializes length and the other instance attributes for each new instance.
8. c. __init__() has one required parameter, conventionally called self, which allows the constructor to access the instance.
9. b. order_id is an instance attribute defined in __init__(). The other instance attribute is cup_size.
10. b. Changing order_1.cup_size does not affect order_3.cup_size. order_1.cup_size changes to 8 and order_3.cup_size is still 16.
11. a. order_1, order_2, and order_3 all share the class attribute CoffeeOrder.loc. Changing loc affects all instances, so Caffeine Cafe is printed as the location.
12. b. Trying to access a class attribute using an instance is unsafe. In __init__(), trying to access the class attribute creates a new instance attribute called cls_id. Though possible, programmers should avoid using the same name for class attributes and instance attributes to avoid confusion.

11.3 Instance methods

1. b. Removing the default parameter value makes bp a required parameter.
2. b. self is the first parameter in __init__() definition, not an explicit argument. self should not be included in the call.
3. c. The second definition overwrites the first as multiple explicit definitions of __init__() aren't allowed. __init__() requires all parameters, so the first two __init__() calls for patient_1 and patient_2

are incorrect.
4. c. `order_1` is originally a coffee without milk or sugar, but the call to `change()` adds sugar to the order by assigning `order_1.with_sugar` with `True`.
5. c. An instance method's first parameter indicates the method can change an instance. `change()` allows a change in whether a coffee order has milk or sugar.
6. b. Unindenting `print_order()` would produce an error. An instance method must be defined in the class.

11.4 Overloading operators

1. c. `__add__()` is a magic method, indicated by the double underscores at the start and end of the method name.
2. b. Magic methods are designed to be invoked internally to perform under-the-hood actions to simplify tasks for the user.
3. c. `__init__()` is defined by the programmer to initialize instance attributes. `__str__()` is defined by the programmer to customize an `Engineer` instance's string representation.
4. a. A programmer can overload an operator to customize the built-in operator's function.
5. b. The addition operation maps the left operand, `acct_a`, to the parameter `self` and the right operand, `acct_b`, to the parameter `other`.
6. c. `-` is a binary operator, so `__sub__()` has two parameters. The parameters' x and y attributes are subtracted from each other, and the resulting values are made into a new `Pair`.
7. a. <, >, and == are overloaded with `__lt__()`, `__gt__()`, and `__eq__()`, respectively.
8. b. `__le__()` is the magic method for the <= operator. `__le__()` takes two parameters for the left and right operand, and returns the correct comparison of the two amount values.
9. b. `__gt__()` overloads the > operator, which makes a comparison and returns `True` or `False`.

11.5 Using modules with classes

1. b. Level and XP are classes imported from the character module into the program. Any other class in the character module is not imported.
2. b. A single class or multiple classes can be imported from a module using the class name(s).
3. c. The number of classes in a module is unlimited, but classes should be grouped in modules to maximize reusability.
4. b. The character module is aliased as game_char, so character is not defined in the program. game_char is used in place of character.
5. c. game_char referred to the imported module, but assigning game_char replaces the imported module with the string `'Ranger'`. game_char can no longer be used to access classes.

Chapter 12
12.1 Recursion basics

1. a. The move of the smaller ring, which is a smaller problem, is done twice on the way to solving for the two rings overall. The task of moving all three rings is broken down into smaller tasks of moving one ring at a time.
2. b. The two-ring solution from question 1 is used in the solution for three rings.
3. b. Once to move two rings to the middle tower following the rules, then to move two rings to the target tower.
4. c. The small ring is moved to the middle tower. The bigger ring is moved to the target tower. Then, the small ring is moved from the middle to the target.
5. c. To solve, the two-ring solution is used twice, and there is one extra step to move the biggest ring from the source to the target. Each solution of two rings requires three steps each. So 3 + 1 + 3 = 7 steps total.
6. a. The four-ring problem uses the three-ring solution twice. The three smaller rings are moved to the

middle tower, taking seven steps as in question 2. One step is needed to move the biggest ring from the source to the target. It takes seven more steps move three smaller rings from the middle to the target. The total is 7 + 1 + 7 = 15 steps.

12.2 Simple math recursion

1. The summation can be calculated using recursion because there is a regular pattern and the summation to n depends on the summation to `n - 1`.
2. Each number in the sequence can be found by adding 2 to the previous number, with the solution at 1 being `1`.
3. A prime number does not depend on a smaller prime number; thus, no recursion can be found to generate new prime numbers based on an existing list of prime numbers.
4. A given number in the Fibonacci sequence is found by summing the previous two numbers in the sequence, so the Fibonacci sequence can be found recursively.
5. c. There is a missing base case, so there is no place for the recursion to end.
6. b. This definition of `rec_fact()` uses a base case of `n == 0`, which works because, just like `1!`, `0! = 1`. However, the base case of `n == 0` returns n, which at this stage is `0`, and therefore zeroes out the rest of the computation.
7. a. The recursive function begins returning correctly at the base case of `n == 0`. `0! = 1`.
8. b. The base case of `n == 1` is not used in the function. When n is `0`, the overall multiplication becomes `0`. The recursion begins returning once the `n < 0` base case is reached, initially returning `-1`. But the previous recursive call would return `0`, thereby zeroing out all computations and leaving an overall result of `0`.

12.3 Recursion with strings and lists

1. b. Once changed to all lower case, the word `"madam"` is a palindrome, so the function will recognize the word as a palindrome.
2. a. When a palindrome has an even number of letters, eventually an empty string is left as pairs of letters are removed. Thus, the base case should include `len(word) == 0`, which is resolved with the condition `len(word) <= 1`.
3. b. The `strip()` function removes a given letter from the beginning and end of the string, including repeated letters. When `strip('m')` is used with `"madamm"`, the resultant string is `"ada"`.
4. a. Both lists have the same items in a different order.
5. b. The two lists have four overlapping items, but `list_num` has an extra 15, and `other_list` has an extra 22.
6. a. Both lists have the same items in a different order. The function works for items of any type.
7. a. Both lists have the same items in a different order. The function works for items of any type, including other lists.
8. a. Both lists have the same items in the same order.

12.4 More math recursion

1. c. `fib(9) = fib(8) + fib(7)`. `fib(9) = fib(8) + fib(7) = 21 + 13 = 34`.
2. c. There are eight calls to base cases as seen in the animation. Those calls result in the recursion returning and the final value being computed.
3. b. The structure that shows which function calls are made is called a recursion tree. A recursion tree can be used to trace how the final values are computed.
4. c. `5 * 3 = 15` and `5 * 7 = 35`, so `5` is a the greatest common divisor of `15` and `35`.
5. a. The first call `gcd(24, 30)` results in `30 - 24 = 6`, so the next call is `gcd(24, 6)`. Thereafter, other calls are `gcd(18, 6)`, `gcd(12, 6)`, and `gcd (6,6)` for a total of four recursive calls after the initial function call.

6. b. When the two numbers have no common divisors, the GCD is 1.
7. b. The first call gcd(13, 23) results in 23 - 13 = 10, so the next call is gcd(13, 10). Thereafter, other calls are gcd(10, 3), gcd(7, 3), gcd (4,3), gcd(3,2), gcd(2,1), and gcd(1,1) for a total of eight calls.

12.5 Using recursion to solve problems

1. c. This array is sorted in ascending order, as is required for using the binary search algorithm.
2. a. mid = (4 + 7) // 2 = 11 // 2 = 5. The operator // is used for floor division.
3. a. The first call results in mid being 3 , next mid becomes 5 , and finally, mid becomes 4 . The element found at index 4 is equal to the key 16 .
4. a. The first call results in mid being (0 + 13) // 2 = 6. The next call has mid (7 + 13) // 2 = 10. The next call has mid (11 + 13) // 2 = 12. At this point, 86 < 99, so the final call is to mid 11, after which there is nowhere else to go.
5. b. As seen in the code example for three rings, the solution requires seven steps. The seven steps are called twice, along with one additional step, for a total of 2 x 7 + 1 = 15.
6. a. The iterative solution to Three Towers requires significantly more code and uses additional programming capabilities.

Chapter 13

13.1 Inheritance basics

1. a. A doughnut is a type of pastry, so Doughnut inherits from Pastry.
2. b. A kitchen has a freezer, so a Kitchen class would contain a Freezer instance. A has-a relationship is also called a composition.
3. b. The Goalkeeper class inherits from the Player class.
4. b. The subclass name is followed by the superclass name in parentheses.
5. a. Deriving CarryOn from Luggage is specified in CarryOn's class definition. Ex: class CarryOn(Luggage): . Instances of a subclass, like CarryOn, are created like other classes and do not require the base class name.
6. c. A SubClass instance has access to func_1(), inherited from SuperClass, as well as to func_2(), a SubClass method.
7. a. A SuperClass instance has access to SuperClass's func_1() but doesn't have access to anything in SubClass, including func_2().

13.2 Attribute access

1. b. dev_1 is the second Employee created. So dev_1 is the second object to call Employee.__init__(), and dev_1.e_id is assigned with 2 .
2. a. SubClass's __init__() is not explicitly defined, so SuperClass's __init__() is executed.
3. b. dc_1 inherits feat_1 and feat_2 from SuperClass.
4. b. dev_display() is a Developer method that accesses dev_1's instance attribute lang_xp.
5. c. dev_display() is a Developer method. emp_1 is not a Developer instance, so emp_1 cannot access dev_display().
6. a. Instance attributes inherited from Employee, the superclass, are accessed the same way as the subclass Developer's instance attributes.

13.3 Methods

1. b. Overriding involves defining a subclass method that has the same name as the superclass method.
2. b. The self parameter is missing from the overridden method's definition.
3. c. The class definition doesn't indicate inheritance. The definition should be class ContractTax(Tax):.

4. b. Square's superclass is Rectangle. Rectangle's __init__() is called on line 6.
5. a. super().__init__(4) calls the __init__() of Rectangle's superclass, Polygon. Control moves to line 3, and num_sides is initialized with 4.
6. b. The instance attribute side is initialized with 5.
7. b. Rectangle's __init__() always calls Polygon's __init__() with num_sides=4.
8. c. Polymorphism allows print_type() to be overridden in subclasses of Polygon.
9. a. The * operator can be used with integer operands as well as strings and other types.

13.4 Hierarchical inheritance

1. a. Class A is the superclass for Class B and Class C.
2. b. Employee would be an appropriate superclass for Developer and SalesRep. Developer and SalesRep are not directly related.
3. a. B(2) resolves to B(2, 0), as b_attr has a default value of 0 . a_attr is assigned with 2 .
4. b. c_inst has access to C's instance attribute, c_attr, as well the inherited attribute from A, a_attr.
5. b. D, which inherits from B, so d_inst inherits b_attr. B also inherits from A, so d_inst inherits d_attr.

13.5 Multiple inheritance and mixin classes

1. a. 1 is the argument passed to C's __init__() for a_attr.
2. b. An argument is not passed to C's __init__() for c_attr, so c_attr is assigned with the default value, 20 .
3. a. 2 maps to b_attr in B's __init__().
4. a. eat() only applies to carnivorous plants, which Pitcher and VenusFlyTrap represent.
5. b. eat() can be moved into a mixin class included in Pitcher's and VenusFlyTrap's inheritance list.
6. b. Good practice is to have a mixin class name end in "Mixin" to identify the class's purpose. The final implementation is:

```
class Plant:
   def photosynth(self):
      print("Photosynthesizing")

class CarnivMixin:
   def eat(self):
      print("Eating")

class Rose(Plant):
   pass

class Pitcher(Plant, CarnivMixin):
   pass

class VenusFlyTrap(Plant, CarnivMixin)
   pass
```

Chapter 14
14.1 Reading from files

1. c. The file is opened and is associated with the fileobj object. Reading from the file will be possible using fileobj.
2. a. The file must exist in the same folder as the Python file in order for the file to be opened.

3. b. Python interprets this command as the programmer trying to print the object details. The object details are printed. Ex: `<_io.TextIOWrapper name='newfile.txt' mode='r' encoding='cp1252'>`.
4. c. The `read()` function is called on `fileobj`. The file's contents will be read into `file_str`.
5. b. The `readlines()` function is called on `fileobj`. `file_lines` is the string list `['Hello world!\n', 'How are you?\n']`.
6. a. The `readline()` function reads the next line of a file. Since `readline()` is called right after opening the file the first line is read. The resulting string `"Hello world!"` is printed. Note that `readline()` includes the `'\n'` character so the print will include an additional newline.

14.2 Writing to files

1. a. The default mode for the `open()` function is read.
2. c. `'a'` indicates append mode allowing additions to the file.
3. b. `'w'` indicates write mode, and *newlog.txt* will be created or overwritten (if *newlog.txt* already exists) and will allow writing.
4. c. *resources.txt* is likely empty, but the state of *resources.txt* is uncertain. To ensure the contents are saved correctly, the `close()` function must be used.
5. a. Write mode will overwrite the existing file. The `close()` statement finalizes changes to the file.
6. b. Append mode adds to the existing file. *resources.txt* is opened such that additions can be made to the file.

14.3 Files in different locations and working with CSV files

1. b. The path followed by the filename enables the file to be opened correctly and in read mode by default.
2. c. The use of forward slashes / replacing the Windows standard backslashes \ enables the path to be read correctly. The path followed by the filename enables the file to be opened and when reading a file read mode is preferable.
3. c. The file is created or overwritten and changes can be written into the file.
4. a. Since the backslashes in the Windows path appear in the string argument, which usually tells Python that this is part of an escape sequence, the backslashes must be ignored using an additional backslash \ character.
5. a. The newline \n character indicates where line breaks are in a file and is used by the `readlines()` function to tell lines apart.
6. b. The cell at the 2nd row and 3rd column contains `'268'`.
7. c. The first line of the *books.csv* is read into `csv_read`. The first line is `'Title, Author, Pages'`, which is the same as the first row.

14.4 Handling exceptions

1. c. The string `"3-4"` is not an integer, so the `int()` function raises a `ValueError` like before.
2. a. The filename should end with .txt, not .text.
3. b. If the line has no spaces, then `len(parts)` will be only 1, and `parts[1]` will be out of range.
4. b. The `int()` function raises a `ValueError` when trying to convert `"one"` to an integer, so the program jumps to the except clause.
5. c. The program crashes and displays this error because the except clause does not handle `ValueError`.
6. b. If an except clause does not specify a specific error type, then any error type is handled.

14.5 Raising exceptions

1. a. `"M"` is a valid size, so the `Pizza` object is constructed.
2. c. `PizzaError` is not a built-in exception type.
3. a. An exception can be raised without providing an error message. In this case, the error message is empty, but the exception name is still printed.

Chapter 15

15.1 Introduction to data science

1. c. Data acquisition is the first stage of the data science life cycle. Data can be collected by the data scientist or gathered previously and provided to the data scientist.
2. b. The data science life cycle has four stages: 1) data acquisition, 2) data exploration, 3) data analysis, and 4) reporting.
3. c. The data exploration stage includes data cleaning and visualization.
4. a. Python is the most popular programming language in data science.
5. b. NumPy is a Python library used in numerical data analysis.
6. a. Google Colaboratory is a Google document that can be shared with other Google accounts for viewing or editing the content.

15.2 NumPy

1. c. To create an m by n matrix of all zeros, `np.zeros((m,n))` can be used.
2. a. `ndarray` is a data type supported by NumPy. When printing the type of an `ndarray` object, `<'numpy.ndarray'>` is printed.
3. d. NumPy array is optimized for computational and memory efficiency while also offering array-oriented computation.
4. b. `2 * arr` multiplies all elements by 2 resulting in:

   ```
   [[2 4]
    [6 8]]
   ```

5. c. `np.array([[1, 2], [1, 2], [1, 2]])` creates an `ndarray` of 3 by 2. The T operator transposes the array. The transpose operator takes an array of m by n and converts the array to an n by m array. The result of applying the transpose operator on the given array is a 2 by 3 array.
6. a. The result of element-wise multiplication between `arr1` and `arr2` is:

   ```
   [[1 0]
    [0 4]]
   ```

15.3 Pandas

1. a. Series is a Pandas data structure representing one-dimensional labeled data.
2. a. A DataFrame object can be considered a collection of one-dimensional labeled objects represented by Series objects.
3. b. The Pandas DataFrame can store columns of varying data types, while NumPy only supports numeric data types.
4. c. The function `head()` returns a DataFrame's top rows. If an argument is not specified, the default number of returned rows is five.
5. c. The `unique()` function when applied to a column returns the unique values (rows) in the given column.
6. a. When the function `describe()` is applied to a DataFrame, summary statistics of numerical columns will be generated.

15.4 Exploratory data analysis

1. a. The element in the first row and the first column is a.
2. c. The element in the second row and the second column is `20`.
3. a. The element at row label `2` and column label A is c.
4. b. `df.loc[0:2, "A"]` returns rows 0 to 2 (inclusive) of column A.

5. c. `loc[1]` returns the row with label `1`, which corresponds to the second row of the DataFrame.
6. b. `iloc[:, 0]` selects all rows corresponding to the column index 0, which equals returning the first column.
7. a. The condition returns all rows where the value in the column with label A is divisible by 2.
8. b. `isnull()` returns a Boolean DataFrame representing whether data entries are `Null` or not.
9. a. `fillna()` replaces all `Null` values with the provided value passed as an argument.
10. c. The function `sum()` is applied to each column separately and sums up values in columns. The result is the number of `Null` values in each column.

15.5 Data visualization

1. b. A histogram is used to plot the distribution of continuous variables.
2. c. A box plot is used to show the distribution of a continuous variable, along with visualizing outliers, minimum, maximum, and quartiles.
3. a. A line plot is used to show trends and changes over time between two variables.
4. c. The function call `plt.scatter(x, y)` creates a scatter plot based on the data stored in the variables x and y.
5. b. The given code plots a bar plot with four bars representing the given categories. The height of the bars corresponds to the values stored in the `values` variable.
6. b. Plotly is a library that creates interactive visualizations.

Index

Symbols
!= 94
< 94
<= 94
= 14
== 94
> 94
>= 94

A
Abstraction 267
Aliasing 282
and 100
append 223
argument 158
Arithmetic operators 21
ASCII 72
assignment operator 14

B
base case 290
bool 92
bool() 93
branch 91
break 134
built-in function 55

C
class 267
class attribute 270
code point 72
Comments 27
Comparison operators 94
computer 8
condition 97
conditional expression 116
container 71, 125
continue 135
Control flow 149
count() 206

D
data analysis 350
Data filtering 364
Data indexing 363
Data science 349
Data Science 349
data science life cycle 350

Data slicing 364
data type 20
DataFrame 355
def 147
delimiter 217
diamond problem 321
dict 242
dictionary 241, 241
Dictionary comprehension 258
docstring 29

E
elif 108
else statement 98
Encapsulation 266
escape sequence 74
explicit type conversion 43
Exploratory Data Analysis (EDA) 362
expression 39

F
f-string 76
feature 362
field width 214
find() 207
float() 43
Floor division 51
for loop 125
format specifier 77
format() 210
formatted string literal 76
Formatting string 209
function 146

G
global scope 153
Google Colaboratory 351
Google Sheets 351

H
Hierarchical inheritance 316

I
identity 81
if statement 97
iloc[] 363
immutable 86, 161, 203

implicit type conversion 43
import statement 55
in 205
index 88
index() 208
infinite loop 134
inner loop 129
Input 12
input() 12
instance attribute 270
instance method 273
instances 267
int() 43
interpreter 40

J
join() 218
Jupyter Notebook 350
JupyterLab 350

K
Kaggle Kernels 351
key-value 241
keyword arguments 168
keywords 15

L
len() 17
library 9
list comprehension 235
list-of-lists 232
loc[] 363
local scope 154
logical operator 100
loop 121
loop else 137
lower() 199

M
Magic methods 276
memory diagram 80
Microsoft Excel 351
Mixin classes 321
mode 331
module 55, 173
modulo operator 51
modulus 52
Multilevel inheritance 316

Multiple inheritance 320
mutable 86, 161

N
name collision 178
named replacement fields 211
ndarray 352
Nested dictionaries 256
nested list 232
nested loop 129
newline 10
not 103
numbered replacement fields 212
NumPy 352

O
object 71
Object-oriented programming 265
open() 327
Operator overloading 277
or 102
outer loop 129
Output 10
overflow error 49
override 310

P
Pandas 354
parameter 158

pass-by-object-reference 161
path 335
PEP 60
Polymorphism 312
positional arguments 168
precedence 22
print() 10
program 8
prompt 12
Python Package Index 191
Python Standard Library 190

R
range() 126
read() 328
readline() 328
readlines() 328
Recursion 287
recursion tree 294
recursive case 290
REPL 41
replacement field 76
Replacement fields 209
return statement 163
round-off error 48
round() 50

S
scope 153
self 269
Series 355

shell 40
snake case 15
Sorting 226
split() 217
statement 7
step size 123
str() 43
string 88, 197
string alignment type 214
String slicing 201
syntax 9

T
Traceback 24
True division 51
try 341
tuple 85
type 81

U
Unicode 72
upper() 199

V
value 81
variable 12

W
while loop 121
write() 332

www.ingramcontent.com/pod-product-compliance
Lightning Source LLC
LaVergne TN
LVHW062244070526
838201LV00093B/174